Real Estate Exam Prep

A Comprehensive Guide to the National/General
Portion of Your License Exam

1st Edition Update

This publication is designed to provide accurate and authoritative information in regard to the subject matter covered. It is sold with the understanding that the publisher is not engaged in rendering legal, accounting, or other professional advice. If legal advice or other expert assistance is required, the services of a competent professional should be sought.

REAL ESTATE EXAM PREP 1ST EDITION UPDATE
©2022 Kaplan North America, LLC
Published by DF Institute, LLC, d/b/a Dearborn Real Estate Education and
Kaplan Real Estate Education
1515 West Cypress Creek Road
Fort Lauderdale, Florida 33309

10 9 8 7 6 5 4 3 2

ISBN: 978-1-5062-8837-6

10 9 8 7 6 5 4 3 2

ISBN: 978-1-5062-8838-3 (custom)

CONTENTS

PREFACE

NATIONAL PORTION REVIEW

The national portion for salesperson contains 80 or 100 questions, depending on the exam provider and state. The national portion for brokers contains 75 or 80 questions and 5 or 10 scenario questions, depending on the exam provider and state. These questions reflect the current national real estate laws, rules, and regulations. Topics covered in the national portion are listed as follows.

Property Ownership

Topics include real versus personal property, encumbrances and effects on property ownership, and legal descriptions.

Forms of Ownership

Topics include freehold estate, leasehold estates, and sole versus co-ownership/multiple owners.

Transfer of Title

Topics include essential elements of a valid deed, types of deeds, title transfer, recording the title, and title insurance.

Land-Use Controls and Regulations

Topics include governmental powers (Rights in Land [PETE])/public controls, zoning, regulation of special land types, environmental hazards, and regulation.

Agency Relationships

Topics include agency and nonagency relationships and licensee-client relationships, creation of agency, the agent's duties to clients, liability for another's acts, disclosure of representation, seller representation—listing agreements, buyer representation agreements, termination of agency, responsibilities of the agent to customers and third parties, Sherman Antitrust Act, and multiple listing service (MLS).

Leasing and Property Management

Topics include basic concepts/duties of property management, property management agreement, leases, and fair housing compliance and ADA in property management.

Practice of Real Estate

Topics include federal fair housing laws, the Americans with Disabilities Act (ADA), Megan's Law, advertising, National Do Not Call Registry, trust/escrow accounts and employing broker responsibilities, mandated disclosures, types of insurance, warranties, and broker responsibilities.

Contracts

Topics include types of contracts, general concepts, sales contracts, option contracts, and amendments, addenda, contingencies, and time is of the essence.

Property Valuation

Topics include appraisals, concepts of value, valuation methods, and reconciliation.

Finance

Topics include lien theory versus title theory, financing instruments, foreclosure, deed in lieu of foreclosure, and short sales, financing terms, methods of debt service (debt repayment), types of loans, primary and secondary mortgage markets, laws affecting financing and lending, and mortgage fraud and predatory lending.

Real Estate Calculations

Topics include measurement, finance, property management calculations, property valuation, investment, and settlement/closing calculations.

Broker Only Topics

Topics include forms of ownership, transfer of title, leasing and property management, practice of real estate, and real estate calculations.

UNIT 1

Property Ownership

LEARNING OBJECTIVE

When you have completed this unit, you will be able to accomplish the following.

> Discuss the characteristics and rights associated with real property, distinguish the difference between real property and personal property, the types of encumbrances and their effect on property ownership, and the methods used to describe real property.

I.   REAL VS. PERSONAL PROPERTY

A. Definitions

1. Real property is land, plus appurtenances that benefit the land. (Appurtenant means *belongs to* or *goes with*.) Appurtenances are things that transfer with the land when the land is transferred to another owner, such as improvements, rights, privileges, and fixtures.

    a. This includes permanent natural objects, such as water and trees.

    b. This includes anything attached to the land with the intent of being permanent, like a building, house, and garage.

    c. This includes the rights of ownership enjoyed by the owner of a parcel of real estate.

    d. This encompasses and includes the rights appurtenant to the following:

        i. Surface

        ii. Subsurface

        iii. Air above the surface

2. <u>Personal property</u> is <u>everything</u> owned <u>that is *not* real property.</u>

   a. Items of personal property are also referred to as <u>chattel</u>.

B. Characteristics of real property

1. The <u>economic characteristics</u> of real property are <u>scarcity</u>, <u>improvements</u>, <u>permanence of investment,</u> and <u>location.</u>

   a. <u>Scarcity</u>—the supply of land is not limitless. Land at a given location, or of a particular quality is finite.

   b. <u>Improvements</u>—<u>an improvement</u> built on a parcel of land <u>affects</u> that land's <u>value and use</u>, as well as that of <u>neighboring tracts</u> of land, and potentially an entire community.

   c. <u>Permanence of investment</u>—because the capital and labor required to build an improvement may be a large investment, the <u>return on an investment tends to be long and stable</u> in comparison to other types of investments.

   d. <u>Location</u>—location is the <u>most important economic characteristic</u> of land. Sometimes called area preference, location refers to people's preferences of an area based on its history, reputation, scenic beauty, and convenience.

C. Physical characteristics

1. The <u>physical characteristics</u> of real property are <u>immobility</u>, <u>indestructibility</u>, and <u>uniqueness</u>.

   a. <u>Immobility</u>—the <u>geographic location</u> of a tract of land <u>is fixed</u>; it is immobile.

   b. <u>Indestructibility</u>—the <u>permanence of land</u> tends to <u>make investments in real property relatively stable</u> compared to other investments. However, improvements on land can <u>depreciate</u> and reduce the land's value.

   c. <u>Uniqueness</u>—no two parcels of land are alike. Each parcel is <u>geographically distinct</u>.

D. Rights

1. Ownership of <u>real estate includes</u> certain rights that pertain to the <u>surface</u> of the land, the <u>subsurface</u> below the surface, and the <u>air</u> above the surface.

   a. <u>Mineral</u> rights—an owner of real estate is entitled to use the <u>natural resources below the earth's surface</u>, provided they're not held by another party or the government.

   b. <u>Air</u> rights—an owner of real estate may use the <u>air above</u> the land, provided the rights have not been eliminated by law.

   c. <u>Mineral and air rights are independent of the surface rights</u> of land ownership. An owner may transfer those rights to another party while still retaining surface rights to the land itself.

   d. <u>Water</u> rights—owners of <u>land adjacent to rivers, lakes, or oceans</u> have special <u>common-law</u> rights.

      i. <u>Riparian</u> rights are granted to owners of land along the course of a stream, <u>river</u>, or similar body of water.

■ An owner has <u>unrestricted rights to use the water</u>, provided the owner <u>does not impede the flow of water</u>.

   ii. <u>Littoral</u> rights are granted to owners of lands that border a standing body of water, like a <u>lake</u>, or the seas and oceans. These owners have the <u>right to use the available waters</u>, but not at the expense or detriment of the other littoral owners.

   iii. <u>Water rights are appurtenant</u> to the land and are not retained when the land is sold; a former owner does not enjoy those rights once that owner sells the land.

   iv. <u>Doctrine of prior appropriation</u>

      ■ Certain states rely on this doctrine, which states that <u>the first user diverting water for beneficial use</u> (like irrigation) <u>has the first claim on the water</u>.

E. Personal property—also referred to as <u>chattel</u>, and must be <u>included</u> in the sale contract if the buyer wishes to receive it

  1. Personal property is all property that does not fit the definition of *real property*.

  2. Personal property is <u>movable</u>, and includes such things as furniture and drapes/curtains but does NOT include anything built in or otherwise attached/affixed to an improvement.

  3. Any <u>manufactured housing that is not permanently affixed to the land</u> is also considered personal property.

  4. An <u>emblement</u> is an <u>annually growing crop</u> that is produced and picked at harvest. Though attached to the land before harvest, emblements are regarded as <u>personal property</u>.

   a. <u>In the case of a tenant growing the crop on leased land</u>, the tenant has the right to take the harvest resulting from the tenant's labor even after the lease is terminated. The crop's <u>harvests are the tenant's personal property</u>.

   b. A landlord cannot terminate a lease without giving the tenant the right to enter the land to harvest any crops belonging to the tenant.

  5. <u>Personal property can become real property</u> if the personal property becomes a <u>fixture</u>.

   a. Fixtures and trade fixtures

     i. A <u>fixture</u> is <u>personal property that has been affixed or attached to land or to an improvement so that it becomes a part of the real property</u> (including such items as heating systems, kitchen cabinets, light fixtures, and plumbing), <u>and transfers with the property unless the contract specifically excludes them</u>.

     ii. <u>Intent is the determining factor</u> in what constitutes a fixture. Intent depends on three factors:

      ■ The method of <u>annexation</u>: how permanent is the attachment of the item?

      ■ <u>Adaptation</u> to real estate: is the item used as real property or personal property?

        – Example: garage door openers and keys to the doors in the home

      ■ <u>Agreement</u>: have the parties agreed to whether a particular item is real or personal property?

      iii. A <u>trade fixture is an article belonging to a commercial tenant</u>, which is attached to a rented space or building <u>and used in conducting the business of the tenant</u> (such as moving clothing racks in a dry-cleaning business or ovens, stoves, food preparation vents, bars, wine racks, and other restaurant equipment in a restaurant).

      iv. A <u>tenant is responsible for removing trade fixtures</u> before the last day of the rental period, or the fixtures may become the real property of the landowner.

  b. Attachment, severance, and bill of sale

      i. <u>Attachment</u>—an item of personal property can become real property when it is <u>affixed</u> to real property. Construction materials used to build a house or other structure become part of real estate through attachment, as well as lighting and plumbing fixtures, for example.

      ii. <u>Severance</u>—this is removing something attached to the land or an improvement, resulting in the object becoming <u>personal property</u>, such as a light fixture the sellers wish to take with them.

      iii. <u>Bill of sale</u>—an item of <u>personal property is transferred through a bill of sale</u>, <u>not with a deed</u>.

II. ENCUMBRANCES AND EFFECTS ON PROPERTY OWNERSHIP

A. Encumbrance (i.e., an imperfection, or cloud on title)

1. An <u>encumbrance</u> is a <u>charge, claim, or liability attached to real property</u>.

2. It is a <u>right or interest held by someone other than the fee owner</u> of the real estate, and therefore is not a possessory interest.

3. Encumbrances are clouds on title that may impair or lessen an owner's rights or property value.

B. Liens and lien priority

1. A <u>lien is a claim or interest in a property to secure payment of a debt</u>. If the debt obligation is not paid, the lienholder may have the <u>debt satisfied</u> from proceeds of court proceedings or a forced sale of the property.

2. A <u>general lien</u> affects all of a debtor's property—<u>both personal and real property</u>. Here are examples:

  a. Judgment lien

  b. Inheritance or estate tax lien

  c. IRS lien

3. A <u>specific lien attaches to a particular property or type of property, making the owner of the real estate responsible for payment</u>. Here are examples:

  a. Mechanics' liens

  b. Mortgage liens

c. Real estate tax liens and special assessment liens

d. Condominium/townhome association liens

4. The <u>creation of a lien</u> may be

a. <u>voluntary</u>, created by action of the property owner (such as a mortgage lien); or

b. <u>statutory (involuntary)</u>, created without the express <u>permission</u> of the property owner (like property tax liens and mechanic's liens).

5. The <u>priority of a lien determines the order in which claims will be paid off (satisfied)</u>:

a. Generally, liens <u>first legally recorded are satisfied first</u>

b. But <u>real estate taxes and special assessments take priority over all other liens</u>

c. Lienholders may establish a subordination agreement that changes order of priority of liens

6. Real estate <u>tax liens include real estate taxes and special assessments</u>.

a. Real estate taxes

i. Referred to as an <u>ad valorem</u> (Latin for "at value") tax

ii. <u>Based on the assessed value</u> of the property, and is an involuntary, statutory (created by law) lien

iii. Ad valorem taxes: levied by government agencies (e.g., school districts or water districts) and municipalities (e.g., states, counties, cities, towns, and villages)

C. Easements and licenses

1. Easements

a. An <u>easement is the right to use another owner's land for a particular purpose</u>.

b. Easements are <u>not revocable</u> once granted.

c. An easement <u>always transfers with the land at closing unless it's released by the holder</u>.

d. They may or may not be paid for, but they <u>must be in writing</u>.

e. They <u>can apply to any part or portion of real property, including a right of way across the property, or even the airspace above the property</u>.

i. <u>Appurtenant</u> easement—always <u>involves two separate properties</u>

- Allows the owner of one parcel of land to use another owner's land for a specific purpose

- Parcel over which the easement runs is called the <u>servient tenement</u> (it "serves" the interests of the other parcel)

- The parcel that benefits from the easement is called the <u>dominant tenement</u> (it "dominates" the interests of the servient parcel)

- An appurtenant easement <u>runs with the land</u>; <u>will transfer with the deed of either parcel</u>, and remains in effect <u>until it is released</u>

ii. <u>Easement in gross</u>

- Has <u>only a servient tenement</u> (e.g., an easement held by a utility, or a railroad's right-of-way)

iii. <u>Easement by necessity</u>—used to help a buyer purchasing a <u>landlocked property</u>

- Arises when an owner sells part of their land that has <u>no access</u> except over the seller's remaining land; this easement is created by a court order

- Only available to private owners; <u>not</u> available to government, utility, cable, telephone, or gas companies

iv. <u>Easement by prescription</u> occurs when a party (or parties) uses another person's property continuously without property owner's permission for a <u>statutory period</u> of time; <u>state laws</u> define the time period required to create this kind of an easement

f. How an easement is created

i. An easement always involves <u>two</u> separate parties, one of whom is the owner of the land over which the easement runs

ii. Easements <u>must be in writing</u>, and are commonly created between the two parties, but may also be created by other means (e.g., court order)

iii. A <u>party wall</u> easement is a <u>commonly shared partition wall</u> between two connected properties (e.g., side-by-side townhomes)

g. The most common ways easements are <u>terminated</u>

i. When the <u>parcels merge</u> (owner of either parcel becomes the owner of both parcels)

- Doesn't terminate the easement, until the owner records a release of the easement in the property records

ii. When the easement is <u>released</u>

iii. If the easement is <u>abandoned</u>

2. License

a. <u>Does not establish a legal interest in real property</u>

b. <u>Revocable permission</u>, granted by the owner, to enter the owner's land for a specific purpose

c. Terminated by the owner, by the death of the owner, or the sale of the property

D. Encroachment

1. <u>Unauthorized use of another owner's land(s)</u>

2. Occurs when all or part of a structure illegally extends beyond the land of its owner or beyond the legal boundary lines

3. Usually <u>disclosed</u> by either a <u>physical inspection</u> of the property, a <u>spot survey</u>, or an <u>ILC (Improvement Location Certificate)</u> showing the location of all improvements on a property and whether they extend over the lot or building lines

4. Neither a standard title insurance policy nor an attorney's title opinion protect against encroachments

E. Lis pendens

1. A recorded document that gives <u>constructive notice of a pending lawsuit regarding title</u> to a property

F. Other potential encumbrances of title

1. <u>Deed restrictions—privately created controls</u> on land use

    a. They are also known as <u>restrictive covenants</u> or <u>CC&Rs (covenants, conditions, and restrictions)</u>.

    b. They are typically imposed by a developer to <u>maintain subdivision standards</u> and are listed in the original development plans for the subdivision (e.g., no RVs are allowed to be parked on driveways, all homes must be painted certain colors, fencing must be of a certain type, there must be minimum square footage of a dwelling structure).

    c. They <u>may not violate fair housing laws</u> (e.g., cannot refuse to sell based on a buyer's race or national origin).

    d. They are <u>binding on all present and future owners</u>.

    e. Property owners could be subject to injunctions if they violate deed restrictions.

2. <u>Homeowners association regulations—privately created controls</u>

    a. Communities managed by an association are restricted by <u>policies or procedures dictated</u> by the association.

    b. A developer transfers the <u>right to enforce any CC&Rs</u> in a community once a certain percentage of the lots or units have been sold.

    c. Individual properties may be <u>restricted</u> to certain lot sizes, square footage, paint color schemes, and other factors affecting homes, condominiums, or townhomes in the community.

3. <u>In the case of deed restrictions, covenants, CC&Rs, regulations, and zoning, most stringent (strictest) requirement always applies</u>

III.   LEGAL DESCRIPTIONS

A.   Definition of a legal description

1. A legal description of real estate is one that is <u>sufficiently specific enough for a surveyor to locate the exact dimensions</u> of a particular property.

2. A <u>street address is not precise enough</u> to be used on documents affecting the <u>ownership</u> of land.

B.   Types of legal descriptions

1. <u>Metes and bounds</u> is the oldest method of legal description in the United States, and the most accurate when used with contemporary global positioning system (GPS) technology. This type of legal description does the following:

   a. Uses compass directions and distances (metes) to <u>describe the perimeter of a property's boundaries (bounds)</u>

   b. <u>Starts and ends at a point of beginning (POB)</u>

      i. The only form of legal description that begins with words such as starting, proceeding, beginning, etc.

   c. <u>Uses monuments</u> (fixed objects or markers) to identify the POB and specific locations where boundaries change directions

      i. Monuments may be natural objects (rocks, trees, or streams) or <u>iron pins</u> or <u>concrete posts</u> placed by U.S. Corp of Engineers or a private surveyor

2. <u>Recorded plat, also known as lot, block, and subdivision</u>, is used in <u>urban residential</u> areas to describe property in a subdivision. This type of legal description does the following:

   a. Divides a large parcel of land into <u>blocks</u> and <u>lots</u> on a <u>plat map</u>, which is filed in the public records of the county where the property is located

   b. To <u>create a subdivision</u>, a developer must first <u>create the plat map, then record the map</u>

      i. Without recording the plat map, there is no record of lot, block, and subdivision

3. The <u>government survey,</u> also known as the <u>rectangular survey system</u>:

   a. Divides land into <u>squares and rectangles</u>

   b. Is measured from the intersections of <u>principal meridians</u> (imaginary north/south lines) and <u>base lines</u> (imaginary east/west lines)

   c. Describes <u>townships</u> relative to their positions east or west from a prime meridian, and north or south from a correlating base line

      i. Townships are <u>6 miles by 6 miles</u>

      ii. And they contain <u>36 square miles, each of which is called a section</u>

         ■ <u>Each section—640 acres</u>

Township 3 North, Range 3 East
(T3N, R3E)

|← 6 miles →|

6	5	4	3	2	1
7	8	9	10	11	12
18	17	16	15	14	13
19	20	21	22	23	24
30	29	28	27	26	25
31	32	33	34	35	36

6 miles

1 mile

|← 1 mile →|

A township is divided into 36 sections.
Each section is 1 mile × 1 mile.

C. Measuring

1. Units and measurements are used to determine the <u>size and square footage</u> of both structures and parcels of land:

   a. Mile = <u>5,280 ft.</u>

   b. <u>Square mile</u> = 5,280 ft. × 5,280 ft., and <u>contains 640 acres</u>

   c. <u>Acre = 43,560 sq. ft.</u>

   d. Square yard = <u>9 sq. ft.</u>

   e. Square foot = <u>144 sq. in.</u>

2. Measuring <u>elevations</u>

   a. <u>Air lots</u>

      i. Air lots are the <u>airspace</u> within specific boundaries located <u>above a parcel of land</u>, which show elevations of floors and ceilings and vertical boundaries of units (like condominiums and offices) referencing an official surface, line, or point from which elevations are measured.

b.   <u>Subsurface</u> rights can be legally described in same manner as air lots (above), but are <u>measured below an official surface</u>, line, or point rather than above it

D.   Livable, usable, and rentable area

1.   The <u>livable area</u> of a home is the total area that is <u>heated</u> or <u>cooled</u>.

2.   <u>Usable</u> area (commonly used for rental property) describes the <u>area a tenant can use for ordinary, daily living</u>.

3.   <u>Rentable</u> area is another term for <u>usable area</u>.

E.   Survey

1.   A <u>licensed surveyor is authorized to locate and confirm, as well as create the legal description of a parcel of land</u>. A surveyor usually prepares two documents:

   a.   A <u>survey</u> that <u>states the property's legal description</u>

      i.   As mentioned previously, surveys are used to create plat maps of subdivisions.

   b.   A <u>survey sketch</u> that <u>shows the location and dimensions of the parcel</u>

      i.   Note: When a survey shows the location, size, and shape of buildings on the lot, it is known as a <u>spot survey</u>.

2.   A <u>survey</u> may be necessary to discover any <u>encroachments</u> on a property.

UNIT 1 REVIEW QUESTIONS

True/False Questions

1. Because a garage door opener is movable, it is considered personal property.
   A. True
   B. False

2. A 20-foot potted tree is chattel.
   A. True
   B. False

3. If a seller wants to take chattel, it must be excluded from the purchase contract.
   A. True
   B. False

4. After a lease of agricultural property terminates, the growing crop of wheat belongs to the landlord.
   A. True
   B. False

5. Emblements are regarded as personal property.
   A. True
   B. False

6. Real estate can include surface rights, subsurface rights, and air rights.
   A. True
   B. False

7. A license is the irrevocable permission of the landowner, allowing a nonowner to use the property without it being a trespass.
   A. True
   B. False

8. An encroachment must touch the property.
   A. True
   B. False

9. Property tax liens take priority over all other liens.
   A. True
   B. False

10. A specific lien, in contrast to a general lien, attaches to a specified parcel of real estate.
    A. True
    B. False

11. To remove an appurtenant easement, the owner of the servient tenement would sign a quitclaim deed.
    A. True
    B. False

12. In the rectangular survey system, a section of land is one square mile and contains 640 acres.
    A. True
    B. False

13. In the government survey system, the grid is formed by a base, a meridian, lots, and blocks.
    A. True
    B. False

14. A developer growing a new residential subdivision in a suburban area would likely use the lot and block method legal description.
    A. True
    B. False

15. In the metes and bounds legal description, *metes* refers to distances and *bounds* refers to boundaries.
    A. True
    B. False

16. In the rectangular survey system, a section contains 36 square miles.
    A. True
    B. False

17. The metes and bounds legal description starts at some point external to the parcel of real estate being described.
    A. True
    B. False

Multiple-Choice Questions

1. In a purchase agreement, fixtures transfer with the title, while personal property must be included to transfer to the buyer. An encumbrance that also automatically transfers with the land is
   A. a freestanding stove or dishwasher.
   B. a freestanding refrigerator.
   C. an appurtenant easement.
   D. a trade fixture currently being used and attached to the property.

2. In the lease agreement, two tenants have agreed to build out a commercial space to meet their needs at their own expense. The chattel fixtures that they add are the property of
   A. the landlord upon the expiration of the lease, because they are now attached to the property.
   B. the tenants, as long as they are removed from the property on or before the expiration of the lease and they leave the property in good repair.
   C. the tenants, as long as they are removed from the property on or before the expiration of the lease because they paid for them.
   D. the landlord automatically upon their addition, and the property must be left in good repair.

3. House keys are considered to be
   A. personal property because they are movable.
   B. personal property because they are not attached.
   C. real property because sale contracts stipulate that they will be transferred.
   D. real property because of the adaptation to the real estate.

4. There are two neighboring parcels. The southern parcel has access to the only road in the area. The northern parcel has no access to any nearby road. The owner of the southern parcel verbally and informally allows the owner of the northern parcel to cross over the southern parcel to get to the road. This arrangement continues for 10 years. Which of these describes this arrangement?
   A. A prescriptive easement
   B. An appurtenant easement
   C. An easement in gross
   D. A license

5. Which lien is given first priority?
   A. A real estate tax lien
   B. A mortgage lien
   C. A trust deed lien
   D. A hospital bill lien

6. A prospective buyer is considering the purchase of a single-family residence. Which of these might dissuade the buyer from purchasing the real estate?
   A. An appurtenant easement over a neighboring parcel for street access
   B. A one-inch encroachment of a neighbor's house
   C. A deed restriction limiting the races to whom the property could be sold
   D. A withdrawal of lis pendens, filed several years ago

7. A seller recently sold a buyer a parcel of real estate. The legal description stated, "Parcel A, reserving therefrom, the west half, and further reserving an easement over the south 10 feet of the property for street access." After the purchase transaction is complete, which of these describes what the seller still holds?
   A. The west half and an appurtenant easement over the south 10 feet of the east half
   B. The east half and an appurtenant easement over the south 10 feet of the west half
   C. The south half and an appurtenant easement over the north 10 feet of the north half
   D. The north half and an appurtenant easement over the south 10 feet of the south half

8. The owner of a large parcel of real estate located in a rural area listed the property for sale. The metes and bounds method of legal description was used to describe this irregularly shaped parcel. The legal description started at an iron spike driven into the center of an immediately adjoining road. Which phrase was MOST likely used at the point in the legal description that began to describe the boundaries of the listed parcel?
   A. Commencing at
   B. Starting at
   C. Point of beginning
   D. Base and meridian

9. A developer was subdividing a large parcel of
   vacant land for a new residential subdivision in a
   suburban area. Before building, the developer was
   legally required to create and file a plat for the new
   subdivision. What type of legal description would
   the developer MOST likely use?
   A. Metes and bounds
   B. Government survey system
   C. Lot and block
   D. Rectangular survey system

UNIT 2

Forms of Ownership

LEARNING OBJECTIVE

When you have completed this unit, you will be able to accomplish the following.

> Summarize the forms of ownership available to clients and customers.

I. FREEHOLD ESTATE

A. Definition

   1. An <u>estate</u> in land is <u>an interest allowing for the right of possession</u>.

   2. <u>Freehold</u> estates last for an <u>indefinite</u> period of time.

B. Types of freehold estates

   1. Fee simple absolute

      a. A <u>fee simple absolute</u> estate (often referred to as <u>fee simple</u> or a <u>fee estate</u>) is the most <u>common freehold estate</u>, and features the <u>maximum rights of ownership and can last forever</u>.

      b. The owner of a fee simple absolute estate

         i. holds <u>title</u> to the property;

         ii. <u>may dispose of the property</u> through <u>a gift or a sale</u>, or through a <u>will or inheritance</u> upon the owner's death; and

         iii. <u>may impose restrictions or conditions</u> on the future use of the property, which would apply to all future owners of the property.

2. <u>Fee simple defeasible</u> (sometimes referred to as a qualified fee estate)

   a. Fee simple defeasible is an estate where <u>ownership is subject to certain conditions</u> that are clearly defined in the deed. The root word of defeasible is *defeat*. Ownership of this kind of estate can be "defeated" if the conditions as stated in the deed are not met.

      i. Therefore, ownership of a fee simple defeasible estate <u>lasts as long as those conditions are met</u>.

   b. A fee simple determinable automatically ends when the purpose for which it was established terminates. However, if the defeasible estate is a fee simple subject to a condition subsequent, the original grantor must physically retake possession of the property to terminate.

3. Life estate

   a. A <u>life estate</u> is a freehold estate that <u>lasts the lifetime of the owner, or</u> the lifetime of <u>some other person</u>.

   b. The individual who receives the estate is called the <u>life tenant</u>. When the life tenant dies, the life estate ends.

   c. <u>Pur autre vie</u> is a life estate based on the lifetime of someone other than the life tenant. When that person dies, the life estate ends.

   d. <u>When a life estate ends, it becomes a fee simple absolute estate</u> and goes to

      i. the party holding the <u>reversionary interest</u> (normally, the original grantor who created the life estate); or

      ii. the <u>remainderman</u>, the party holding the <u>remainder</u> interest (someone designated by the original grantor to receive ownership upon the death of the life tenant or the measuring life).

C. Bundle of rights

1. <u>Real property includes the legal rights of ownership</u> attached to a parcel of real estate, known as the bundle of rights.

2. These include the rights to

   a. <u>possess</u> the property,

   b. <u>control</u> the use of the property,

   c. <u>enjoy</u> using the property in any legal manner,

   d. <u>exclude</u> others from using the property,

   e. <u>improve</u> the property,

   f. <u>encumber</u> the property,

   g. <u>sell</u> the property,

h.   <u>lease</u> the property, and

i.   <u>transfer ownership of the property</u>.

II.   LEASEHOLD ESTATES

A.   Definition

1.   A <u>leasehold estate</u> is <u>an interest</u> in real estate <u>that allows a tenant to possess the property for a fixed time period</u>.

   a.   It lasts for a <u>definite duration</u> and <u>can be terminated</u>.

   b.   The <u>tenant</u> is the <u>lessee</u> and the <u>landlord</u> is the <u>lessor</u>.

B.   Estate for years and from period to period (periodic estate)

1.   An <u>estate for years</u> is a leasehold estate that <u>lasts for a definite time period</u>; that period may be years, months, weeks, or even days. It's a lease arrangement between the owner (lessor) and the tenant (lessee) that has a <u>definite beginning and ending date</u>.

2.   A <u>periodic estate</u> has no specific expiration date. Rent is payable at intervals defined in the lease agreement.

   a.   It <u>automatically renews upon receipt of payment</u>.

   b.   It is commonly known as <u>month-to-month</u> in residential leases.

   c.   It sometimes becomes a <u>holdover tenancy</u> when a tenant with an estate for years remains in possession after the expiration date, and the landlord accepts rent payments (<u>the tenant remains in possession with the landlord's consent</u>).

   d.   It <u>ends upon notice</u> from either the owner or the tenant.

3.   In both an estate for years and a periodic estate, a <u>purchaser gets possession "subject to the lease"</u> with the tenant retaining possession until the lease expires.

C.   Estate at will and estate at sufferance

1.   An <u>estate at will</u> has <u>no specific initial term</u>, and it continues until it's terminated by either the landlord or the tenant with proper notice.

2.   An <u>estate at sufferance</u> is created when the <u>tenant retains possession of the property after the termination of the lawful and permissive time period without the landlord's consent</u>.

   a.   The <u>landlord</u> can treat the tenant as a trespasser and <u>begin eviction</u> proceedings according to state laws.

   b.   If the landlord accepts any payment from a tenant at sufferance, a <u>holdover tenancy</u> is created.

III.   **SOLE VS. CO-OWNERSHIP/MULTIPLE OWNERSHIP**

   A. <u>**Tenants in common—co-ownership with no rights of survivorship among the co-owners**</u>

      1. <u>Each co-owner holds an undivided fractional interest</u> in the property (the ownership is divided, not the property).

      2. The <u>co-owners</u>, each of which is a <u>tenant in common</u>, <u>enjoy unity of possession</u>, which is their <u>right to occupy the entire property</u>.

      3. Each co-owner's <u>interests can be sold, conveyed, mortgaged, or transferred independent of the other co-owner(s)</u>.

      4. Because there is <u>no right of survivorship</u> among the co-owners, <u>each co-owner's interest passes to their heirs or devisees when the co-owner dies</u>.

      5. This <u>allows for unequal shares of ownership</u>, but must be specifically stated in the deed.

      6. All co-owners are responsible for the real estate taxes and special assessments.

      7. <u>Default type of ownership</u>:

         a. If no form of ownership is stated in the deed, the law presumes the owners are tenants in common.

   B. <u>**Joint tenancy—co-ownership with the rights of survivorship among the co-owners**</u>

      1. In a joint tenancy, co-owners enjoy four unities of title (PITT) in some states.

         a. Unity of <u>possession</u>—all joint tenants (co-owners) have an undivided right to possess the entire property.

         b. Unity of <u>interest</u>—all joint tenants have <u>equal</u> interests in the property.

         c. Unity of <u>time</u>—all joint tenants acquire their interests at the same time.

         d. Unity of <u>title</u>—title is conveyed to all joint tenants by the same document.

      2. Co-owners enjoy the <u>right of survivorship among them</u>.

         a. The <u>interests of any deceased co-owner pass to the other co-owner(s) upon death without going through probate</u>.

         b. This <u>overrides a will</u>.

      3. A joint tenancy is terminated upon the death of all but one co-owner, who then will become the sole owner of the property and have an estate in severalty.

         a. Joint tenancies can also be terminated as a result of a <u>partition suit</u>, which is a <u>court action forcing the division or sale of the property</u>.

C. Tenancy by the entirety

    1. This is a form of joint tenancy applying only to married couples in some states.

        a. The spouses own the entire property together as a unit and have the right of survivorship between them.

        b. This form of ownership protects the property from debts contracted outside the marriage.

D. <u>Common-interest ownership properties</u>—condominiums, townhomes, and time-shares

    1. <u>Condominiums and townhomes</u>

        a. A form of real estate, portions of which are designated for separate ownership (units), and the remainder of which—including the physical structure(s)—is designated for common ownership and use among all the unit owners.

        b. Owners purchase and finance their own units.

        c. Units are transferred with a deed.

        d. Each unit, along with its percentage share of common elements, is taxed as a separate parcel.

        e. All condominiums and town homes comprise <u>four basic components</u>:

            i. The <u>units</u> are owned by individual owner(s) holding <u>fee simple title</u> to the <u>interior</u> of a unit.

                ■ Owners finance their own units and a default does not affect other units or the association.

                ■ Ownership interests are transferred with a deed.

            ii. The <u>common elements</u> include the <u>remainder of the building(s) and the land</u> (e.g., hallways, elevators, recreational areas such as a pool or an exercise facility, parking lot).

                ■ All <u>common elements are owned by all current unit owners as tenants in common with one another</u>.

                ■ Unit owners may not partition any common area.

            iii. The <u>limited common elements</u> are <u>common elements reserved for the exclusive use by one or more unit owners</u> to the exclusion of all other unit owners (e.g., balcony, storage unit, or an assigned parking space).

            iv. An <u>association</u> that governs:

                ■ May <u>charge fees (a.k.a. monthly dues) one each unit owner to pay for the maintenance of the common elements, and assessments to pay for extraordinary expenses</u>.

                ■ <u>May hire an outside property management firm to administer the property</u>.

                ■ May have a right of first refusal when a unit owner decides to sell.

        f. The <u>Uniform Condominium Act (UCA)</u>, defines how condominiums are created and owned. It has been adopted by many states, however, <u>each state creates its own condominium laws</u>.

2. <u>Time-shares</u>

    a. Time-shares are a form of common-interest ownership in which <u>multiple owners have a possessory interest in a property for a certain time period each year.</u>

    b. Most commonly used for <u>resort-type properties</u>

3. Cooperatives (co-ops)

    a. In a <u>cooperative</u>, a <u>corporation owns the land and building</u>, and it <u>leases space to a shareholder who owns stock</u> in the corporation.

    b. The <u>corporation sells shares of stock to prospective tenants.</u>

        i. The <u>purchaser</u> of stock <u>becomes a shareholder</u> in the corporation and <u>receives a proprietary lease</u> to a specific space (usually an apartment) for the life of the corporation.

            ■ Because there is <u>no ownership of the space</u>, the <u>buyer does not receive a deed.</u>

            ■ The stock is <u>personal property</u>, not real property; it does not establish a real property interest. In other words, <u>the buyer does not own any real estate.</u>

        ii. Shareholders elect <u>officers and directors</u> who are responsible for operating the cooperative according to the corporation's bylaws.

        iii. Funds for the budget are <u>assessed</u> to individual shareholders, generally in the form of <u>monthly fees or dues.</u>

        iv. A <u>lender</u> may accept <u>stock</u> as collateral for financing, expanding the pool of potential owners.

        v. The cooperative may have a <u>right of first refusal</u> when a unit owner wants to sell.

        vi. Note: The <u>IRS</u> treats cooperatives the same as houses and condominiums with respect to <u>deductibility</u> of loan interest, property taxes, and homesellers' tax exclusions.

E. Ownership in <u>severalty/sole ownership</u>

1. <u>When a single party</u>, either an individual or an entity (e.g., company, corporation, partnership, LLC) <u>holds title to real estate</u>, that ownership is known as <u>ownership in severalty</u>. (The root word of severalty is *sever*, meaning other parties' interests are "severed" from those of the owner.)

2. Ownership in severalty involves the following:

    a. <u>Sole rights</u> to ownership

    b. <u>Sole discretion to transfer</u> all or part of all ownership rights to another party or parties

3. Partnerships take title in severalty:

    a. General partnership—all partners share equal profits, liability

    b. Limited partnership—<u>limited partners are responsible only for the amount they invested</u>, so their liability equals amount invested

UNIT 2 REVIEW QUESTIONS

True/False Questions

1. A fee simple defeasible estate is an example of a freehold estate of ownership that can be inherited from the owner and might last forever.
   A. True
   B. False

2. The fee simple defeasible estate is an estate of ownership without conditions.
   A. True
   B. False

3. A life tenant under a life estate is a lessee.
   A. True
   B. False

4. A lessee holds a leased fee estate.
   A. True
   B. False

5. An estate for years must be for multiple years.
   A. True
   B. False

6. Under the common law, an estate at will could be terminated at any time by either party.
   A. True
   B. False

7. The term *severalty* refers to one parcel being owned by several people or entities.
   A. True
   B. False

8. There are four unities in a joint tenancy: possession, interest, time, and title.
   A. True
   B. False

9. Unmarried couples can own property as tenants by the entirety.
   A. True
   B. False

10. *Fractional, but undivided interests* means that concurrent owners have equal rights of possession.
    A. True
    B. False

Multiple-Choice Questions

1. What type of estate exists when a tenant continues to occupy an apartment without the consent of the landlord after the lease has expired?
   A. A canceled leasehold
   B. A remainder estate
   C. An estate at sufferance
   D. A hostile estate

2. Which of these is an example of an inheritable freehold estate that might last forever?
   A. Leasehold estate
   B. Periodic estate
   C. Estate at will
   D. Fee simple defeasible estate

3. What type of a leasehold exists if a tenant without a lease sends the landlord monthly rent checks and the landlord continues to accept them?
   A. Estate for years
   B. Estate from period to period
   C. Estate will
   D. Estate at sufferance

4. A lessor and lessee entered into a rental agreement. Both agreed that the tenancy would end when either decided to terminate it. Both also agreed that no notice would be required to terminate the tenancy. Which of these BEST describes this form of less-than-freehold estate?
   A. Tenancy for years
   B. Periodic tenancy
   C. Tenancy at will
   D. Tenancy at sufferance

5. Which of these owns a parcel of real estate in severalty?
    A. One married couple
    B. One divorced couple
    C. One multinational corporation
    D. One pair of identical twin siblings

6. Person A, Person B, and Person C are co-owners of property. When Person C dies testate, the property is probated, and Person A and Person B acquire Person C's one-third interest in the property as devisees. How do Person A and Person B own the property?
    A. Joint tenancy
    B. Tenancy in common
    C. Severalty
    D. In trust

UNIT 3

Transfer of Title

LEARNING OBJECTIVE

When you have completed this unit, you will be able to accomplish the following.

› Explain the essential elements of a deed, the types used, how property is transferred, and how to record the title to real estate.

I.   ESSENTIAL ELEMENTS OF A VALID DEED

A.   A <u>deed</u> is the <u>written instrument by which an owner of real estate voluntarily conveys rights, title, and/or interests in parcel of real estate to another party</u>.

1.   The <u>statute of frauds</u> requires that all deeds be <u>in writing</u>.

2.   In a deed, the <u>grantor</u> is the <u>owner</u> who transfers the title; the <u>grantee</u> is <u>the party who acquires the title</u>.

3.   A <u>valid deed</u> must include the following elements:

   a.   The <u>grantor</u> must be <u>legally competent</u> to convey title.

      i.   <u>Mental impairment</u> at time of signing makes the deed <u>voidable</u>.

      ii.   A deed signed by a <u>minor</u> is <u>voidable</u>.

      iii.   If a grantor is declared <u>incompetent</u> by a judge, the deed is <u>void</u>.

      iv.   The deed should include <u>all names</u> used by the grantor.

23

b. It must include <u>an identifiable grantee</u> named in the deed with reasonable certainty of their identity.

c. There must be <u>consideration</u>, which is <u>anything of value</u>, and a clause acknowledging that the grantor has received consideration.

d.   It must include a <u>granting clause</u> stating the grantor's intention to convey the property.

  i. With the <u>habendum clause</u>, *habendum* means to have and to hold. The clause begins with the words *to have and to hold*, which identifies the type of estate being conveyed to the grantee.

  ■ *To have and to fold forever* indicates a fee simple absolute estate is being conveyed.

  ■ *To have and to hold for as long as you live* indicates a life estate is being conveyed.

  ■ *To have and to hold as long as the following conditions are met* indicates a fee simple defeasible estate is being conveyed.

e. There must be an accurate <u>legal description</u> of the property being conveyed.

f. It must include a signature of all grantors conveying title, which must be acknowledged (some states also required witnesses).

g. There must be <u>delivery of the deed and acceptance</u> by the grantee.

  i. Title and possession typically pass to the grantee upon acceptance of the deed.

h. When the deed has been delivered to an agent of the grantor, such as a settlement or escrow officer, delivery is completed when the deed is <u>given to the agent</u>.

i. While it is customary to record deeds, they do not need to be recorded to be valid between the parties.

II.   TYPES OF DEEDS

A. General warranty deed

1. A <u>general warranty deed</u> provides the <u>greatest protection to the grantee</u> in the transfer of real property, and <u>includes</u> the following <u>five covenants (promises)</u> made by the grantor:

a. Covenant of <u>seisin</u>—grantor promises they <u>own the property and has the right to convey</u> title

b. Covenant <u>against encumbrances</u>—grantor promises there are no <u>encumbrances</u> or <u>liens</u> affecting title to the property <u>other than those on the property's public records</u>, unless expressly stated otherwise

c. Covenant of <u>quiet enjoyment</u>—grantor promises that <u>no other party has a legal ownership interest in the property</u>

d. Covenant of <u>further assurance</u>—the grantor's promise to obtain any other document(s) necessary to convey good title

e. Covenant of <u>warranty forever</u>—the grantor's promise to compensate <u>the grantee if title fails at any future time</u>

2.   In a general warranty deed, the grantor promises to defend the title against any claim arising from the time the grantor owned the property, as well as during the time all previous parties owned the property.

B.   Special/limited warranty deed

1.   This deed warrants only against title defects that occurred during the grantor's period of ownership, and makes NO promises regarding any claims that occurred BEFORE the grantor(s) initially took title.

C.   Bargain and sale deed

1.   This deed implies that the grantor holds title and possession of the property, but there are no express warranties against encumbrances.

D.   Quitclaim deed

1.   A quitclaim deed provides the least protection of any deed, carries no covenants or warranties (no promises), and conveys whatever interest the grantor has when the deed is delivered.

E.   Deed of trust

1.   A deed of trust is used in some states as a security instrument instead of a mortgage.

2.   A trustee holds title to the property for the beneficiary until the loan is paid.

F.   Reconveyance deed

1.   Once a buyer pays off a loan secured with a deed of trust, a trustee uses a reconveyance deed to convey legal title to the buyer.

G.   Trustee's deed

1.   This deed is used when a trustee conveys ownership to a property held in trust.

H.   Deed executed pursuant to a court order

1.   These deeds are established by state statute and used to convey title to property that is transferred by a court order or a will:

   a.   Examples: executor's deeds, administrator's deeds, sheriff's deeds

III.   TITLE TRANSFER

■   Private parties transfer title to other private parties using a deed.

■   Government transfers ownership to private parties using a land patent.

■   Private parties transfer ownership to government using a dedication.

Unit 3

A. Definitions

1. Title is ownership or the rights of ownership of land and evidence of that ownership.

2. Alienation is the act of transferring title. When a grantor transfers title to another party, it's said that the grantor is "alienating" themselves from their interests in the property and transferring them to another party.

B. Types of transfers

1. Voluntary alienation

   a. Voluntary alienation is the voluntary transfer of real property.

   b. To transfer real property during one's lifetime, the owner must use some form of deed for conveyance.

   c. Types of voluntary alienation include the following:

      i. Transfer of title by will occurs when someone dies testate, which means they had a valid will.

         ■ A will takes effect only after death of the property owner.

         ■ A gift of real property by will is called a devise. A gift of personal property is called a bequest. In a will, a person "devises" real property, and "bequeaths" personal property.

         ■ A will must be filed with the court and probated for title to pass upon the death of the property owner. Wills cannot supersede any state laws protecting the inheritance rights of a surviving spouse (dower or curtesy) or benefits granted by homestead laws.

            – Probate is the process of distributing all of a deceased person's assets.

            – A will must go through probate for both real and personal property to transfer.

      ii. When a person dies intestate (without leaving a valid will), a probate transfer of title occurs according to a state's statute of descent and distribution. The property distribution is governed by the laws of the state where the real property is located.

2. Involuntary alienation

   a. Involuntary alienation is the transfer of real property interests without the owner's consent.

   b. Forms of involuntary alienation include the following:

      i. Escheat—property is taken by the state when an owner dies intestate with no heirs capable of inheriting the property or the property is abandoned.

      ii. Eminent domain—property is taken for public good or use by a government agency.

      iii. Foreclosure—property is taken by a creditor for nonpayment of debt secured by real property.

    iv. <u>Adverse possession</u>—this is <u>title granted by the court</u> to a party who possesses the property in an <u>open, continuous, exclusive, actual, and notorious/hostile (meaning without the owner's consent)</u> manner for a minimum statutory period of time as set by state law.

        ■ **Memory aid OCEAN: possession must be Open (visible), Continuous, Exclusive (distinct), Actual, and Notorious (hostile)**

    v. <u>Easement by prescription</u>—this is an easement <u>prescribed by the court</u> due to open, continuous, actual, and notorious/hostile USE of a portion of another party's property for a minimum statutory period of time as set by state law.

    vi. <u>If all parties recognize, accept, and permit the possession or use of the property, it cannot be adverse possession or become an easement by prescription.</u>

IV. RECORDING THE TITLE

A. <u>Recording</u>

1. This is the <u>act of placing a document into the public record</u>.

    a. The specific rules for recording are governed by state laws.

    b. The records are held in the county (or sometimes the city) in which the property is located.

2. The public records are <u>critical in establishing ownership, giving notice of encumbrances, and establishing priority of liens</u>.

    a. The order in which interests (e.g., liens) are recorded may determine the <u>priority of interests</u> in the property (<u>first in time, first in right</u>).

3. <u>State laws</u> govern specific recording processes, and generally include the following:

    a. Recorded deeds and mortgages <u>must be executed (signed)</u> by the grantors and mortgagors.

    b. Documents <u>must be dated</u>.

    c. Signatures <u>must be notarized</u>.

        i. There must be legal acknowledgment that the signatures are <u>genuine and not made under duress</u>.

4. Recording is generally not required for validity.

B. <u>Constructive notice</u>

1. Properly recording documents in the public record serves as <u>constructive notice</u> to the world of an individual's rights or interest.

2. Constructive notice is the <u>legal presumption that information about a property may be obtained by anyone through diligent inquiry</u>, and the entire world knows.

3. A <u>deed that is not recorded</u> creates the risk that a later interest could take priority because the deed <u>does not have constructive notice of ownership</u>.

Unit 3

C. Actual notice

1. Also known as <u>direct knowledge</u>, *actual notice* means a <u>party has searched the public records and inspected the property</u> and thereby has direct and actual knowledge of the property and its characteristics.

V.   TITLE INSURANCE

A. What is title insurance a.k.a. title insurance policy?

1. It is a contract under which the <u>policyholder (buyer) is protected from losses arising from defects in the title</u>.

2. It protects the policyholder (buyer) from events occurring <u>before the policy is issued</u>.

B. What is insured?

1. A <u>title insurance policy</u> determines if the title is insurable based on a review of the public records. The company will defend any lawsuit based on an insurable defect and pay claims if the title proves to be defective.

2. A <u>standard coverage</u> policy <u>insures the title as it is known in the public records. It also insures against hidden defects</u> such as forged documents, conveyances by incompetent grantors, incorrect marital statements, and improperly prepared and delivered deeds.

3. An <u>extended coverage</u> policy protects the policyholder against all defects covered by a standard policy, <u>plus defects that may be discovered by an actual inspection of the property</u> (like the rights of parties in possession [tenants], <u>examination of the survey</u> [which would reveal any encroachments], <u>and certain unrecorded liens</u>).

4. A <u>lender's/mortgagee's policy</u> is issued for the benefit of the lending institution for the amount of the mortgage loan, and it is normally paid by the buyer.

5. An <u>owner's policy</u> is issued for the benefit of the <u>owner (new buyer) and the owner's heirs or devisees</u> for as long as they have an ownership interest in the property.

6. Title insurance <u>premiums are only paid once</u> at closing.

7. <u>A broker who is</u> a partner or otherwise <u>affiliated with a title insurance company may refer someone</u> to that title insurance company, but <u>only after written disclosure of the broker's relationship</u> to the title insurance company has been made.

C. Chain of title, title search, abstract of title

1. The <u>chain of title</u> is the <u>record of a property's ownership</u>.

2. A <u>title search</u> is an <u>examination of all the public records to determine whether any defects exist in the chain of title</u>. The search involves <u>tracing the ownership backward</u> to its origin, or for a specific number of years as defined by state law.

   a. If a title search reveals any <u>liens or judgments</u> attached to a property, these <u>must be cleared up before a property is transferred</u>.

3. An <u>abstract of title</u> is an <u>historical summary of all conveyances and encumbrances that have ever been recorded on a property</u>.

a. Prepared by an abstractor, it includes all recorded liens and encumbrances and lists the records searched.

b. It does not indicate forgeries and interests that are unrecorded, or that could be discovered by an actual property inspection.

D. Marketable title

1. <u>Marketable title</u> is title to real property that

    a. <u>does not have serious defects or doubtful questions</u> of law or fact to prove its validity,

        i. Such defects and questions are <u>often referred to as "clouds" on title</u>

            ■ For instance, if ownership cannot be traced through an <u>unbroken chain</u>, there is a <u>gap in the title</u>.

            ■ Other examples of "clouds" include any encumbrance, claim, document, unreleased lien, or other matter that <u>may impair title</u> to a property <u>or cast doubt</u> on the title's validity.

    b. does not expose the purchaser to litigation or threaten quiet enjoyment of the property, and

    c. can convince a reasonably well-informed and prudent purchaser that the property could be sold or mortgaged at a later time.

2. Every buyer's goal is to obtain marketable title when they close on their property purchase and is generally required by lenders.

E. Quiet title action

1. It is sometimes necessary for the courts to resolve title issues ("clouds") found in the abstract or in a title report.

2. A quiet title suit is a <u>legal action (lawsuit) to clear title problems</u>.

UNIT 3 REVIEW QUESTIONS

True/False Questions

1. A valid deed can be verbal, provided it is a conveyance between family members.
   A. True
   B. False

2. A valid deed must be signed by the grantor.
   A. True
   B. False

3. A special warranty deed warrants title even before the grantor acquired ownership.
   A. True
   B. False

4. A quitclaim deed contains several warranties that the grantor makes to the grantee.
   A. True
   B. False

5. For title to transfer, the deed must be delivered by the grantee to the grantor.
   A. True
   B. False

6. Title transfers when a valid deed is filed for the record.
   A. True
   B. False

7. The general rule that says, "First in time, without notice, is first in right" means that recording first, without actual notice of someone else's paramount priority, is the way to achieve lien priority.
   A. True
   B. False

8. A lender's policy of title insurance protects both the lender and the borrower from defects of title.
   A. True
   B. False

9. Title insurance premiums are paid once each year.
   A. True
   B. False

10. A mortgagee's policy of title insurance also protects the buyer.
    A. True
    B. False

11. A lender's policy of title insurance expires when the loan is paid in full, while an owner's policy of title insurance remains valid while the owner owns the property.
    A. True
    B. False

Multiple-Choice Questions

1. To have a valid deed, all of these are required EXCEPT
   A. legal capacity to execute.
   B. written deed.
   C. proof of heirship.
   D. words of conveyance.

2. A buyer purchased a property and accepted a quitclaim deed. The buyer can be certain that
   A. the seller had a good title to the property.
   B. whatever the seller's interest currently may be, it is being transferred.
   C. the seller will convey after-acquired title.
   D. there are no liens against the property that adversely affect marketable title.

3. A seller and buyer entered into a purchase contract for the sale of a single-family residence. The seller executed a deed and gave it to the settlement officer. The seller died before the closing. Which of these is correct?
   A. Because the seller died before the closing, there was no delivery of the deed.
   B. Delivery must always occur while the grantor is living.
   C. Delivery occurred at the time the seller and buyer entered into the purchase contract.
   D. Delivery was effective when the deed was given to the settlement officer.

4. Normally, the priority of general liens is determined by
   A. the order in which they are filed or recorded.
   B. the order in which the cause of action arose.
   C. the size of the claim.
   D. the clerk of the court.

5. A borrower purchased mortgagee's title insurance on a property. After the final payment was made on the mortgage, a title defect was found. The borrower may have recourse through
   A. the previous owner, if a general warranty deed was transferred at the closing.
   B. the previous owner, if a quitclaim deed was transferred at the closing.
   C. the title insurance company, because a title policy was secured when the property was purchased.
   D. the title insurance company, because a mortgagee's title insurance was secured when the property was purchased.

UNIT 4

Land-Use Controls and Regulations

LEARNING OBJECTIVE

When you have completed this unit, you will be able to accomplish the following.

› Discuss the types of public and private land-use controls that affect the ownership and use of real property.

I.   GOVERNMENTAL POWERS (RIGHTS IN LAND [PETE])/PUBLIC CONTROLS

A. Police power

1. The <u>police power</u> of the state is its <u>authority to create regulations to protect the public health, safety, and general welfare of its citizens</u>.

2. A state's police power is passed down to cities, municipalities, and other local governing authorities, each of which can

   a. <u>enact and enforce laws governing land use</u>, which are <u>public controls</u> on land.

      i.   Examples include zoning, building codes, and comprehensive/master planning safety codes.

      ii. They are enforced by requiring things like building permits, building inspections, and certificates of occupancy.

B. <u>Eminent domain</u>

1. This is the <u>right of government to "take" (acquire) privately owned real estate for public use</u>.

2. <u>Condemnation</u> is the <u>process</u> by which the property is acquired.

3. The property owner must be paid fair compensation for the value of the property, plus damages if the property is used to produce income (e.g., farmland).

4. A property owner may claim compensation under <u>inverse condemnation</u>, if <u>an adjacent public land use negatively affects the value of the owner's property</u>, even when the owner's own property has not been condemned for public use.

C. <u>Assess and collect property taxes and special assessments</u>

1. <u>Property taxes</u> are <u>ad valorem</u> taxes, meaning they're based on the <u>assessed value</u> of the property, not on the current market value.

   a. County or township tax assessors or appraisers conduct periodic (often yearly) assessments (valuations).

   b. <u>Property owners</u> who believe the assessment is incorrect <u>may appeal to an assessor's appeal board</u>.

2. The <u>tax rate may be expressed as a mill rate</u> (one mill is 1/1,000th of a dollar, or $0.001), as a percentage rate, or as a decimal.

3. <u>Special assessments</u> are <u>charges against specific benefitting properties to fund public improvements</u> (e.g., new streets and sidewalks).

   a. <u>Pending special assessments</u> are improvements that have been <u>approved, but the work has not yet begun</u>.

   b. <u>Levied special assessments</u> are improvements that have been <u>completed, and the lien has been placed on the property</u>.

      i. These liens are <u>statutory</u> (by law) <u>specific</u> (attach to specific properties) <u>liens</u>.

   c. Special assessments are usually paid in annual installments over a period of time.

      i. They are paid at the same time property taxes are paid.

   d. They are normally levied by local governments (cities and counties).

   e. Reading the assessment roll will tell if there is a special assessment lien on a property.

4. Remember—Property taxes and special assessments are both statutory specific liens. They take priority over all other liens.

D. <u>Escheat</u>

1. This is government's <u>reversionary right</u>.

   a. Because all land was first owned by the government, <u>when there is no party to take ownership of real property, it "reverts" to the government</u> through its right of escheat.

i. Here are examples:

- Abandoned property

- Property owned by someone who died intestate with no heirs

II. ZONING

A. Local governments have the authority to create a <u>master, or comprehensive, plan</u>.

  1. It is used to <u>control growth</u>.

    a. It normally covers land use, housing needs, the movement of people and goods, community facilities and utilities, and energy conservation.

  2. To implement and enforce the master plan, local governments enact zoning laws and ordinances covering items such as permitted uses of land, lot sizes, types of structures, building heights, setback distances, the style and appearance of structures, structural density, and the protection of natural resources.

B. <u>Zoning classifies property by uses and types, such as residential, commercial, industrial/ manufacturing, agricultural, or mixed</u>.

  1. Special land types can include floodplains, coastal preservation, and other special-use classifications that can be regulated at a local, state, or federal level.

  2. These can also specify certain types of architecture for new buildings and require certain uses in new developments.

  3. Rezoning, or an amendment, is a zoning change for an entire area.

C. <u>Buffer zones</u> are <u>areas of land</u> (like a park or a four-lane road) <u>that separate two drastically different land-use zones</u>.

D. <u>Nonconforming use</u> allows an owner to <u>continue the present use of a property that no longer complies with current zoning</u>.

  1. This is sometimes referred to as being "grandfathered in."

  2. For example, a retail store surrounded by residential property would have been grandfathered in when the zoning changed from commercial to residential.

  3. The owner typically can't expand or rebuild a nonconforming use if the improvements on the property are destroyed.

E. <u>Setbacks</u>—front, side, and rear setbacks <u>restrict and limit the location of improvements</u> in relation to the boundaries of the property.

F. A <u>variance</u> allows an individual owner to <u>"vary" or deviate to prevent an economic hardship</u>. **Variances are most commonly used when an owner wants to vary from building codes or build into a setback.**

G. A <u>special/conditional use permit</u> (sometimes referred to as a special exception) is a <u>permitted exception</u> to the zoning ordinance, which is <u>given to the property owner and does not automatically transfer when the property is sold.</u>

    1. An <u>example</u> would be a <u>day care located in a residentially zoned neighborhood</u>.

        a. It allows a property owner to deviate from zoning regulations, but not from deed restrictions (private controls on property) or building codes.

        b. Buyers who want to purchase such a property and continue its use, or who are not sure if a particular use is allowed, should always check with the local zoning department before buying.

H. Governments enforce zoning laws and ordinances by <u>issuing permits</u>.

I. Individual cases for exceptions to zoning are considered by a zoning hearing board (or zoning board of appeals) that has the authority to, among other things,

    1. allow a nonconforming use to continue,

    2. grant a variance, and

    3. grant a special/conditional use permit.

J. <u>Any special-use zoning *must be disclosed* to buyers.</u>

    1. Examples include a property that is located in a special tax district, or is in an airport flight path.

K. Building codes

    1. <u>Building codes</u> specify <u>construction standards</u> required when erecting or repairing buildings.

        a. They <u>deal with structural integrity and safety</u> for a building.

            i. Examples include the minimum number of bathrooms per square foot in a commercial building.

        b. They <u>determine the types of construction materials</u> that can be used.

            i. There are standards for <u>types</u> of materials and <u>how</u> they are used.

            ii. There are separate codes for plumbing, electrical, fire, and so forth.

    2. Local jurisdictions require and issue <u>building permits</u> for new construction and remodeling of homes and buildings.

    3. Local municipalities or governments often require periodic inspections of construction work after some specific work has been completed (such as electrical or plumbing construction).

4. A <u>certificate of occupancy</u> is issued after the <u>completion</u> of the work for which the building permit was issued.

    a. This <u>confirms that the building meets minimum required standards</u>.

III.   REGULATION OF SPECIAL LAND TYPES

A.   Floodplains/flood zones

1. These are flat portions of land located along rivers, streams, or other waterways that may be prone to flooding.

2. Flood insurance policies may be required by lenders for homes or structures constructed in flood-prone areas.

    a. <u>Flood insurance is separate from homeowners (hazard) insurance</u>.

3. The <u>Federal Emergency Management Agency (FEMA)</u> administers the flood program.

B.   <u>Wetlands</u>

1. Wetlands are ponds, swamps, estuaries, and marshes where the groundwater is at or near the surface of the land, creating a wetland plant community.

2. These areas are <u>subject to federal, state, and local controls</u> because they are susceptible to flooding. These controls include <u>environmental protection</u> and <u>zoning</u> that ensures special preservation and conservation of wetland areas.

IV.   ENVIRONMENTAL HAZARDS—<u>REGULATED BY THE EPA (ENVIRONMENTAL PROTECTION AGENCY)</u>

■ All known <u>environmental issues may impact value</u>, and they <u>must be disclosed</u> by a seller and the broker or salesperson.

A.   Types of hazards/hazardous substances

1. <u>Lead-based paint</u>

    a. Lead-based paint could be used in <u>housing built before 1978</u>.

    b. It requires <u>disclosure</u> of known lead-based paint hazards <u>to potential buyers and renters</u> (Lead-Based Paint Hazard Reduction Act of 1992).

        i. <u>Sellers and landlords of homes built before January 1, 1978</u> must give a copy of the EPA pamphlet *Protect Your Family From Lead in Your Home* to potential buyers and renters <u>before accepting an offer to buy or rent</u>.

        ii. <u>Buyers</u> have a <u>10-day</u> opportunity to have the home tested after receiving the disclosure, and they <u>may waive their right to have an inspection</u>.

        iii. <u>The seller is not required to do a lead inspection or removal</u>, but is required to disclose the locations of any known lead-based paint.

   c.   Brokers are responsible for making sure the disclosures are made.

   d.   Lead is not typically found in wall insulation, but it can be in paint, pipes, and soils.

2. Asbestos—a mineral used in building materials that can cause respiratory disease, the worst of which is mesothelioma

   a.   It was used for its fireproofing and insulating qualities.

   b.   It becomes a health hazard when it breaks down into microscopic fibers (friable) and inhaled.

   c.   It was banned for use in insulation as of 1978.

   d.   In buildings being demolished or renovated.

      i.   Abatement (removal) is often required and needs to be done by a licensed professional.

      ii. Encapsulation (sealing in place) is sometimes a better choice than removal because it prevents the fibers from becoming airborne and inhaled.

3. Radon—an odorless, tasteless radioactive gas created by the decay of Uranium 238 and occurs naturally in the ground

   a.   It is suspected of causing lung cancer.

   b.   It can enter homes through cracks in the basement floors.

   c.   It is typically mitigated by sealing cracks and adding a ventilation system to move the gas outside the home.

   d.   It is relatively inexpensive to detect and mitigate.

      i.   Testing is not a federal requirement, but may be required by local jurisdictions.

      ii. In most states, brokers must disclose known radon problems.

4. Carbon monoxide (CO)—an odorless gas that's the byproduct of combustion

   a.   It can lead to death.

   b.   If combustible appliances, furnaces, and wood stoves are working properly and have proper ventilation, CO is not an issue.

   c.   Many states mandate that properties have CO detectors.

5. Mold

   a.   Toxic mold is created by excess moisture.

   b.   Not all molds are hazardous. Mold is present in the air, and all molds require moisture to grow.

      i.   If a home has a mold problem, it has an excess moisture problem.

   c.   Some molds can cause serious health problems.

d.   If found in walls or other areas of a home, it may be considered toxic and would require <u>remediation</u>.

    i.   <u>Remediation</u> must be performed per EPA and individual state regulations.

e.   There is no federal disclosure law; however, some states require mold disclosures.

f.   All sellers must disclose if they know of a mold issue in their home.

g.   Licensees should be aware of indications of mold, like musty smells, indications of water damage, high inside humidity levels, and visible water leaks.

h.   Licensees should recommend a mold inspection if mold is visible or is suspected because of water/moisture problems with a property.

6. Groundwater, which is subject to contamination

a.   Any water source, other than a public supply, along with any septic system, should be tested before a property ownership transfer.

    i.   The federal <u>Safe Drinking Water Act</u> of 1974 (designed to help protect the nation's public water supply) <u>regulates the public drinking water supply</u>.

b.   <u>Underground storage tanks (USTs)</u>

    i.   When USTs containing <u>petroleum products or industrial chemicals</u> leak, this causes serious groundwater contamination.

        ■   USTs <u>are subject to both federal and state laws</u>.

        ■   The Leaking Underground Storage Tank (LUST) Trust Fund oversees cleanups of USTs by responsible parties and pays for cleanups when the owner is unwilling or unable to respond.

        ■   The <u>EPA</u> regulates the federal UST program.

7. Waste disposal sites

a.   These may be owned and/or operated by cities and other municipalities, or part of a commercial enterprise, or may simply be found on farms or other rural properties.

b.   They can be <u>excavated, or be a previously mined property</u>.

c.   Requirements:

    i.   They must be <u>lined</u> to prevent seepage.

    ii.   They must be <u>capped</u> with soil for aesthetic reasons.

    iii.   They must be <u>vented</u> to release gases created by decomposing waste.

8. <u>Brownfields</u>

a.   A brownfield is a <u>polluted industrial site</u> due to the presence or potential presence of hazardous substances or contaminants.

    i.   This creates problems in the expansion or redevelopment of a polluted property.

Unit 4

    b.   There was federal brownfields legislation from 2002:

        i.   It <u>encourages</u> the development of abandoned, contaminated properties.

        ii.   It <u>shields</u> innocent developers from liability for brownfield sites after purchase.

            ■   A <u>buyer's liability is limited by law</u>.

9.   Other environmental issues

    a.   Formaldehyde, chlorofluorocarbons (CFCs), electromagnetic fields, and methamphetamine labs all pose potential environmental problems.

B. Disclosure of hazards/hazardous substances

1.   States require <u>sellers</u> to <u>disclose</u> all known <u>material facts</u>, including environmental issues affecting a property with one to four dwelling units

2.   State laws also require real estate <u>licensees</u> to <u>disclose</u> any <u>known material facts</u>, including hazardous materials or conditions in a real estate transaction

3.   In some states, <u>licensees may be liable if they should have known of a condition</u>, even if the condition is not disclosed by seller

V.   REGULATION

    ■   Licensees are expected to be knowledgeable about their state's laws and regulations regarding environmental issues.

A. Clean air and water acts

1.   Most states have enacted legislation to ensure clean air, water

2.   A licensee must be knowledgeable about their state's or municipality's laws or regulations regarding environment

B. <u>Environmental Protection Agency (EPA)</u>

1.   This is the <u>federal agency</u> empowered to regulate and enforce federal clean air and water legislation

2.   Comprehensive Environmental Response, Compensation, and Liability Act (<u>CERCLA</u>)

    a.   Established a <u>Superfund</u> to clean <u>up uncontrolled hazardous waste and respond to hazardous waste spills</u>

    b.   <u>Identified responsible parties</u> and established that the <u>landowner is liable</u> for cleanup of the landowner's and other affected properties

3.   Superfund Amendments and Reauthorization Act (SARA)

    a.   Clarified the obligations of lenders who might become property owners through foreclosure

    b.   Established that innocent landowner immunities apply when pollution was caused by a third party, and the property was acquired after the fact

    c.   States that an <u>innocent landowner must have had no actual or constructive knowledge</u> of the damage, and exercised due care in the purchase of the property

C. <u>**Environmental impact statement (EIS)**</u> **and environmental site assessment**

    1. <u>EIS</u>—a report that assesses the probable <u>impact of a proposed federal project on the environment</u>

        a.   Required for all federal agencies on proposed projects

        b.   Must include a discussion of any direct or indirect impacts of the project on the environment, and an assessment of any feasible alternative to the proposed action

        c.   Because environmental issues can impact value, <u>the fact that an EIS is being done would have to be disclosed</u>, even if report hasn't been finalized

    2. <u>Environmental site assessments</u> (including Phase I and Phase II studies)

        a.   May be requested by a lender, developer, or buyer to show that due care was exercised in determining if any environmental impairments exist

        b.   Phase 1—<u>determines if any potential environmental problems exist</u> near or at a subject property that may cause an impairment to its purchase or use

        c.   Phase 2—may involve further testing and analysis of the seriousness of environmental <u>issues that may impose future financial liability</u> for the purchaser

    3. Wetlands protection

        a.   National Resources Conservation Service (NRCS) identifies wetlands on agricultural lands so farmers can rely on a single wetland determination

        b.   Federal, state, local governments have issued laws and regulations protecting wetlands

Unit 4

UNIT 4 REVIEW QUESTIONS

True/False Questions

1. Zoning is one aspect of the government's power of eminent domain.
   A. True
   B. False

2. An escheat occurs after an owner dies without a will and without heirs.
   A. True
   B. False

3. With both escheat and eminent domain, title to real estate ends up held by a governmental entity.
   A. True
   B. False

4. The four governmental powers over land are police power, escheat, taxation, and eminent domain.
   A. True
   B. False

5. Zoning laws are passed by the state.
   A. True
   B. False

6. All private deed restrictions on residential properties are now illegal in the United States.
   A. True
   B. False

7. Ad valorem taxes are based on the current market value of the property.
   A. True
   B. False

8. Some properties are exempt from real estate taxes.
   A. True
   B. False

9. A nonconforming use allows an owner to continue the present use of a property that no longer complies with current zoning.
   A. True
   B. False

10. Zoning codes specify construction standards required when erecting or repairing buildings.
    A. True
    B. False

11. Industrial properties referred to as brownfield sites are contaminated with environmental hazards.
    A. True
    B. False

12. The development of wetlands is strictly prohibited by both federal and state law.
    A. True
    B. False

13. An environmental hazard is one that occurs without any human intervention.
    A. True
    B. False

14. For target housing, both prospective tenants and prospective buyers must be given the opportunity to test for lead-based paint.
    A. True
    B. False

15. Asbestos poisoning may occur when the microscopic particles become airborne and are inhaled.
    A. True
    B. False

16. Radioactive radon gas is only created by human beings artificially in a laboratory.
    A. True
    B. False

17. A property owned by one family for over 78 years is shielded from the government's power of eminent domain.
    A. True
    B. False

18. The government's power of eminent domain is effectuated through a legal procedure known as condemnation.
    A. True
    B. False

19. A buffer zone is one way that a municipality can separate two drastically different types of land use.
    A. True
    B. False

Multiple-Choice Questions

1. All of these are governmental powers over land EXCEPT
   A. taxes.
   B. police power.
   C. eminent domain.
   D. condemnation.

2. Which of these types of privately owned real estate is shielded from the government's power of eminent domain?
   A. Agricultural property farmed by the same family for 105 years
   B. Residential property owned by the same family for 50 years
   C. Commercial property used for research and development of new antibiotics
   D. None of these

3. A city wishes to acquire some properties to widen a highway. It initiates legal proceedings to acquire the properties and begin construction. The city is exercising what type of government power?
   A. Police power
   B. Eminent domain
   C. Escheat
   D. Building codes

4. How does a local government's master plan and zoning work?
   A. The master plan eliminates the need for zoning ordinances.
   B. Master planning is a state level function while zoning is handled by local governments.
   C. The master plan is a summary of the of the zoning laws.
   D. Zoning ordinances are a primary way to implement the master plan.

5. In states that mandate the disclosure of material facts, which of these must be disclosed about a property placed on the market?
   A. Mortgage balance
   B. The asking price of other homes in the neighborhood
   C. That the property is in a floodplain zone
   D. Original cost of the property

6. Abandoned factories, former dry cleaner buildings, and vacant gas stations may contain environmental hazards that are classified as
   A. wetlands.
   B. brownfields.
   C. greenfield sites.
   D. beigefields.

7. Because the cost of cleanup and removal of hazardous waste can be greater than the value of the property, an agent is expected to have
   A. technical expertise in possible hazardous substances found within buildings.
   B. technical expertise in the area of asbestos, which is present in many buildings.
   C. taken a class on how to identify asbestos, because it is present in many buildings.
   D. basic knowledge of hazardous substances in a real estate transaction.

8. Construction on a single-family residence started before 1978. Which of these statements regarding lead-based paint (LBP) is correct?
   A. LBP warnings for this property are not legally required.
   B. The prospective buyer of the property must be given an opportunity to test for LBP.
   C. The prospective tenant of the property must be given an opportunity to test for LBP.
   D. If LBP is discovered, the seller is legally required to pay for its removal.

9. An owner seeks relief from zoning regulations on the grounds of nonconforming use. Effective arguments to the zoning authorities would include all of these EXCEPT
    A. that the nonconforming use existed before the passing of the zoning ordinance.
    B. that the property would generate more income if it were exempt from zoning.
    C. that the nonconforming use didn't harm the public's health, safety, and welfare.
    D. that conforming to the zoning ordinance would create an undue hardship.

10. Zoning ordinances and building codes are forms of local land use controls known as
    A. escheat.
    B. condemnation.
    C. preemptive rights.
    D. police powers.

UNIT 5

Agency Relationships

LEARNING OBJECTIVE

When you have completed this unit, you will be able to accomplish the following.

> Explain the various types of agency relationships and the duties owed by an agent to a client.

I.   AGENCY AND NONAGENCY RELATIONSHIPS AND LICENSEE-CLIENT RELATIONSHIPS

- Agency is the <u>relationship between a real estate licensee and the party the licensee represents</u> in a transaction.

A.   Types of agency relationships

1.   Agency relationship is <u>created when a party</u> (such as a seller, buyer, landlord or tenant) <u>hires a licensed real estate broker to represent them</u> in a real estate transaction

2.   How an agency relationship is created

a.   <u>Express agency</u> is <u>created through a formal written or oral/verbal agreement</u> between the parties.

   i.   A real estate agency relationship requires a real estate agency <u>contract</u> (real estate brokerage agreement) <u>that expresses the intentions of the parties to establish an agency relationship.</u>

   - It <u>defines the terms and conditions of the agency relationship.</u>

   - It authorizes the broker and the broker's agents to act for (<u>to represent</u>) the principal in a particular type of real estate transaction.

   - It may be called a real estate agency contract, a real estate agency agreement, a real estate brokerage agreement or contract, or simply an agency contract or agreement, depending on state law and practice.

       ii. Representation contracts should always be express contracts, preferably in writing, and are owned by the brokerage.

    b. <u>Implied agency is created through the unintentional, inadvertent, or accidental actions or behavior of the parties.</u>

B. Parties to an agency relationship

  1. Principal

    a. This is <u>the party who employs</u> another to represent them.

    b. The <u>principal</u> is referred to as an agent's <u>client</u>.

       i. The agent owes fiduciary duties to the principal who <u>employs</u> them.

          ■ This may or may <u>not</u> be the party who pays them.

  2. Agent/fiduciary

    a. This is the <u>party employed</u> to represent a principal.

       i. The <u>broker is always the agent</u>.

          ■ Licensed <u>salespersons</u> working for the broker represent the broker and <u>are not agents of the client</u>.

             – A salesperson signing a listing is <u>not</u> the seller's agent. The listing creates an agency agreement between the salesperson's broker and the seller.

          ■ <u>All licensees employed by the broker owe all clients of the broker the same obligations as the broker owes all clients.</u>

  3. Subagent

    a. This is an agent who represents another broker's client through the cooperation with, and the consent of, the representing broker. Due to brokers' memberships in multiple listing services, subagency has been changed to an offer of cooperation and sharing of compensation.

  4. <u>Facilitator/transaction broker—nonagency relationship</u>

    a. This is a real estate <u>licensee who provides services</u> to parties in a transaction without representing any party's interests. The <u>licensee is a nonagent</u> in the transaction and only <u>assists parties with the mechanics of a transaction</u> (i.e., <u>provides services without representing</u> any party).

       i. Facilitators/transaction brokers <u>cannot advocate</u> for anyone because they represent no one.

5. <u>Third party/customer—nonagency relationship</u>

   a. This is <u>a party who is not represented by the agent in a transaction.</u>

   b. <u>At first substantive contact</u> with a customer, <u>an agent must disclose they are not an agent of the customer and may share the customer's confidential information with their client.</u>

      i. Agents are required to share such information with their clients <u>because of agents' fiduciary duties.</u>

6. Note: <u>agents represent clients and work with customers</u>

   a. When representing the seller, the seller is a <u>client</u> and the buyer is a <u>customer.</u>

   b. When representing the buyer, the <u>buyer</u> is a <u>client</u> and the <u>seller</u> is a <u>customer.</u>

   c. When representing the landlord or owner, the <u>landlord or owner</u> is a <u>client</u> and the <u>tenant</u> is a <u>customer.</u>

   d. When representing the tenant, the <u>tenant</u> is a <u>client</u> and the <u>landlord or owner</u> is a <u>customer.</u>

C. Types of agency

1. <u>Special agency</u>

   a. This is created when an <u>agent is authorized to perform one particular act without the ability to legally bind the principal.</u>

      i. Examples:

         ■ <u>Broker is a special agent for a seller</u> in a listing agreement

            – Broker promises to find a ready, willing, and able buyer for the seller's property

         ■ <u>Broker is a special agent for a buyer</u> in a buyer representation agreement

            – Broker promises to find a suitable property for the buyer

2. <u>General agency</u>

   a. This is created when an <u>agent is authorized to perform a series of acts</u> associated with the continued operation of a particular business, <u>with limited authority to bind the principal.</u>

      i. Examples:

         ■ <u>Salespersons and broker associates are general agents of a broker</u>

         ■ <u>Property manager is a general agent of a property owner</u>

3. <u>Universal agency</u>

    a. This is created when an <u>agent is authorized to perform IN PLACE OF a principal</u>, empowering the agent to do anything the principal could do personally.

        i. This type of authority can only be <u>created by a general power of attorney</u>, which makes the agent <u>an attorney-in-fact</u>.

    b. A special power of attorney authorizes an agent to carry out <u>a specific act or acts</u> not authorized under an agency agreement.

D. Other brokerage relationships

1. Single agency and dual agency

    a. A <u>single agency</u>—when <u>one broker represents only one party</u> in a transaction

    b. A <u>dual agency</u>—when <u>one broker represents two principals</u> in the same transaction

        i. An inherent <u>conflict of interest</u> exists between the seller's and buyer's respective interests, and it <u>limits the level of fiduciary duties the broker can provide to both parties</u>.

           ■ Dual agency <u>must always be disclosed</u>.

           ■ To create a dual agency, <u>parties must give their consent in writing</u>.

        ii. A <u>designated</u> agent is a <u>salesperson authorized by the broker to act as the agent of a specific client of the broker</u> in a dual agency situation.

           ■ The broker remains a dual agent of both parties in the transaction.

        iii. <u>State laws determine if dual agency is permitted</u>.

II. THE AGENT'S DUTIES TO CLIENTS

A. Governed by

1. <u>Common law—established by tradition and court decisions</u>

    a. Most states define agency relationships by statutory law, but <u>you may see common law of agency</u> on the national test.

2. <u>Statutory law—specific real estate agency laws</u>, rules, and regulations enacted by state legislatures and other governing bodies

    a. Some state laws <u>replace</u> the concepts of common law with <u>state agency laws</u>.

    b. In states where the statutory law does not replace the common law, real estate brokers and agents are subject to both common law and the agency laws of that state.

3. Agency agreements—establish a <u>fiduciary relationship of trust and confidence</u> with the client and require broker to provide the client <u>six specific fiduciary duties (OLD CAR)</u>

4. Remember—An agent always owes fiduciary duties to the party who employs them (This may or may not be the party who pays them for services performed.)

B. Fiduciary responsibilities (OLD CAR)

1. <u>Obedience</u>

   a. The agent must act in good faith at all times, and <u>obey the client's lawful instructions</u> in accordance with the agency contract.

   b. The <u>agent may not obey instructions that are unlawful or unethical.</u>

2. <u>Loyalty</u>

   a. The <u>agent must place the principal's interest above all others</u>, including the interests of the agent.

   b. The negotiation of contracts must be conducted without regard to how much commission the agent will earn.

3. <u>Disclosure</u>

   a. An <u>agent is duty-bound to inform the principal of all knowledge the agent has about the transaction</u> including, but not limited to, material facts.

      i. Here are examples:

         ■ The listing agent must share concerns with the seller about a buyer's ability to qualify for a loan.

         ■ The buyer's agent must share concerns with the buyer about the property's condition and recommend expert evaluation.

   b. Inform the client of the benefits of a transaction, as well as any concerns about the risks or defects.

4. Remember—agents must also disclose all known material facts about the property to all parties.

5. <u>Confidentiality</u>

   a. An <u>agent must keep confidential a client's price, terms, and motivations (PTM)</u> unless the client gives written permission to disclose or disclosure is required by law.

      i. Divulging such information would jeopardize a client's ability to negotiate.

         ■ Here are examples:

            – Lost employment

            – Income tax obligations

            – Terminal or debilitating illness

            – Circumstances surrounding a divorce

            – Financial difficulties

    b. State laws determine if the duty of confidentiality <u>remains forever,</u> or if it terminates upon completion, expiration, or termination of the agency contract.

6. <u>Accounting</u>

    a. <u>Agents must account for all money and personal property</u> (e.g., house keys, garage door opener) received from or given to them on behalf of their clients.

7. <u>Reasonable care and skill</u>

    a. <u>Agents must be knowledgeable in the areas of real estate they are practicing.</u>

        i. They must exercise reasonable care when representing a client.

       ii. They must use their skill and knowledge on behalf of a client.

    b. <u>Agents must do as the seller requests to make sure that all parties, even third parties, are protected.</u>

        i. For example, a listing broker must follow the seller's directions to prevent harm to others, especially for setting showings (e.g., if the house has a hazard that the seller warned the listing broker about, the listing broker is responsible to make certain no one enters).

III.   LIABILITY FOR ANOTHER'S ACTS

A. General

1. Each employing broker is responsible for all professional acts and conduct performed by the broker and by any licensee the broker employs. Liability created not because of a person's acts but because of the their <u>relationship to the acts of others is called vicarious liability.</u>

2. <u>The broker or any licensee employed by the broker may not misrepresent property or conceal material facts.</u>

3. Broker can be liable for any promises made by them or by any licensee employed by them.

    a. Example: If a broker or licensee employed by the broker promises something like, "I know the new light rail will run here," when in fact it doesn't, the broker would be guilty of material misrepresentation.

IV.   DISCLOSURE OF REPRESENTATION

A. General

1. Many states require that a broker disclose the types of agency offered by their brokerage firm before working with a consumer as a client or a customer, but no later than before a purchase offer is either written or accepted.

2. <u>Brokers and licensees</u> employed by brokers <u>must disclose who they represent before showing</u> a property <u>or receiving any confidential information from a party they don't represent.</u>

3. A <u>licensee</u> (broker or salesperson/associate broker) <u>must disclose to all parties</u> involved in a transaction when

    a. <u>they are a principal</u> in the transaction,

    b. <u>they are representing a relative or a business associate</u>, and

    c. <u>they have an ownership or financial interest in the property, or in the proceeds</u> resulting from the sale of the property.

4. When representing both parties (dual agency), disclosure of dual agency and written consent from both parties is required.

    a. Disclosure must state the source of any expected compensation to the broker.

V. SELLER REPRESENTATION—LISTING AGREEMENTS

A. General

1. A <u>listing agreement</u> is an <u>employment contract appointing a broker as a special agent</u> for the specific purpose of finding a buyer who is ready, willing, and able to buy according to the terms contained in the listing contract.

    a. In most states, the agreement <u>must be in writing</u> to be enforceable in court.

    b. The listing is a contract <u>owned by the broker</u>.

B. Types of listing agreements

1. <u>Exclusive right-to-sell listing</u>

    a. <u>Listing broker is paid the commission if the property sells</u> during the term of the listing

        i. <u>Authorizes only one broker</u> as the seller's sole agent

        ii. Broker is paid even if the seller or someone else brings in the buyer

        iii. Gives maximum broker protection by eliminating procuring cause disagreements

2. Exclusive agency listing

    a. <u>Listing broker is paid the commission if the property sells during the term of the listing, unless the seller finds the buyer</u>

        i. Still <u>authorizes only one broker</u> as the seller's sole agent

        ii. But <u>allows the seller to retain the right to sell the property without the obligation of paying a commission to the broker</u>

        iii. If anyone other than the seller brings in the buyer, listing broker is paid the commission

3. Open/nonexclusive listing

    a. Default type of listing if a listing agreement does not specifically create an exclusive agency agreement

    b. <u>Seller may list the property with multiple brokers at the same time</u>

c. Obligate the seller to pay a commission only to the broker who produces a ready, willing, and able buyer

d. Seller is not obligated to pay a commission if the seller personally sells the property without the aid of any broker

e. Sale to a buyer automatically terminates all other open listings

4. Net listing

a. Specifies that the seller will receive a net amount of money from the sale of a property, with any excess money going to the listing broker as a commission

i. Broker is free to offer the property at any price greater than the net amount

ii. Either illegal or discouraged in most states because it creates a conflict of interest between broker and property owner

C. Essential elements of listing agreements

1. Express—in writing and signed

2. Amount and method of compensation

a. Flat fee

b. Percentage of sales price

c. Remember—commissions are negotiable in all cases; the broker earns the commission when the seller accepts a purchase contract and the broker is paid the commission at closing.

3. Price the seller is willing to accept

4. Legal description of the property

5. Financing terms the seller is willing to accept

6. Specific termination date

7. Protection clause/extension clause/holdover clause/safety clause

a. An optional clause in a listing that allows a broker to collect a commission for a certain length of time after the listing terminates, if a buyer procured by the broker purchases the property

i. Not to be confused with loan clauses such as alienation or acceleration

ii. Many states have laws that terminate this clause in residential listing agreements when seller signs a new listing with another broker, thereby preventing a residential seller from having to pay a commission to two different brokers

D.   Obligations of the listing broker (including licensees employed by the listing broker)

1. <u>Present all written offers as soon as possible, unless otherwise specified in writing</u>

   a.   Multiple offers should be presented simultaneously

2. Complete a written offer from a buyer, even if buyer isn't represented by the listing broker

   a.   This is done because listing broker owes loyalty to their client, the seller

3. Only pay referral fees to other brokers, never to another broker's salesperson or broker associate

   a.   <u>No fees or commissions can be paid to unlicensed people</u>

4. Make certain all agreements are in writing, signed, and that copies are given to all parties

5. Complete a visual inspection of the property, looking for material defects, and request that seller complete their property disclosures

   a.   <u>Recommend the buyer have an inspection</u> to check for <u>latent</u> (<u>hidden, not easily discoverable</u>) defects, environmental issues

   b.   Point out any red flag issues that may represent potential problems (sagging floors, water stains, etc.)

6. Verify that all marketing is correct and truthful

   a.   This includes disclosure of all known material facts, and property information such as property taxes, HOA dues and rules, and other important information, such as:

      i.   Proposed uses or changes in uses that trigger inquiry about public or private land-use controls

         ■   Zoning changes or variances that may affect a property's value or desirability

         ■   Changes in zoning from industrial to residential or commercial should trigger broker to discover if there are any environmental issues or other circumstances that may require disclosure to potential buyers

         ■   When land is developed into a subdivision or planned use community, broker should inquire about any private deed restrictions or any covenants that must be disclosed to potential buyers

7. Make certain that a buyer has received the seller's property disclosure before making offer

   a.   <u>If a seller misrepresents a latent defect</u> in their disclosure

      i.   <u>As long as the broker or a licensee employed by the broker had performed a visual inspection and found no obvious defects, broker would not be held liable for misrepresentation</u>

8. Verify information and statements made by buyer seller, especially if they appear to be untrue

9. Complete a CMA to verify value, even if licensee believes they know the current value

10. Disclose all material facts immediately to all parties—up to and including the day of closing

   a.   Examples: hail damage from a recent storm, and pending special assessments

11. Answer third-party questions with honesty and clarity

VI.   BUYER REPRESENTATION AGREEMENTS

A. General

1. A <u>buyer representation agreement</u> is an <u>employment contract appointing a broker as a special agent</u> for the specific purpose of representing a buyer in a real estate transaction.

   a.   In most states, agreement <u>must be in writing</u> to be enforceable in court

   b.   Buyer representation agreement is a contract owned by the broker

2. <u>A licensee who shows a property to a buyer they represent based on the potential commission rather than the buyer's needs would be violating their fiduciary obligation of loyalty</u>.

   a.   <u>Exclusive right to represent</u> a buyer agreement

      i.   Buyer promises to work with <u>only one</u> broker

      ii. Unless agreed that the seller pays the commission, the buyer compensates the broker when the buyer purchases a property of the type described in the agency agreement

      iii. <u>Broker is entitled to payment regardless of whether the broker locates the property</u>

   b.   <u>Exclusive agency</u> buyer agreement

      i.   Buyer promises to work with <u>only one</u> broker

      ii. Broker is entitled to payment only if the broker locates a property the buyer ultimately purchases

      iii. <u>Buyer is entitled to find a suitable property without any obligations to the broker</u>

   c.   <u>Open agency</u> buyer agreement

      i.   Buyer can be represented by <u>more than one broker</u>

      ii. <u>Buyer compensates only the broker who locates the property the buyer ultimately purchases</u>

      iii. Buyer is not obligated to pay a commission if the buyer purchases a property without the aid of any broker

VII.   TERMINATION OF AGENCY

A. Expiration

1. An agency relationship expires when the agreement's time period (term) expires without a successful transfer of property or the completion of the purposes given in the agreement.

B. Completion/performance

1. This is when the purpose of the contract is completed or performed, such as the closing of a purchase transaction.

C. Termination by force of law

1. The agency relationship may be terminated when the title to the property is transferred by an operation of law, as in the case of an owner's bankruptcy, or bankruptcy of the broker.

D. Destruction of property/death of a principal

1. The agency relationship is terminated if the property is destroyed, or if either party to the agreement (broker or client) dies or is incapacitated.

    a. Note: The death of a salesperson or broker associate does <u>not</u> affect the representation agreement, because the broker owns the contract.

E. Mutual agreement

1. The agreement may be terminated if both the broker and the client agree to terminate the contract.

F. Unilateral termination or breach of contract

1. One party fails to uphold the agreement, and the other party <u>unilaterally ends</u> the contract.

    a. The party unilaterally ending the contract may be liable for damages.

2. If either the broker or the client <u>breaches</u> the contract.

VIII. RESPONSIBILITIES OF THE AGENT TO CUSTOMERS AND THIRD PARTIES, INCLUDING DISCLOSURE, HONESTY, AND INTEGRITY

A. General

1. Brokers and their licensees must adhere to state and federal consumer protection laws, as well as <u>ethical requirements</u> imposed by professional associations or by state regulations.

2. State laws generally require that licensees' duties to those they don't represent include the following:

    a. <u>Honesty and fair dealing</u>

        i. Even if the licensee's client asks the licensee to lie or keep silent, licensee is obligated to disclose all known material facts

    b. <u>Integrity</u> in all dealings and negotiations, including exercising <u>reasonable skill and care</u>

    c. <u>Accounting</u> for any monies received from a customer

    d. <u>Disclosure</u> of all known material facts regarding the condition of the property that <u>might affect its value or desirability</u>

IX.   SHERMAN ANTITRUST ACT

A. Antitrust laws—<u>designed to prohibit anticompetitive behavior such as price-fixing, illegal boycotting, and illegal tie-in arrangements</u>

B. <u>Price-fixing</u>—occurs when <u>competitors all agree to charge the same rates/prices</u>

1. This is <u>illegal</u>, as it <u>inhibits competition</u>.

2. This is why the <u>amount and method of compensation paid to brokers is always negotiable</u>.

    a. Brokers must not be a party to discussions of commissions with those outside their offices, such as with other brokers.

    b. Brokers who overhear such commission discussions of other brokers should "shout and get out."

3. Employing brokers may have commission side agreements with their own licensees, but never with someone outside the firm.

C. <u>Illegal boycotting</u>

1. Competitors cannot conspire to cut out or not use another firm in an effort to reduce competition.

D. <u>Illegal tie-in arrangements</u>

1. A broker cannot offer one type of service to a client with a requirement that the client contract for a different service with the broker at the same time.

E. <u>Criminal and civil penalties</u> for antitrust violations can be severe and <u>involve monetary fines</u> plus <u>jail time</u>.

X.   MULTIPLE LISTING SERVICE (MLS)

A. How it works

1. Brokers may belong to a <u>marketing organization</u> known as the <u>multiple listing service</u> <u>(MLS)</u>.

   a.   <u>Members make their own exclusive listings available to other brokers</u>.

   b.   <u>Brokers have access to a wide variety of properties</u> for buyers.

   c.   <u>Brokers make a unilateral offer of cooperation and compensation to other member brokers</u>.

2. A broker <u>must have written consent of the seller</u> for the seller's property <u>to be included in the MLS</u>.

   a.   That consent may be included in the listing agreement.

3. A buyer's broker whose client is interested in a property listed on the MLS must notify the listing broker before any communication with the seller takes place.

UNIT 5 REVIEW QUESTIONS

True/False Questions

1. The listing is a contract owned by the salesperson who is working with the seller.
   A. True
   B. False

2. Fiduciary duties are owed by the agent to the principal.
   A. True
   B. False

3. Because of the fiduciary duty of obedience, agents must obey all commands of the principal.
   A. True
   B. False

4. The listing agreement establishes an agency relationship, but the power of attorney (POA) does not.
   A. True
   B. False

5. The promise to use due diligence to fulfill the terms of the listing contract is the promise that the principal makes to the agent.
   A. True
   B. False

6. A listing agent has to disclose to all interested parties that a train station near the subject property will be permanently closing in two years.
   A. True
   B. False

7. An exclusive right-to-sell listing agreement is a unilateral contract.
   A. True
   B. False

8. The listing agreement may be terminated if both the broker and the client agree to terminate the contract.
   A. True
   B. False

9. An agent holding only a 1% ownership interest in a listed property need not disclose that to interested parties.
   A. True
   B. False

10. If an implied agency is created accidentally or unintentionally by the actions or speech of the parties, then the agent does not owe fiduciary duties to the principal.
    A. True
    B. False

11. The statute of frauds requires certain contracts to be in writing (and signed) to be enforced in a court of law.
    A. True
    B. False

12. Agency relationships are only created through an expressed agreement between the parties.
    A. True
    B. False

13. A seller only interacted with a real estate salesperson. If that salesperson dies, the listing contract terminates.
    A. True
    B. False

14. If a single-family residence burns down, the listing contract terminates.
    A. True
    B. False

15. If a seller becomes mentally incapacitated, the listing agreement terminates.
    A. True
    B. False

16. If a listing broker files for bankruptcy, the listing agreement terminates.
    A. True
    B. False

17. The duty of disclosure to a third party is the same as the duty of disclosure to a principal.
    A. True
    B. False

18. Because of the fiduciary duty of obedience, a listing agent can conceal material facts about the listing property.
    A. True
    B. False

19. When it concerns the listed property, listing agents owe the duty of honesty to third-party buyers.
    A. True
    B. False

20. A net listing is illegal in many states because of the potential conflict of interest between the seller and the listing agent.
    A. True
    B. False

21. Assuming a net listing is legal, the listing broker may end up without a commission if the sales price is the same as the net profit that the sellers stated they wanted to gain through the transaction.
    A. True
    B. False

22. In a net listing, the listing broker earns anything over what the seller stated was the net profit goal.
    A. True
    B. False

23. Cooperating agents must split commissions 50/50.
    A. True
    B. False

24. A listing posted to the MLS is a promise to pay that must be honored in the event a buyer's broker performs.
    A. True
    B. False

25. If a property is listed on the MLS, the listing agent cannot change the percentage split offered to the selling agent.
    A. True
    B. False

26. A broker representing two principals in the same transaction is practicing dual agency.
    A. True
    B. False

Multiple-Choice Questions

1. All of these establish an agency relationship EXCEPT
   A. power of attorney.
   B. listing agreement.
   C. buyer representation agreement.
   D. purchase and sale agreement.

2. Both a listing agreement and a power of attorney (POA) establish an agency relationship between a principal and an agent. All of these set forth reasons a real estate broker would have a seller sign a listing agreement, rather than a POA, EXCEPT
   A. the listing agreement details the compensation the broker hopes to earn.
   B. the listing agreement details the scope of the broker's authority.
   C. the listing agreement allows the broker to act in place of the seller.
   D. the listing agreement allows the broker to act on behalf of the seller.

3. One week before a closing, a listing broker heard that a noisy train station located near the subject property would be permanently closing within a year. What, if any, responsibility does the broker owe to disclose this newly acquired information?
   A. One week before the close, the broker does not need to disclose this information to either party.
   B. The broker must disclose this information to the seller because of the fiduciary duty of disclosure.
   C. The broker must disclose this information to both the seller and the buyer because of the fiduciary duty of disclosure.
   D. The broker must disclose this information to the buyer because of the fiduciary duty of disclosure.

4. A broker has listed a home for a neighbor. What is the relationship between the broker and the seller?
   A. The broker is a subagent of the seller.
   B. The seller is the broker's client.
   C. The seller is the broker's customer.
   D. The seller is the broker's agent.

5. A buyer's agent found a property that a buyer wanted to buy. Which of these would the buyer's agent need to disclose to the buyer?
    A. The agent was a remainderman on that property.
    B. The agent's sibling owned a 1% interest in the property.
    C. The agent also represented the seller.
    D. All of these need to be disclosed.

6. A listing broker was holding an open house on 123 Apple Tree Lane. A prospective buyer—who was also a friend of the listing broker—came to look at the property. Because no one else was at the open house, the listing broker verbally advised the friend on how to raise a credit score and how to submit a winning offer. The following day, the friend submitted an offer that the seller accepted on 123 Apple Tree Lane. The friend knew nothing about agency, and it was never discussed at the open house. A court later finds that there was an undisclosed dual agency. What type of agency was established at the open house?
    A. An express agency
    B. An implied agency
    C. An ostensible agency
    D. An agency by estoppel

7. Which of these would NOT terminate the fiduciary duties in a listing agreement?
    A. Death of the seller
    B. Death of the listing broker
    C. Death of a buyer
    D. Destruction of the premises

8. A broker and a seller entered into a listing agreement for the sale of a multifamily residence. A tornado destroyed the improvements, but to a large extent left the land itself untouched. Which of these is incorrect regarding the listing agreement?
    A. The destruction of the improvements terminated this listing agreement.
    B. The seller does not need to approve the termination of this listing agreement.
    C. The seller and the listing broker can mutually decide to rescind the contract.
    D. The listing agreement terminates only if both the land and the improvements are destroyed.

9. An agent lied to a third party. The principal had not instructed the agent to lie, and had not known about the lie until sued by the third party. If the principal loses the lawsuit, it will MOST likely be a result of
    A. lis pendens.
    B. caveat emptor.
    C. vicarious liability.
    D. ad valorem.

10. A seller orders a listing broker to lie to all prospective buyers about the leaky roof of the subject property. Which of these is correct?
    A. Because of the fiduciary duty of obedience, the listing broker must lie about the leaky roof.
    B. Because of the fiduciary duty of disclosure, the listing broker must disclose the leaky roof.
    C. Because of the fiduciary duty of loyalty, the listing broker must lie about the leaky roof.
    D. None of these are correct.

11. A broker enters into a listing agreement where the seller wants to make $120,000 as the net profit from the sale of a vacant lot. The broker agrees to receive as compensation any proceeds over and above that amount. The broker and seller entered into
    A. a gross listing.
    B. an exclusive right-to-sell listing.
    C. an exclusive agency listing.
    D. a net listing.

12. Many states have discouraged or outlawed which of these listing agreements between two parties?
    A. Dual agency
    B. Net
    C. Open
    D. Exclusive

13. Real estate listing brokers belonging to the multiple listing service (MLS)
    A. must split the commission evenly.
    B. may split the commission evenly.
    C. must list FSBO properties.
    D. must not list FSBO properties.

14. Which of these would NOT be listed on the multiple listing service?
    A. Business opportunities for sale or lease
    B. Commercial properties for sale or lease
    C. Residential properties for sale or lease
    D. Seller's chattels not included in a sale

UNIT 6

Leasing and Property Management

LEARNING OBJECTIVE

When you have completed this unit, you will be able to accomplish the following.

› Discuss the basic elements of a property management agreement, the key elements in a lease agreement, the types of leases, and ADA and fair housing compliance.

I. **BASIC CONCEPTS/DUTIES OF PROPERTY MANAGEMENT**

A. **Definition**

1. A <u>property manager</u> is a <u>licensed broker</u> (either a licensed real estate brokerage employing licensees, or simply an independent licensed broker) <u>who functions as a general agent of an investment property owner</u>.

B. **Obligations**

1. Generate income for the owner.

2. Maintain the physical condition of the property to preserve and increase the property's value.

3. Market space to attract tenants:

   a. <u>Most important is careful selection of the highest-qualified tenants</u>

4. Collect rents and security deposits.

5. Investigate applicants' qualifications.

6. Negotiate leases.

7. Depending on the property/properties being managed for the property owner, property managers <u>may</u> also be actively involved in the following:

    a. <u>Helping decrease the owner's liability by assisting the owner in risk management</u>

        i. <u>Avoiding</u> a risk by removing the source, such as a swimming pool in an apartment complex

        ii. <u>Controlling</u> a risk by helping the owner prepare for emergencies before they happen, such as <u>installing smoke detectors</u>, sprinkler systems, fire door, and security systems

        iii. <u>Transferring</u> the risk by shifting it to another party, such as taking out insurance policies

        iv. <u>Retaining</u> the risk by helping the owner decide the chances of an event occurring are too small to justify the expense of doing one of the above

    b. Engaging in asset management

        i. Helping an owner determine the type of real estate in which to invest (residential or commercial)

        ii. Helping an owner decide the best property/properties to purchase

        iii. Helping an owner secure the financial resources to fund purchases

        iv. Helping an owner decide the best time to sell an investment property or properties

8. Property managers renting <u>industrial/manufacturing property</u> should be <u>very concerned about environmental issues</u>.

C. Property manager's fiduciary responsibilities

1. <u>These are fiduciary duties owed to the property owner (**OLDCAR**)</u>:

    a. <u>Obedience</u>—complying/following the <u>lawful</u> instructions of the owner

    b. <u>Loyalty</u>—placing the owner's interests above that of the property manager

    c. <u>Disclosure</u>—informing the owner of any known material facts or environmental hazards

    d. <u>Confidentiality</u>—not divulging client's price, terms, or motivations

    e. <u>Accounting</u>—faithfully accounting for all funds received for or distributed by the owner

    f. Reasonable care and skill

II.   PROPERTY MANAGEMENT AGREEMENT

A. General

1. There must be a <u>management contract establishing the duties of the property manager and the property owner</u>:

    a. <u>Creates a general agency</u> relationship with the property owner

    b.   Signed by the broker

        i.   <u>May not be signed by a salesperson or broker associate without permission of the employing/managing broker</u>

  2. It establishes the fees and commissions to be paid to the property manager.

  3. It establishes the extent of the manager's authority over expenses and payments of expenses:

    a.   <u>Property managers cannot spend the owner's profits or unilaterally approve capital expenditures</u>

  4. It specifies the time period the agreement covers, and specific provisions for terminating the agreement.

III. LEASES

A. Definition

  1. <u>Lease</u>—a <u>bilateral contract</u> between the <u>lessor</u> (the owner) and the <u>lessee</u> (the tenant)

    a.   <u>Transfers possession and use</u> of the property

    b.   Lasts for a <u>specific length of time</u>

    c.   <u>Signed</u> by both the lessor and the lessee

    d.   Lessor has a leased fee estate

    e.   <u>Lessee has a leasehold estate</u>

B. Key elements and provisions of lease agreements

  1. Description of the leased premises

  2. Tenant's possession and use of the premises including any restrictions

  3. Rent amount and when it is due and payable

  4. Term (the period of time of the lease)

  5. Amount of security/damage deposit

  6. Responsibilities of both parties

  7. Parties' option(s) for renewal or a right of first refusal

C. Types of leases

  1. <u>Gross lease</u>

    a.   The tenant pays <u>fixed rent</u> and usually all of their utilities (e.g., gas, electric, cable, telephone, trash and recycle); <u>landlord pays all other property expenses</u> (e.g., taxes, insurance, repairs)

    b.   This is <u>typical of residential</u> leases, but can be used for commercial or industrial properties

2. <u>Net lease</u>

     a. The <u>tenant pays fixed rent plus</u> all or some of property <u>expenses,</u> such as utilities, taxes, special assessments, etc.

     b. Most common for commercial or industrial properties

3. <u>Percentage lease</u>

     a. The <u>tenant pays fixed rent plus a percentage of tenant's gross sales or income</u>

     b. Typical of retail leases

4. <u>Ground lease</u>

     a. Used to lease <u>unimproved property (raw land)</u>

         i. Any improvements added by tenant usually become the owner's property at the end of the lease

             ▪ Tenant would want a long-term lease if they plan to add improvements

     b. Very common with farmland when property owners lease portions of their land to other parties who farm the land

     c. Could also be a short-term lease, like renting small parcels of raw land to pumpkin vendors at Halloween and Christmas tree vendors during the Christmas season

D. Constructive eviction

1. Lease may be terminated if the <u>tenant must vacate because of the landlord's actions or failure to act</u>

E. Actual eviction

1. Used by a landlord to evict a <u>tenant who is in breach of the lease contract</u>

F. Landlord and tenant rights and obligations

1. Most states—have adopted all or part of the Uniform Residential Landlord and Tenant Act (URLTA) or have enacted similar legislation

     a. Considers a tenant to have a periodic tenancy based on the terms of the lease, so long as the terms are not grossly unfair to the tenant

     b. Requires the lessor and the lessee to make a joint inventory detailing the conditions of the premises within five days after the lessee takes possession

     c. Limits the amount of security deposit to one month of rent for an unfurnished unit and one-and-a-half months of rent for a furnished unit; additional half-month of rent may be charged as a pet fee

d. Allows the landlord to set rules governing the use of the property; tenant may not unreasonably withhold permission for the landlord to enter the premises

e. Permits the landlord to enter the premises after giving reasonable notice and at a reasonable time; landlord is obligated to make all repairs necessary to keep premises habitable and in good operating condition

f. Requires the tenant to comply with local building and housing code provisions concerning health and safety, keeping premises clean, and using facilities provided by the landlord in a safe and reasonable manner

g. Provides various provisions related to termination of a lease when a tenant has not paid rent and prohibits a landlord from restricting service to or raising the rent of a tenant who has made a complaint against the landlord

IV. FAIR HOUSING COMPLIANCE AND AMERICANS WITH DISABILITIES (ADA) IN PROPERTY MANAGEMENT

A. Fair housing

1. Federal and state <u>fair housing laws apply to landlords and tenants</u> just as they do to parties in a purchase and sales transaction.

2. The Fair Housing Amendments Act of 1988 prohibits discrimination on the basis of race, color, religion, national origin, sex, handicap or disability, or familial status.

3. State and local governments may add more protected groups.

B. The Americans with Disabilities Act

1. The <u>Americans with Disabilities Act (ADA) prohibits discrimination in commercial properties and public accommodations.</u>

2. Property managers must ensure that people with disabilities have <u>full and equal access to facilities and services</u> (such as access to a property's rental office).

UNIT 6 REVIEW QUESTIONS

True/False Questions

1. A property manager's duties are solely on site.
   A. True
   B. False

2. A property manager should keep the owner informed of any major renovations needed to be performed in the near future.
   A. True
   B. False

3. The property manager owes the owner the fiduciary duties of obedience, loyalty, disclosure, confidentiality, accounting, and reasonable skill and care.
   A. True
   B. False

4. Because of the fiduciary duty of obedience, the property manager must obey the owner's order to exclude tenants belonging to a particular race.
   A. True
   B. False

5. The property manager typically does not have the authority to sign tenants, and bind the owner to the property manager's decision.
   A. True
   B. False

6. Even if the owner has hired a property manager, a lease is a bilateral contract between the owner of the rental property and the tenant.
   A. True
   B. False

7. The areas of a residential apartment building open to the public must be ADA compliant.
   A. True
   B. False

8. Property managers can exclude HIV/AIDS patients from housing.
   A. True
   B. False

9. A listing broker owes the fiduciary duty of confidentiality, while a property manager does not.
   A. True
   B. False

10. A property manager's fiduciary duties can be summarized as follows: obedience, loyalty, disclosure, confidentiality, accounting, and reasonable skill and care.
    A. True
    B. False

11. The owner of rental property and the property manager owe fiduciary duties to each other.
    A. True
    B. False

Multiple-Choice Questions

1. The owner of a 15-unit, multifamily apartment building hired a property manager. The duties of the property manager would typically include all of these EXCEPT
   A. finding and signing well-qualified tenants.
   B. staying current with applicable environmental law.
   C. evaluating rental rates of nearby properties.
   D. evaluating the owner's estate planning.

2. The typical property manager acts on behalf of the property owner as
   A. a special agent.
   B. a general agent.
   C. an attorney-in-fact.
   D. an implied agent.

3. Conduct that may result in constructive eviction is when a
   A. tenant is given notice to pay overdue rent.
   B. landlord stops the tenant's water and heat.
   C. tenant refuses to pay rent.
   D. tenant remains in possession of the property after the lease has ended.

4. All of these properties are under the supervision of a property manager. Which would, per the Americans with Disabilities Act (ADA), require special accommodations for the handicapped and/or disabled?
   A. Hotels
   B. Sports stadiums
   C. Shopping centers
   D. All of these

5. At the end of a 40-year ground lease, a building and other structures erected by the tenant
   A. become the property of the lessor.
   B. are considered trade fixtures.
   C. must be removed by the tenant.
   D. remain the property of the lessee.

6. Addison, a property manager of a 10-unit apartment building, was directed by the owner to limit new tenants to members of a particular religion. The owner assured Addison that this was legal because the owner lived in one of the 10 units. Addison must
   A. obey, because of the fiduciary duty of obedience.
   B. obey, because the owner is living in one of the units.
   C. disobey, because Addison would be violating federal fair housing laws.
   D. disobey, because Addison owes the tenants the fiduciary duty of loyalty.

UNIT 7

Practice of Real Estate

LEARNING OBJECTIVE

When you have completed this unit, you will be able to accomplish the following.

› Explain the protections afforded by fair housing laws and the role of the broker in management and supervision in a real estate firm.

I.   FEDERAL FAIR HOUSING LAWS

A.   History

1. The <u>Civil Rights Act of 1866</u> prohibited any type of discrimination based on <u>race.</u>

2. The Federal Fair Housing Act of <u>1968</u> prohibited discrimination in housing based on <u>race, color, religion, or national origin</u>.

3. The Housing and Community Development Act of <u>1974</u> added <u>sex</u> to the list of protected classes.

4. In <u>1988</u>, the Fair Housing Amendments Act included <u>handicap/disability and familial status</u> to the classes protected under federal law.

   a. <u>Familial status protects pregnant women and families with children.</u>

      i. <u>This does not apply to retirement communities in which 80% of the units are occupied by residents age 55 and older.</u>

   b. <u>Handicap/disability</u> protects those with any <u>physical or mental impairment that substantially limits one or more major life activities</u>.

      i. This includes those suffering from HIV/AIDS.

    ii. Alcoholics and drug addicts are protected if seeking treatment.

        ■ They are not protected if they are using illegal substances.

    iii. This law specifically <u>excludes those convicted of dealing drugs</u>.

    iv. <u>Landlords must allow a disabled tenant to make changes to a unit to accommodate a disability at the tenant's expense</u>.

        ■ Landlords can require the tenant to return the property to its original condition upon conclusion of the lease.

B. Equal opportunity in housing

1. Equal opportunity in housing is intended to create a marketplace in which all persons of similar financial means have a similar range of housing choices.

2. Equal opportunity laws apply to owners, real estate licensees, property management companies, real estate organizations, lending agencies, builders, and developers.

3. The laws also prohibit discrimination against individuals because of their <u>association</u> with persons in the protected classes.

4. Failure to comply with fair housing laws is civil violation and constitutes grounds for disciplinary action against real estate licensees.

C. Protected classes

1. Memory aid—FReSH CoRN

    a. **F**amilial status

    b. **R**ace

    c. **S**ex (includes sexual orientation and gender identity)

    d. **H**andicap/disability

    e. **C**olor

    f. **R**eligion

    g. **N**ational origin

D. <u>Nonprotected classes</u>

1. <u>Age</u>

2. <u>Marital status</u>

3. <u>Occupation</u> (e.g., student)

4. Note: these laws also prohibit discrimination against individuals because of their <u>association with persons in the protected classes</u>

E. Prohibited conduct

1. <u>Redlining</u>

   a. This is the practice of <u>refusing to make mortgage loans or issue insurance policies in specific areas or neighborhoods because of the nature of the area (e.g., high crime rate) and/or the protected classes who live there.</u>

      i. Redlining is done for <u>reasons other than the economic qualifications</u> of applicants.

2. <u>Blockbusting</u> (sometimes called panic peddling)

   a. A licensee <u>encourages property owners to sell or rent their homes by claiming that protected classes of people are moving into the neighborhood, which will have a negative impact</u> on property values.

      i. It's illegal for licensees to assert that the presence of certain protected classes of people will cause property values to decline, that crime or antisocial behavior will increase, or the quality of schools will suffer.

3. <u>Steering</u>

   a. This occurs when a licensee attempts to <u>"steer" or "channel" potential homebuyers to particular neighborhoods, or discouraging them from considering some areas based on protected classes who live there.</u>

F. Exceptions

1. There are <u>never</u> exceptions in regard to <u>racial discrimination</u>.

2. It is not a violation to discriminate against other protected classes in the following situations:

   a. A nonlicensed owner when renting or selling their single-family home

      i. There can be no broker involvement and no discriminatory advertising

   b. A nonlicensed owner renting a four-unit property, as long as the owner occupies one of the units

      i. There can be no broker involvement and no discriminatory advertising

   c. <u>Senior housing may discriminate against familial status</u> (families with children)

      i. <u>Buildings with at least 80% of the occupants age 55 or older</u>

      ii. <u>Housing restricted to persons age 62 or older</u>

   d. Housing expressly operated by organizations or private clubs that limit occupancy to their members only

G. Prohibited advertising

1. In the sale or rental of real property, <u>no advertisement may include language indicating either a preference or a limitation based on protected classes</u>:

   a. Cannot indicate a discriminatory limitation or preference based on <u>race</u>

   b. Must avoid any religious preference or limitation

   c. Must avoid any explicit preference based on sex

   d. Cannot display any exclusions or limitations based on handicap or disability

   e. Cannot show a preference or limitation based on family size or nature

   f. Cannot represent nonexclusive groupings in photographs or illustrations of people

2. When advertising, it is best to describe the property, <u>not</u> who should or should not live there.

3. Media used in advertising cannot target one population to the exclusion of others:

   a. Real estate advertisements should appear in general-circulation media, even if appearing in publications designed for one ethnic or racial group

H. <u>Enforcement and penalties</u>

1. Whenever policies or practices result in unequal treatment of persons in the protected classes, they are considered discriminatory regardless of whether there was any intent to discriminate.

2. Regulatory agencies consider the effect of policies and actions in determining whether an individual has been discriminated against. This is called disparate impact.

3. The U.S. Department of Housing and Urban Development <u>(HUD) administers and enforces federal fair housing laws.</u>

   a. HUD establishes rules and regulations to further clarify the law, and creates and distributes the <u>Equal Opportunity poster</u> required for businesses, including real estate brokerage firms.

   b. <u>HUD will first investigate all incidents</u> of wrongdoing.

4. Complaints must be made within <u>one year</u> of the alleged act of discrimination.

   a. In a complaint, <u>HUD will consider if the equal opportunity poster is displayed in the broker's office(s)</u>.

   b. <u>HUD will not consider the licensee's intentions,</u> even if the licensee felt they were working in the client's best interest.

      i. Example: <u>Only showing a family with children homes in neighborhoods with other children.</u>

   c. <u>Violations could involve financial penalties.</u>

5. An aggrieved party may <u>file a civil action directly in federal court within two years</u> of the alleged act of discrimination

6. <u>A broker's best protection is to keep good records</u>

7. A broker could file a complaint and request the commission as damages if a client seller refuses to accept an offer from a member of a protected class.

II.   THE AMERICANS WITH DISABILITIES ACT (ADA)

A.   Purpose

1. The purpose is to <u>ensure equal access to public accommodations for disabled people</u>.

    a.   Public accommodations include commercial properties, and places accessible to the public, <u>including broker offices</u> and retail stores.

        i.   <u>Access</u> to facilities and services <u>must be provided when reasonably achievable</u> in existing buildings, and in all new commercial construction.

2. The purpose is also to provide guidelines for accessibility requirements in buildings.

III.   MEGAN'S LAW

A.   Description

1. <u>Megan's Law requires the registration of sex offenders</u>.

2. Licensees should inform buyers to contact the local law enforcement offices if they're concerned about a registered offender in the area.

3. States vary on licensees' disclosure requirements, and how to inform buyers of this law.

IV.   ADVERTISING

A.   Truth in advertising

1. In general, <u>advertising</u> by real estate brokers and their associates <u>must be truthful and fair</u>.

    a.   It <u>may not mislead</u> the public with false information.

    b.   It must comply with nondiscriminatory federal, state, and local laws.

2. <u>Exaggerating a property's benefits</u> is called <u>puffing</u>.

    a.   Superlative statements about the quality of a property that should not be considered assertions of fact.

    b.   <u>Puffing is not illegal</u>, but licensees must be careful not to commit fraud in statements or advertisements.

        i.   <u>Fraud is an intentional or negligent misrepresentation or concealment of a material fact</u>, which is relied on by another (who is "taken advantage of"), and who is then induced to enter into a transaction and is harmed as a result.

3. Federal and state laws regulate advertising by real estate licensees.

   a. Most state laws provide that advertising rules and regulations apply to both written and to internet advertising.

      i. Written and electronic <u>advertising</u> by licensees <u>must include the following</u>:

         ■ <u>Licensee's name</u>, office address, <u>and broker affiliation</u>

            – Advertising a salesperson's or broker associate's name without broker's name is prohibited

            – Advertising that does not include the name and address of the person placing the ad is called <u>blind advertising</u>.

   b. No property may be advertised without the written permission of the property owner.

B. Confidential Information

1. In the general daily practice of real estate and the use of any technology (such as websites, blogs, emails, or texts), real estate licensees must not reveal confidential information about any client unless permitted by law.

2. <u>Agency laws require brokers and their agents to keep a seller's or buyer's personal and privileged information confidential to avoid harm to their clients.</u>

3. Confidential and private, privileged information deals with the seller's or buyer's personal life and motivation for selling, such as:

   a. lost employment,

   b. income tax obligations,

   c. terminal or debilitating illness,

   d. income tax obligations,

   e. circumstances surrounding a divorce, or

   f. financial difficulties.

V.   NATIONAL DO NOT CALL REGISTRY

A. General

1. The registry is a list of <u>telephone numbers of consumers who have indicated their preference to limit telemarketing calls</u>.

   a. Real estate licensees must <u>check this list before cold-calling</u>.

2. <u>Licensees may contact consumers</u> on this list <u>for up to three months after the consumer has made the first contact</u>, such as an inquiry on a listing.

3. Licensees may call consumers on this list with whom they have an established business relationship <u>for up to 18 months after the consumer's last purchase, delivery, payment, and so on.</u>

VI.   **TRUST ACCOUNTS AND EMPLOYING BROKER RESPONSIBILITIES**

A.   **Purpose and definition of <u>trust accounts</u>, including monies held in trust accounts**

1.   Escrow and trust accounts

a.   <u>Escrow</u> is the <u>process whereby money and documents</u> related to a real estate transaction <u>are held by a broker or other escrow agent until all the terms and obligations</u> of the transaction have been met.

b.   A <u>trust account is a demand account</u> (which allows for free deposit and withdrawal of funds) set up by a broker <u>to hold other people's money separate</u> from the broker's own personal or operating accounts.

   i.   It is designed to have a <u>safe place with additional protection for funds that don't belong to the brokerage</u>.

   ii.   It is used for funds held "in trust" for others, such as the following:

   ◼   Down payments

   ◼   <u>Earnest money</u> deposits

   –   Unless otherwise agreed to, <u>earnest money is given to the listing broker</u> as soon as possible after an offer has been accepted, and the time limit for depositing earnest money into broker's trust account is set by state law

   –   <u>If an earnest money check is returned due to insufficient funds, broker must immediately inform the seller</u>

   ◼   Rental security deposits

   ◼   Rental payments collected on behalf of an owner

   ◼   Monies advanced by buyers or sellers to cover closing costs in a transaction

   iii.   The <u>trust account may also be called an earnest money account or an escrow account.</u>

c.   Broker is responsible for trust monies, including commingling and conversion.

   i.   The <u>principal broker</u> is the <u>trustee</u> of the trust account and is <u>ultimately responsible</u> for the account:

   ◼   Brokers must keep accurate records of all money deposited into and disbursed from trust account

   ii.   A broker may not <u>commingle</u> (mix) personal or business monies with any funds in a trust account.

   ◼   The only times brokers can keep their own funds in a trust account

   –   To <u>maintain a required minimum balance</u>

   –   To <u>pay bank service fees/charges</u>

        iii. A broker <u>may not convert trust account funds to pay for personal or company operating expenses (conversion)</u>.

B. Supervision practices

1. The <u>employing broker</u> (also called principal/primary broker) <u>is responsible for, and owns all the contracts</u> (listings, buyer representation contracts, purchase agreements, etc.), and has the agency relationship with all clients.

    a. When licensees leave an employing broker, they cannot take contracts with them.

2. The employing broker is <u>responsible for supervising the actions of all licensees and employees</u>.

3. The employing broker is <u>responsible for providing training and supervision</u> for licensees affiliated with the firm.

    a. This typically includes providing a <u>written company policy manual</u> outlining the firm's practices and policies and its compliance with federal, state, and local laws.

        i. Policies and procedures must <u>encourage and ensure due diligence</u> in all real estate transactions.

            ■ This includes providing proper, fair, and appropriate levels of care and activity on behalf of a client:

                – Proper and complete drafting of all agreements and contracts

                – Good-faith efforts to perform all obligations under any agreement

                – Providing true and accurate information to clients and customers

4. Especially in larger firms, the employing broker may authorize associate brokers to act as supervising brokers in branch offices.

    a. The <u>employing broker still retains ultimate accountability for supervision</u>, and for the actions of all licensees and employees—even in branch offices managed by an associate broker.

5. <u>Salespersons and associate brokers are employed to represent the employing broker.</u>

    a. <u>They all owe duties to each of the employing broker's clients equivalent to the duties owed by their employing broker.</u>

    b. There is an <u>employment agreement between the employing broker and every affiliated licensee defining the nature, obligations, and responsibilities of each party in the relationship</u>.

    c. They can be employees or independent contractors.

        i. For <u>employees</u>, the employing <u>broker must withhold</u> Social Security <u>taxes</u>, as well as state and federal income and unemployment <u>taxes</u> from pay.

            ■ A broker can also require an employee to follow rules governing work hours, office routine, obligatory meetings, an assignment of quotas, and a dress code.

            ■ A <u>broker may</u>, but is not required to, <u>offer benefits to employees</u>.

ii. <u>Independent contractors</u> must have a written and signed agreement with the employing broker stating they may <u>set their own work hours</u> and will <u>pay their own taxes</u>.

- ◼ The <u>broker does not exercise the same degree of control over an independent contractor's work or activity as they could a licensed employee</u>.

- ◼ Independent contractors <u>receive no benefits</u> from their employing broker.

- ◼ The Internal Revenue Service (IRS) requires that a real estate agent acting as an independent contractor does the following:

  – Has a current real estate license

  – Has a written agreement with their broker stating that they will <u>not</u> be treated as an employee for tax purposes

  – Income is based on sales production, and not on the number of hours they work

C. Fraud and misrepresentation

1. Employing brokers must discourage any and all <u>fraud or misrepresentation</u> by their licensees.

   a. <u>Fraud</u> is an <u>intentional or negligent misrepresentation form of deceit,</u> which is relied upon by another party who is induced to enter into a transaction and harmed as a result.

      i. Here are examples:

         ◼ Making <u>false statements</u>

         ◼ <u>Intentionally concealing</u> material facts

   b. <u>Misrepresentation is typically misleading another party unintentionally</u>.

      i. Although normally unintentional, misrepresentation <u>can still result in a licensee being liable for any ill effects</u> caused by their misrepresentation.

D. Vicarious liability

1. A real estate <u>broker is vicariously liable</u> for the acts of an associate broker or salesperson even if the broker did nothing to create liability.

2. <u>Vicarious liability is responsibility created not because of the broker's actions but because of the relationship between the broker and affiliates.</u>

VII. MANDATED DISCLOSURES

A. <u>Seller's property disclosure</u>

1. It should <u>cover all issues that might influence a buyer's decision</u>.

2. <u>Sellers</u>—never the broker—<u>complete</u> the disclosure <u>to the best of their current actual knowledge</u>.

   a. Most states require sellers to disclose any known <u>latent</u> (<u>not easily discoverable</u>) material defects as well, which is anything affecting structural soundness or personal safety.

3. Even if selling the property "as is," sellers and brokers must disclose all known material defects, both visible and latent, to all buyers.

4. Regardless of what a seller discloses, licensees must always disclose any known material facts, including any known defects that may affect the property's value or desirability.

B. Material facts

1. A material fact is an important fact—so important that it could influence a party's decision, and therefore must be disclosed.

   a. It must first be disclosed to the party the licensee represents, and then to the other licensee(s) and parties to the transaction.

   b. "Stigmatized" property disclosure requirements are determined by state laws.

      i. Examples: death having occurred on a property, paranormal activity, occupants with AIDS/HIV, etc.

   c. The licensee is not responsible for discovering latent facts that the seller didn't disclose.

   d. A licensee who withholds or lies about material facts may be guilty of misrepresentation or fraud, which could render a contract voidable.

      i. Remember—"puffing" is an exaggerated opinion, and does not constitute misrepresentation.

   e. A buyer's ability to get a loan is considered a material fact. The buyer and the buyer's agent have to disclose if the buyer is unable to get a loan.

   f. All environment issues, even those outside the property boundaries, are considered to be material facts and must be disclosed because they could impact a property's value.

   g. Buyers' agents have a duty to recommend a professional property inspection to look for any defects, especially with older properties.

VIII. TYPES OF INSURANCE

A. Errors and omissions (E&O)

1. Errors and omissions insurance is liability insurance that covers a broker's liability for errors and omissions in their listing and selling activities.

2. A broker may purchase the insurance for everyone in the firm, or require each of the firm's licensees to purchase their own E&O insurance.

B. General liability

1. Besides E&O insurance, brokers carry general liability insurance, which covers the risk the broker assumes when the public enters the firm's building.

2. Covers claims made for hospital expenses and medical bills submitted by a person who was injured in the building or on the firm's property.

   ■ No insurance policy will protect a real estate licensee from a lawsuit or prosecution arising from criminal acts, and most insurance companies normally exclude coverage for fraud and violations of civil rights and antitrust laws.

IX.   WARRANTIES

A.   New home construction warranties

   1.   <u>Covers failures</u> of workmanship and materials, <u>and physical defects</u> such as faulty roofing, HVAC, electrical, and plumbing systems.

     a.   <u>Does not cover structural damage</u> from outside forces

   2.   Requirements for new home warranties are set at the state or local level, and must meet strict underwriting guidelines.

B.   Existing home construction warranty programs

   1.   Warranties for existing homes are <u>private insurance programs</u> for homeowners and home buyers.

   2.   Often provided as part of a listing as an incentive to buyers

     a.   May be paid by the licensee, the seller, the buyer, or the cost may be shared.

   3.   They usually feature a deductible, and may exclude some items from coverage.

   4.   <u>The term and length of the warranty are determined by the contract with the warranty company.</u>

C.   Licensees should make certain that buyers fully understand the limits of any warranty.

X.   BROKER RESPONSIBILITIES

A.   <u>Ethics</u> for real estate professionals

   ■   *Ethics* refers to <u>a system of moral principles, rules, and standards of conduct</u>. All licensees must adhere to the ethical requirements imposed by professional associations or by state regulations.

   1.   <u>Expectations of licensees</u>

     a.   They <u>must exhibit a higher level of knowledge and competence than a nonlicensed person</u>.

     b.   They must protect the interests of clients, and <u>treat all parties fairly and honestly</u>.

     c.   They must complete all federal and state mandated disclosures in a timely fashion.

     d.   They must fully explain to the client their obligations and the obligations of the broker in the transaction.

   2.   Disclosure and practicing within levels of competence and expertise

     a.   Association codes of ethics, as well as license laws, state that <u>a licensee must practice within their area(s) of expertise and competence</u>.

     b.   <u>Licensees are expected to know when they are not competent to perform tasks</u>:

       i.   Practicing outside their area(s) of expertise

- ■ Residential licensee selling commercial property

- ■ An urban (city) licensee selling farm land

    ii. Completing and presenting legal documents they do not fully understand

c. <u>Licensees become competent by completing education and working with other licensees who are knowledgeable</u> in specific areas of expertise.

d. Licensees are expected to fully disclose the following:

    i. Who they represent in a transaction

    ii. The obligation of all parties regarding disclosure of material facts

    iii. Whether the licensee is a principal in the transaction

    iv. Any environmental, material, or other issues requiring disclosure that might impact a property

e. <u>Licensees must know when they need to recommend that the party they are dealing with should seek legal advice</u>:

    i. Licensees who are not attorneys are <u>not allowed to give legal advice on any aspect of real estate transactions</u>

    ii. Licensees are not permitted to create contracts on their own

    iii. Licensees should always encourage both clients and customers to contact a licensed attorney for legal advice and how to interpret real estate contracts

f. <u>Licensees should not give tax advice</u>:

    i. Refer party to a <u>tax advisor or CPA</u> for advice on tax implications for real estate transactions

g. <u>Licensees should always recommend</u> buyers and sellers obtain the services of the following:

    i. <u>Attorneys</u> for legal advice, including how to <u>interpret</u> real estate contracts

    ii. <u>Tax advisors or CPAs</u>

    iii. <u>Accountants</u>

    iv. <u>Qualified mortgage brokers or lenders</u> for information on lending practices or on the types and characteristics of various loans

UNIT 7 REVIEW QUESTIONS

True/False Questions

1. Convicted drug addicts are not protected under federal fair housing laws.
   A. True
   B. False

2. Recovering drug addicts are protected under federal fair housing laws.
   A. True
   B. False

3. Poor individuals applying for rental apartment units are protected under federal fair housing laws.
   A. True
   B. False

4. Prohibition of discrimination on the basis of race is found only in the Civil Rights Act of 1968, as amended.
   A. True
   B. False

5. The primary goal of the ADA was to make private dwellings accessible to handicapped and disabled people.
   A. True
   B. False

6. Making new construction for public accommodations ADA compliant is based on the wealth of the builder.
   A. True
   B. False

7. Landlords must allow a disabled tenant to make changes to a unit to accommodate a disability at the tenant's expense.
   A. True
   B. False

8. Redlining is the practice of refusing to make mortgage loans or issue insurance policies in specific areas or neighborhoods because of the nature of the area.
   A. True
   B. False

9. A licensee who encourages property owners to sell or rent their homes by claiming that protected classes of people are moving into the neighborhood, which will have a negative impact on property values, is practicing steering.
   A. True
   B. False

10. Public accommodations under the Americans with Disabilities Act pertains only to residential properties.
    A. True
    B. False

11. In the sale or rental of real property, no advertisement may include language indicating either a preference or a limitation based on protected classes.
    A. True
    B. False

12. Exaggerating a property's benefits is called fraud.
    A. True
    B. False

13. It is the responsibility of the broker of record to supervise brokerage firm licensees, ensuring compliance with federal fair housing rules.
    A. True
    B. False

14. Written policies related to brokerage firm advertising policies frequently fall within the purview of risk management and/or supervision.
    A. True
    B. False

15. Regarding sex discrimination, compliance with state law is sufficient to protect a brokerage firm against a future lawsuit.
    A. True
    B. False

16. Different types of insurance may be included in a brokerage firm's approach to risk management.
    A. True
    B. False

17. If a real estate brokerage firm does not withhold taxes for associate licensees, it indicates that the broker of record has less control over how the work at the brokerage firm is done.
    A. True
    B. False

18. Confidential and private, privileged information deals with the seller's or buyer's personal life and motivation for selling.
    A. True
    B. False

19. Written policies for addressing a complaint from a member of the public are both risk management and good supervision practices.
    A. True
    B. False

20. Under the National Do Not Call Act, licensees may contact consumers on the do not call list for up to three months after the consumer has made the first contact, such as an inquiry on a listing.
    A. True
    B. False

21. Puffing in real estate is illegal.
    A. True
    B. False

Multiple-Choice Questions

1. All of these are exemptions from the federal Fair Housing Act of 1968 as amended EXCEPT
    A. the sale of a single-family home where the listing broker does not advertise the property.
    B. the rental of a unit in an owner-occupied, three-family dwelling where no advertisement is placed in the paper.
    C. the restriction of noncommercial lodgings by a private club to members of that club.
    D. the property is a state or local housing program designed specifically for the elderly.

2. A house was listed for $47,900. A Hispanic couple saw the house and was interested in purchasing it. When they asked for the list price of the house, the listing agent said it was $53,000. Later in the day, the listing agent told an Asian couple that the list price was $47,900. Under the federal Fair Housing Act of 1968, the statement to the Hispanic couple was
    A. legal because all that is important is that everyone be given the right to buy the house.
    B. legal because the statement was made by the agent and not the owner.
    C. illegal because the difference in the listed price and the quoted price was greater than $2,000.
    D. illegal because the terms of the sale were changed for the Hispanic couple.

3. The Americans with Disabilities Act (ADA) provides protection to those who
    A. smoke tobacco.
    B. are receiving treatment for alcoholism.
    C. have been convicted of selling drugs.
    D. have suffered financial hardship because of health costs.

4. Which of these would NOT be a requirement under the Americans with Disabilities Act (ADA) or federal fair housing laws?
    A. A landlord must allow disabled tenants to make changes to the property and may not charge the tenants or force them to move.
    B. The owner of a commercial building could refuse to make changes to the "first-come, first-serve" parking to accommodate a disabled tenant.
    C. A building with a no-pets policy would have to allow service animals without an additional charge.
    D. A tenant who makes changes to an apartment to accommodate a disability can be required to return the unit to its original condition upon lease expiration.

5. The federal fair housing laws prohibit discrimination on the basis of
   A. age.
   B. occupation.
   C. marital status.
   D. sex.

6. Persuading homeowners to sell their homes by telling them minorities are moving into the neighborhood is the illegal practice called
   A. testing.
   B. blockbusting.
   C. redlining.
   D. steering.

7. A licensed salesperson is authorized by law to
   A. sign a closing statement.
   B. collect a commission directly from a principal for performing assigned duties.
   C. advertise listed property under the salesperson's own name.
   D. act under the supervision of a real estate broker.

8. An unlicensed employee with an extensive background in managing businesses is overseeing a real estate brokerage firm. The unlicensed assistant will have ultimate responsibility over
   A. licensees.
   B. unlicensed assistants.
   C. IT professionals.
   D. no one.

9. Under the provisions of the fair housing laws, a real estate broker may
   A. change the terms of a sale for a minority buyer.
   B. solicit listings in a minority neighborhood.
   C. refuse to rent to a qualified prospective tenant who is a minority.
   D. refuse to negotiate with a buyer who is a minority.

UNIT 8

Contracts

LEARNING OBJECTIVE

When you have completed this unit, you will be able to accomplish the following.

> Discuss general concepts of contracts and the types of contracts used in the real estate industry.

I. TYPES OF CONTRACTS

A. Definition of contracts

1. A <u>contract</u> is a <u>voluntary, legally binding and enforceable agreement</u> between parties to do or not do something(s) specific.

2. <u>The issue</u> in contracts <u>is NOT the number of parties!</u> The issue is the number of PROMISES being made. <u>Contracts are all about PROMISES.</u>

B. Express vs. implied contracts

1. An <u>express contract</u> may be <u>oral or written</u>; it exists when the parties "express" the terms and show their intentions in words.

   a. <u>The statute of frauds requires that contracts transferring real property interests must be express written contracts to be enforceable.</u>

2. <u>An implied contract is not in writing</u>; it exists when the agreement between the parties is <u>demonstrated by their actions and/or conduct</u>.

C. Bilateral and unilateral contracts

1. A <u>bilateral contract</u> is a <u>promise exchanged for another promise</u>; it exists when <u>both parties</u> make promises to do or not to do something.

2. A <u>unilateral contract</u> is a <u>promise exchanged for performance</u>; it exists when only one party makes a promise, often in an attempt to induce a second party to do something, but the second party is <u>not legally obligated</u> to act.

    a. An <u>option contract</u> (discussed later in this study) is a <u>unilateral</u> contract.

    b. An <u>open listing</u> (discussed previously) is a <u>unilateral</u> contract.

D. Executed vs. executory contracts

1. An <u>executed </u>contract is one in which <u>all parties have fulfilled all the promises</u> they made in the contract; the contract has been fully performed.

2. An <u>executory</u> contract exists when <u>one or both parties still have an act or promise to fulfill.</u>

    a. <u>A real estate sales contract that has been accepted is an executory contract until closing</u>. Once closed, the sale contract has been executed.

II.   GENERAL CONCEPTS

A. Statute of frauds and statute of limitations

1. Statute of frauds

    a. Under the <u>statute of frauds</u>, a <u>real state contract must be in writing</u> to be <u>enforceable</u> in a court of law.

    b. *Enforceable* means the <u>parties may be forced to comply</u> with the contract's terms and conditions.

    c. The statute of frauds <u>does not apply to leases of 12 months or less.</u>

    d. Its <u>purpose is to prevent problems associated with oral/verbal contracts</u>.

2. <u>Statute of limitations</u>

    a. This law sets the <u>length of time parties are given to file a claim or a lawsuit</u>.

    b. The length of time is determined by state law.

B. Factors affecting validity, enforceability of contracts

1. Contracts—must contain <u>five essential elements</u> to be legally valid

    a. <u>Offer and acceptance</u> (also called <u>mutual agreement</u> or a <u>meeting of the minds</u>)

      i. It is an offer by one party (<u>offeror</u>) that is accepted by the other (<u>offeree</u>).

      ii. An <u>offer is a proposal containing a promise and requesting something in exchange</u>.

      iii. <u>Acceptance is a promise made by the offeree to be bound by the terms proposed by the offeror</u>.

      iv. An offer may be <u>withdrawn</u> by either party <u>before communication of acceptance</u>.

      v. A <u>counteroffer</u> (also called <u>qualified acceptance</u>) is a <u>rejection and terminates the original offer</u>.

- A buyer who receives a counteroffer is not obligated to respond, and can make an offer on another property.

- A seller who makes a counteroffer, but then receives a new offer from another party, must first withdraw the counteroffer before accepting the new offer.

b.   Consideration

   i.   This is something of value offered by one party and accepted by the other.

   ii.   It is also anything of value that the parties agree to.

   iii.   Consideration in a sales contract is the promises made by both parties (promises have value).

   - Earnest money is not required, therefore it is not consideration in a sales contract.

c.   In writing and signed (required by the statute of frauds)

d.   Legal purpose

   i.   A contract must have a lawful objective.

e.   Legally competent parties

   i.   All parties to the contract must have legal capacity (at least age 18 in most states, and with mental capacity to understand the consequences of their actions).

   ii.   A contract with a minor is voidable.

C.   Valid, void, and voidable contracts

1.   A contract is valid when it contains all the essential elements, which makes it legally sufficient and enforceable.

2.   A contract is void when it has no legal force or effect because it lacks one or more of the essential elements of a contract.

   a.   An example is a verbal contract for the sale of real property.

3.   A voidable contract appears valid, but it may be rescinded or disaffirmed by one of the parties because

   a.   they are a minor, or

   b.   they were subject to duress, fraud, or misrepresentation.

D.   Assignments and novations

1.   An assignment is a transfer of rights and duties in a contract, but NOT the liability.

   a.   The transfer may be to a third party and can be made without the consent of the other party unless the contract includes a clause that forbids an assignment.

   i.   An example is a sublease.

2. A <u>novation</u> is a <u>new contract</u> replacing the original contract, <u>transferring rights, duties and liability</u>. Both parties to the original contract must consent to the novation.

E. Notice, delivery, and acceptance of contracts

1. <u>Delivery</u> refers to the <u>intent of a party to transfer a document</u> to another party.

2. <u>Acceptance</u> is the <u>expression of a party receiving an offer to be bound</u> by the terms of the offer.

   a. The acceptance must be made within the <u>time limit stated</u> in the offer.

   b. Some offers specify that the acceptance is not effective unless a <u>signed or initialed copy</u> is received by the broker or the offeror <u>within a certain time</u>.

F. Breach of contract and remedies for breach

1. A <u>breach</u> of contract is <u>a violation of any of the terms of the contract without a legal excuse</u>.

   a. An injured party to a real estate contract may <u>sue for specific performance</u> (unless the contract states otherwise), asking a court to <u>force the other party to perform the duties or responsibilities they promised</u> in the contract.

   b. An injured party may <u>sue for damages</u>, asking a court to order the other party to pay for any <u>costs and hardships</u> suffered by the person seeking damages because of the breach.

   c. An injured party may sue for <u>compensatory damages</u>—money awarded by a court for actual damages.

      i. Compensatory damages are limited to the amount of money lost or denied because of breach.

   d. Accept <u>liquidated damages</u>

      i. This is the amount of money available to "liquidate" or "settle" any damages.

      ii. A sales contract may limit liquidated damages for a seller to the <u>earnest money</u> provided by the buyer.

      iii. <u>Liquidated damages are only available to the seller in a real estate sale contract</u>.

   e. Sue for <u>punitive damages</u>

      i. These are <u>exemplary or vindictive</u> damages, designed to punish the party being sued.

G. Termination, rescission, and cancellation of contracts

1. Besides a breach of contract, a <u>contract may be discharged or terminated</u> for other reasons.

   a. <u>Impossibility of performance/legal impossibility</u>

      i. <u>An act required by the contract cannot be legally accomplished</u>.

   b. <u>Mutual rescission: a written and signed agreement by all parties to cancel</u>

    i. <u>Rescission means terminating or canceling</u> a contract as if it had never been made, returning the parties to their original positions before the contract—and any monies exchanged are returned.

    ii. Mutual rescission would be <u>acceptable if there are major problems</u>, such as

        ■ the house burns down before closing, or

        ■ substantial issues that need repairs are discovered and the seller can't afford to fix them.

    iii. It would not be acceptable if the buyer simply decides that they don't like the home any longer and the buyer wants to purchase a different home.

  c. <u>Death</u>

    i. Some contracts can be canceled by the death of a party, but <u>only if no one is left to perform</u>.

  d. <u>Operation of law</u>

    i. Voiding of a contract by a minor

    ii. A party was subject to duress, fraud, or misrepresentation

    iii. Expiration of a statute of limitations

        ■ A law that sets the length of time parties are given to file a claim or lawsuit

    iv. Alteration of a contract without consent of all parties

H. Electronic signatures and paperless transactions

1. The statute of frauds requires that all real estate contracts be in writing to be enforceable. State laws currently recognize <u>paperless transactions as legitimate transactions</u> equivalent to paper transactions.

2. <u>Documents transmitted electronically are considered written documents</u>.

3. <u>Electronic signatures</u> of the parties to a transaction are considered <u>legal and binding</u>.

III.   SALES CONTRACTS

A. Definition

1. A sales contract <u>establishes the legal obligations</u> of the buyer and seller.

  a. It may also be called a <u>purchase agreement</u>, an <u>offer to purchase</u>, or <u>a contract for purchase and sale</u>.

2. A typical sales contract includes

  a. the <u>sales price</u> and terms,

  b. a <u>legal description</u> of the land,

  c. all the <u>terms and conditions</u> of the agreement between the parties, and

       d. any <u>contingencies</u> to the agreement.

          i. A contingency <u>allows a buyer to terminate the contract under certain conditions and get a refund of the earnest money</u>.

             ■ The most typical contingency is for financing.

          ii. Brokers are <u>not paid</u> if a sales contract terminates per a contingency.

B. Offer and counteroffer

1. A real estate sales transaction <u>normally</u> begins when a buyer signs an offer for a seller's property, and the offer is presented to the seller.

    a. The parties are the <u>offeror</u> (buyer) and the <u>offeree</u> (seller).

2. The seller may <u>accept</u> the buyer's offer, or the seller may <u>change</u> a buyer's offer, which creates a <u>counteroffer</u>.

    a. Legally, the <u>original offer</u> has now been <u>rejected</u> and <u>ceases to exist</u>.

       i. The seller has <u>rejected</u> it by <u>changing</u> it.

    b. The <u>original offeree (seller) now becomes the offeror</u>, and the <u>original offeror (buyer) now becomes the offeree</u>.

3. The buyer may accept or reject the counteroffer, and the parties may continue the process by <u>making additional counteroffers</u> to one another until the parties either <u>reach an agreement</u> or one of them <u>walks away</u>.

4. An offer or counteroffer may be revoked at any time before communication of acceptance is made to the offeror (the party making the offer).

C. When an offer becomes binding

1. <u>When a seller agrees to accept a signed offer</u> (either the original offer or a counteroffer) and <u>signs</u> it, a valid and <u>legally binding, bilateral contract</u> is formed.

    a. The seller becomes the <u>vendor</u>—who <u>holds legal title until closing</u>.

    b. The buyer becomes the <u>vendee</u>—who <u>holds equitable title</u>.

2. An <u>offer is not considered accepted until communication of acceptance has been made</u> to the offering party.

    a. This notification can be made in person, through an agent, or by electronic means.

3. A copy of the signed contract must be provided to each party, and it is usually provided to any brokers involved in the transaction.

D. Earnest money

1. <u>Earnest money</u> is a <u>good-faith deposit</u> made by a buyer when making an offer to purchase real estate.

2. The <u>amount</u> of the earnest money is a matter <u>agreed to by the parties</u>.

    a. <u>Earnest money is not required</u>, but it is normally provided

        i. to <u>discourage</u> the buyer from defaulting, and

        ii. to <u>compensate</u> the seller for removing the property from the market.

3. Earnest money is <u>usually given to a broker who holds it for the parties in a designated trust account</u>, unless otherwise agreed to by the parties.

IV.   OPTION CONTRACT

A. Definition

1. It is a contract in which an <u>optionor</u> (generally an owner) gives an <u>optionee</u> (a prospective purchaser) the <u>right to buy or lease</u> the owner's property at a <u>fixed price for a certain period of time</u>.

    a. The <u>optionee pays a fee as consideration</u> for this right, but has no other obligation until they decide to either exercise the right to buy or lease, or allow the option to expire.

    b. The <u>optionor keeps the option fee if the optionee decides not to exercise the option</u>.

2. An option is a <u>unilateral</u> contract <u>binding only on the optionor</u>.

    a. The <u>optionor</u> is the only party making a <u>promise</u>.

    b. If the optionee (who did <u>not</u> make a promise) decides not to purchase, the optionor would have no legal recourse against them.

    c. If the option is exercised by the optionee, it becomes bilateral (a sales contract).

3. A lease may include an option for a tenant to purchase the property.

V.   AMENDMENTS, ADDENDA, CONTINGENCIES, AND TIME IS OF THE ESSENCE

A. Amendments

1. An <u>amendment</u> is a <u>change to the content of a contract</u>, and it occurs any time words or provisions are added or deleted from a contract.

2. Amendments <u>must be written, signed, and accepted by all parties</u> to the contract.

B. Addenda

1. An <u>addendum</u> is any <u>provision added and attached to an existing contract</u> without altering the content of the original contract.

2. Addenda <u>must be written, signed, and accepted by all parties</u> to the contract.

C. Contingencies

1. A <u>contingency</u> is a <u>condition that must be satisfied</u> before a contract is fully enforceable.

2. A contingency must be included as part of the contract, either as a clause or an addendum.

3. The <u>most common contingencies</u> in real estate sales contract include

   a. a mortgage or <u>finance contingency</u>, which protects the buyer's earnest money until a lender commits to finance the sale;

   b. an <u>inspection contingency</u>, providing the buyer the right to have professional inspections conducted on the property; and

   c. a <u>property sales contingency</u>, making the contract contingent upon the sale of the buyer's current home.

4. <u>Contingencies create a voidable contract, because the contract is void if the contingencies are not satisfied</u>.

D. "Time is of the essence"

1. Some contracts provide that "<u>time is of the essence</u>," which means <u>either the entire contract, or specific elements of the contract, must be performed within the time limits specified</u>.

2. A party who fails to perform on time can be liable for <u>a breach of contract</u>.

Parties to a contract

Offer	One receiving offer = offeree (ee's receive)	One giving offer = offeror (or's give)	**Only document where the parties can change**
Lease	Tenant = lessee	Landlord = lessor	
Option	Buyer = optionee	Seller = optionor	
Purchase agreement	Buyer = vendee	Seller = vendor	
Land contract or contract for deed	Buyer = vendee	Seller = vendor	
Mortgage	Lender = mortgagee	Buyer = mortgagor	
Deed of trust	Lender = beneficiary	Buyer = trustor	Third party = trustee
Deed	Buyer = grantee	Seller = grantor	

UNIT 8 REVIEW QUESTIONS

True/False Questions

1. An executed contract is a contract signed by all parties, but not yet completed.
    A. True
    B. False

2. A valid contract can be made for an unlawful purpose, provided all parties are aware of the illegality.
    A. True
    B. False

3. A valid contract has all these elements: consent, capacity, consideration, and lawful object.
    A. True
    B. False

4. Either party can exit a voidable contract.
    A. True
    B. False

5. Consideration is another term for *meeting of the minds*.
    A. True
    B. False

6. A promise may serve to satisfy the element of consideration.
    A. True
    B. False

7. A bilateral contract is the exchange of a promise for a promise.
    A. True
    B. False

8. A unilateral contract is the exchange of performance for performance.
    A. True
    B. False

9. A sales contract is a unilateral contract.
    A. True
    B. False

10. As long as the two parties agree on most terms, the sales contract is valid and binding.
    A. True
    B. False

11. If there are real estate agents involved in a transaction, they sign the sales contract.
    A. True
    B. False

12. If a buyer exits a sales contract via a contingency, the seller can sue for damages.
    A. True
    B. False

13. The owner is the optionee and the potential buyer is the optionor.
    A. True
    B. False

14. An option fee is typically refundable if the potential buyer decides not to buy the property.
    A. True
    B. False

15. An option contract is a bilateral contract.
    A. True
    B. False

16. An option contract can be used for sales or leases.
    A. True
    B. False

17. The buyer would sign an amendment to a listing agreement.
    A. True
    B. False

18. Parties to a contract typically have a wide latitude as to the time they must perform.
    A. True
    B. False

19. An amendment changes something in a contract, while an addendum adds something to a contract.
    A. True
    B. False

20. A common amendment is change of the sales price.
    A. True
    B. False

Multiple-Choice Questions

1. All of these are contracts between a real estate brokerage firm and a principal EXCEPT
   A. an open listing.
   B. a net listing.
   C. a multiple listing (MLS).
   D. an exclusive listing.

2. Which of these contracts would become void upon the death of one of the principals?
   A. Listing contract
   B. Sales contract
   C. Option contract
   D. Lease with termination date

3. Which of these lists contains only the essential elements of a valid contract?
   A. Consent, capacity, consideration, lawful purpose
   B. Consent, compensation, consideration, lawful object
   C. Negotiation, consent, counteroffers, legal purpose
   D. Consent, consideration, compensation, mutual agreement

4. Two old friends meet to discuss the sale of a parcel of real estate. Because they had been friends for decades, the buyer and seller decide they can dispense with a written purchase contract. One friend then backs out of the deal. Which of these laws will protect the friend who wants to proceed with the verbal agreement?
   A. Statute of frauds
   B. Statute of limitations
   C. Sherman Antitrust Act
   D. None of these

5. Something of value offered by the parties entering into a contract is called
   A. reality of consent.
   B. meeting of the minds.
   C. consideration.
   D. offer and acceptance.

6. A buyer made a written, noncontingent offer of $2,500,000 on a property, and the seller communicated acceptance. The buyer planned to build a shopping center but never mentioned it to the agent or the seller. Just before the closing, the buyer discovered that zoning prohibited a shopping center. What is the status of the sales contract?
   A. Valid
   B. Void
   C. Voidable
   D. Unenforceable

7. A prospective buyer and a seller enter into a written binding contract in which the seller agrees to sell at a specific price for a set term. Later, the buyer decides not to buy the property, and the seller has no recourse against the buyer. The contract is
   A. an estoppel agreement.
   B. an option agreement.
   C. an implied agreement.
   D. a bilateral agreement.

8. Who is the optionee in an option contract?
   A. Prospective vendor
   B. Prospective vendee
   C. Prospective trustor
   D. Prospective trustee

9. Which of these statements is FALSE?
   A. A land contract is also called an installment contract.
   B. If the "time is of the essence" clause is in a contract, the duties are expected to be performed on time.
   C. An equitable title is transferred when the deed is signed by the grantor at the closing table.
   D. Liquidated damages are agreed to in advance by the parties.

10. After a long period of negotiation, the seller and the buyer are under contract. The buyer's lender has some issues with finalizing the loan, so the buyer asks to postpone the closing by three days. The seller agrees to the change. To make the change binding and enforceable, the seller and the buyer should sign
    A. an accretion.
    B. an amendment.
    C. an addendum.
    D. an ad valorem.

11. A single-family residence is listed on the market. The seller communicates acceptance of the buyer's offer, and escrow is opened. The seller is represented by a real estate licensee, and the buyer is represented by a different real estate licensee. In the event the purchase contract is amended, who will sign that amendment?
    A. The seller and the seller's agent
    B. The buyer and the buyer's agent
    C. The seller and the buyer
    D. The seller, the seller's agent, the buyer, and the buyer's agent

UNIT 9

Property Valuation

LEARNING OBJECTIVE

When you have completed this unit, you will be able to accomplish the following.

› Explain appraisal concepts and the processes used by appraisers.

I. APPRAISALS

A. Purpose and use of appraisals for valuation

1. An <u>appraisal</u> is an estimate or <u>opinion of market value</u> and must be based on supportable evidence and approved methods.

    a. Appraisals are regulated at both a state and federal level.

    b. They are <u>required for all federally related loan programs</u>, such as FHA, VA, and conventional loans.

        i. A federally related loan is <u>any real estate financial transaction involving a federally regulated lender or financial institution</u>.

    c. Appraisals are <u>not required for cash transactions</u> or a <u>seller-carry loan</u>, such as a contract for deed (also called land contract or installment land contract).

2. Appraisals <u>must be done by a licensed or certified appraiser</u>.

    a. Appraisers must be licensed or certified according to state law, and in accordance with federal regulations.

        i. State appraisal regulations must conform to federal requirements that follow the criteria for certification by the Appraisal Qualifications Board of The Appraisal Foundation.

      ii. Appraisers are expected to follow the *Uniform Standards of Professional Appraisal Practice* (<u>USPAP</u>) established by the foundation's Appraisal Standards Board.

   b. Appraisers may obtain further designations, such as Member of the Appraisal Institute (<u>MAI</u>) or Senior Residential Appraiser (<u>SRA</u>).

B. Competitive market analysis (CMA)

   1. A <u>competitive market analysis (CMA)</u> is a <u>report</u> prepared by a licensed real estate professional <u>designed to assist a seller to determine a listing price or a buyer with determining an offering price for a property</u>.

      a. Even though real estate professionals can charge a fee for a CMA, they must be certain the CMA <u>cannot be considered an appraisal</u>, and <u>may not be used in the financing of a property</u> transaction.

   2. The CMA is modeled after the sales comparison approach in appraisal and arrives at a price by comparing data from comparable properties that have sold or are on the market.

C. Broker price opinion (BPO)

   1. A <u>broker price opinion (BPO)</u> is similar to a CMA, but is normally commissioned by a lender who wants to sell a property acquired through the foreclosure process, or an attorney handling a divorce or estate matter.

      a. Even though real estate professionals can charge a fee for a BPO, they must be certain the party paying them understands that a BPO <u>cannot be considered an appraisal</u>, and <u>may not be used to finance a property</u> transaction.

II. CONCEPTS OF VALUE

   ■ The best way for sellers to determine the market value of their property is to obtain an appraisal.

A. Market value vs. market price

   1. <u>Market value</u> is what a property <u>SHOULD</u> sell for when taking into account the following items:

      a. Value assumes the following:

         i. A competitive and open market

         ii. Both buyers and sellers assumed to be acting prudently and knowledgeably

         iii. Price is not being affected by unusual circumstances

   2. <u>Market price</u> is <u>what the property DOES sell for</u>—the actual price paid.

B. Effect on value of <u>economic principles</u> and property <u>characteristics</u>

   1. <u>Demand</u>—generally, the higher the demand for something, the greater its value.

   2. <u>Utility/usefulness</u>—the more useful something is, the more value it tends to have.

3. <u>Scarcity</u>

    a. Land is finite in supply, and land in specific areas may be scarce.

    b. Scarcity tends to increase value.

4. <u>Transferability</u>—if a property's title has several "clouds," it's not as easily transferred, and generally will lose some value as a result.

5. Memory aid DUST: demand, utility/usefulness, scarcity, and transferability

C. <u>Economic principles of value</u>

1. <u>Highest and best use</u>

    a. It is the use of the property that produces the greatest net return over time.

    b. It may not be the present use of the property.

    c. Appraisers <u>must show the current highest and best use of a property in every appraisal</u>:

        i. Highest and best use—<u>NOT included in a CMA or BPO</u>

2. Substitution

    a. When several similar properties are available for sale, demand will be greatest for the lowest-priced property.

    b. <u>An appraiser</u>, or a licensed real estate professional creating a CMA <u>using "comps" is using the principle of substitution.</u>

    c. Substitution <u>is used in all approaches to value</u>—especially the sales comparison approach.

        i. This is why substitution is <u>the most important principle to an appraiser.</u>

3. Supply and demand

    a. <u>Supply and demand sets both rental and listing prices.</u>

    b. <u>Supply</u> is the number of properties available.

        i. <u>Prices move opposite of supply</u>.

        ii. If there is a large number of properties for sale or rent, prices tend to go down.

    c. <u>Demand</u> is the number of properties that will be purchased.

        i. <u>Prices move with demand</u>.

        ii. If properties for sale or rent are scarce, prices tend to go up.

4. Contribution

    a. The <u>value of an improvement is based on its increasing or decreasing return, not</u> on the cost to make the improvement.

        i. An <u>increasing return</u> is when the <u>improvement adds more value than the cost</u> to do it.

        ii. A <u>decreasing return</u> is when the <u>improvement adds less value than the cost</u> to do it.

    b. Beyond a property's maximum value, additional improvement(s) may not contribute additional value.

5. Conformity

    a. <u>Values tend to move toward the surroundings.</u>

        i. <u>Regression</u>—the <u>value of an overimproved property declines</u> because of the properties surrounding it.

        ii. <u>Progression</u>—the <u>value of an underimproved property increases</u> because of the properties surrounding it.

III.   VALUATION METHODS

A.   <u>Sales comparison (market data) approach</u> (primarily residential)

1. An estimate of value is obtained by <u>comparing the property being appraised (subject) with recently sold properties (comparables/comps), which are similar</u> to the subject property.

    a. <u>Subject</u>—the <u>property being evaluated</u>

        i. <u>Adjustments are never made to the subject property.</u>

    b. <u>Comparables/comps</u>

        i. These are <u>similar properties that have recently sold.</u>

    c. Selecting comparables/comps

        i. The appraiser selects recently sold properties that are as close as possible to the subject in terms of size and characteristics.

        ii. The comps should be in, or as close as possible, to the subject's neighborhood.

        iii. Especially <u>in a rapidly changing market, an appraiser always uses the most current comps,</u> preferably those that have sold within 6 months but no longer than 12 months.

    d. <u>Adjustments</u>

        i. These are <u>always made to the sale price of the comparables/comps.</u>

        ii. Appraisers normally adjust for features, square footage, and location.

■ Market cycles, appreciating markets, and depreciating markets <u>can create the need for date of sale adjustments</u>.

iii. Because no two properties are alike, the appraiser makes <u>adjustments</u> for features in the <u>comparable properties</u> that either appear or are absent from the subject property, in an effort to make the comparables look as much like the subject as possible.

■ <u>If a feature of the comp is better</u> than the subject, the <u>appraiser subtracts</u> the value of that feature from the sale price of the comp.

■ <u>If a feature of the comp is worse</u> than the subject, the <u>appraiser adds</u> the value of that feature to the sale price of the comp.

■ Sometimes, the value of a feature being adjusted can be determined by <u>comparing properties with and without the feature</u> (paired sales analysis).

– Example: The value of a fireplace or an attached garage could be determined by finding two very similar comps—one with and the other without the fireplace or attached garage. The difference in their sale prices would give the appraiser the value of the fireplace or the attached garage.

iv. The adjusted sales prices of the comparable properties provide the probable range in value of the subject property, from which a fair market value can be determined for the subject property.

B. <u>Cost approach/summation approach</u>

1. This is the <u>most effective method for new construction and special-purpose or single-purpose buildings</u>.

a. <u>Cost to build new – accrued depreciation + value of the land = estimated value</u>

i. Estimating new construction cost

■ <u>Reproduction cost</u> is constructing a <u>replica</u> (duplicate) of the building using the same or highly similar materials.

■ <u>Replacement cost</u> is constructing a building similar to the subject, with the same function and utility, but <u>using current construction materials and methods</u>.

ii. Estimating the amount of accrued depreciation

■ <u>Depreciation is a loss in value for any reason</u>.

– <u>Physical depreciation</u> is <u>wear and tear</u> on a property resulting in deterioration, which may be <u>curable</u> (economically feasible to be repaired) or <u>incurable</u> (not economically feasible with little benefit for the value).

– <u>Functional obsolescence</u> is a loss in value due to <u>features that are outdated, outmoded, or no longer desirable</u> for purchasers, some of which may be replaced to contribute to the property's value.

    –   <u>Economic (external) obsolescence</u> are negative factors <u>not on the subject property</u>, such as environmental, social, or economic forces, which are <u>always incurable</u> because the loss in value cannot be cured by spending money on the property.

C. <u>Income approach</u>—for <u>income (rent)-producing properties</u> like apartments, office buildings, and shopping centers

1. <u>Capitalization</u> is the <u>process of future income to present value</u>.

     a.   Calculating <u>net operating income (NOI)</u>

         i.   Potential yearly gross income (rent) minus allowances for vacancies and bad debt equals effective gross income.

             ▪   Bad debt examples: money owed, NSF/bounced rent checks, etc.

         ii.   <u>Effective gross income minus operating expenses equals net operating income (NOI)</u>.

             ▪   Operating expenses do <u>NOT include debt service</u> (mortgage payments)

                 –   Debt service is used in determining cash flow: NOI – debt service = +/– cash flow

2. The appraiser then estimates the rate of return (or yield) that an investor would demand for investing in this property. This <u>rate of return</u> is called the <u>capitalization rate (cap rate)</u>.

3. <u>NOI divided by the capitalization rate</u> gives the appraiser an estimate of the <u>property's value</u>.

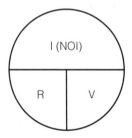

Income (net operating income) = Cap rate × Present Value

4. Certain formulas are important in dealing with income property:

     a.   Net operating <u>**i**ncome</u> (NOI) ÷ cap <u>**rate**</u> = <u>**value**</u>

     b.   Net operating <u>**i**ncome</u> (NOI) ÷ <u>**value**</u> = cap <u>**rate**</u>

     c.   Cap <u>**rate**</u> × <u>**value**</u> = net operating <u>**i**ncome</u> (NOI)

5. The gross <u>rent multiplier (GRM)</u> is a tool that an appraiser sometimes uses when appraising income-producing single-family properties such as homes, town homes, and condos, as well as duplexes.

     a.   The appraiser identifies the values of comparable leased properties in the area (normally four or more), along with the actual or estimated monthly rents they generate.

i. Dividing the individual comparable properties' values by the monthly rents they generate gives an appraiser a GRM.

ii. Here are examples:

- Value of one of the comparable properties is $250,000, divided by the $2,000 monthly rent it generates, equates to a GRM of 125

- Value of another comparable property is $225,000, divided by the $1,800 monthly rent it generates, equates to a GRM of 125

- Value of another comparable property is $240,000, divided by an estimate of $1,900 monthly rent it generates, equates to a GRM of 126

- Value of another comparable property is $265,000, divided by the $2,100 monthly rent it generates, equates to a GRM of 126

iii. Doing this, the appraiser determines that the average GRM in the area is 125.

b. The <u>estimated rent of the subject</u> property is then multiplied <u>by the GRM in the area to arrive at a rough estimate of the subject property's value</u>.

<u>GRM × **MONTHLY** GROSS RENT = ESTIMATED VALUE</u>

i. Remember—If you're given a GRM problem to solve, be certain to use <u>monthly</u> rent.

IV.   STEPS IN THE APPRAISAL PROCESS

A.   <u>State the problem.</u>

1. The first step of the appraisal process is to state the problem or the purpose for conducting the appraisal.

   a. Is the property being appraised to determine the market value because it is being sold?

   b. Is it being appraised to determine the cost to rebuild for insurance purposes?

B.   <u>Determine the scope of the work and data needed.</u>

C.   <u>Gather, record, and verify the necessary data.</u>

1. <u>General data</u> refers to information that covers the region, city, and neighborhood. This includes outside factors, such as social, economic, environmental/physical, and government forces that would affect the value of the property.

2. <u>Specific data</u> refers to the information used in the analysis of the subject property and the comparable properties that will be used in the valuation process. The legal description, environmental reports, and survey are gathered on the subject property.

D.   <u>Analyze the data and determine the highest and best use.</u>

E.   <u>Estimate the land value.</u>

F.   <u>**Estimate the value by the three approaches of estimating value.**</u>

G.   <u>**Reconciliation of values.**</u>

     1.   Use the estimated value received from the sales comparison, cost, and income approaches to arrive at a final value estimate for the subject property.

     2.   Analyze and weigh the effects of the three approaches to determine a final value estimate for the property.

     3.   Appraisers must consider and comment on all three approaches to value when completing an appraisal.

     4.   <u>Reconciliation is NOT averaging.</u>

H.   <u>**Report the final opinion of value.**</u>

UNIT 9 REVIEW QUESTIONS

True/False Questions

1. Appraisals are required for federally related loan programs.
   A. True
   B. False

2. An appraisal is an estimate or opinion of value supported by data in the appraiser's workfile.
   A. True
   B. False

3. The broker of record at a real estate brokerage firm can complete an appraisal.
   A. True
   B. False

4. Market value is the most recent purchase price for a property.
   A. True
   B. False

5. Appraisals are not required for cash transactions.
   A. True
   B. False

6. A competitive market analysis (CMA) is the same as an appraisal.
   A. True
   B. False

7. A property's highest and best use can change over time.
   A. True
   B. False

8. The principle of substitution is only used in the market data approach.
   A. True
   B. False

9. For appraisers, the most important aspect to an improvement is what it cost in terms of permits, materials, and labor.
   A. True
   B. False

10. Prices move with demand; prices move opposite of supply.
    A. True
    B. False

11. The principle of substitution posits that, if all other things are equal, the less expensive property will sell before the more expensive property.
    A. True
    B. False

12. Per the principle of regression, a mansion in a neighborhood of small, older homes will be less expensive.
    A. True
    B. False

13. The market data approach uses either the reproduction cost or the replacement cost.
    A. True
    B. False

14. Recently sold comparables are the basis of the sales comparison approach.
    A. True
    B. False

15. In the cost approach, there is only one way to estimate the cost of new construction.
    A. True
    B. False

16. Capitalization is the process of converting estimated future income into a property's present value.
    A. True
    B. False

17. In the income approach, debt service is included when calculating operating expenses.
    A. True
    B. False

18. Potential annual gross income (rent plus other income from the rental property) minus vacancies and collection losses equals effective gross income.
    A. True
    B. False

Multiple-Choice Questions

1. What would an appraiser consider external obsolescence in the cost approach to estimating value?
   A. An older building with small rooms
   B. Leaky windows, making the building unrentable
   C. Vacant and abandoned structures in the area
   D. Numerous ceiling support pillars in a commercial property

2. A married couple was divorcing and planned to sell the single-family residence they had used as their principal residence. Before the split, in order to generate rental income from the property, the couple had legally remodeled the master bedroom and bathroom into an accessory dwelling unit (ADU). The remodeling work cost $150,000. Why might the ADU have cost more than it added to the market value of the property?
   A. The property was situated in a very affluent area.
   B. The property was situated in an area where many owners had young children.
   C. The market for rental properties was depressed.
   D. All of these are correct.

3. What is the most effective method for estimating the value of new construction?
   A. Sales comparison approach
   B. Cost approach
   C. Income approach
   D. Gross multiplier

4. The principle of supply and demand means what?
   A. When supply is up, prices are up.
   B. When supply is up, rents are up.
   C. When demand is up, prices are down.
   D. When demand is down, rents are down.

5. The principle of value that is used in all three approaches to value is
   A. conformity.
   B. contribution.
   C. substitution.
   D. scarcity.

6. A broker met with a client looking to purchase a new home. The client said, "Find me the worst home in the best neighborhood." This reflects which of these principles of value?
   A. Conformity and regression
   B. Conformity and progression
   C. Contribution and regression
   D. Contribution and progression

7. When appraising a single-family home using the sales comparison approach to estimating value, an appraiser might have to make adjustments for
   A. a change in possible rental income.
   B. a change in the capitalization rate.
   C. the date of sale.
   D. assessed valuation changes.

8. Which of these is NOT found in the appraisal report relying upon the market data approach?
   A. Date of the inspection
   B. Condition of the subject property
   C. Adjustments of the subject property
   D. Signature of the appraiser

9. Reconciliation is an appraisal term used to describe
   A. the appraiser's determination of a property's highest value.
   B. the average values for properties similar to the one being appraised.
   C. the appraiser's analysis and comparison of the results of each appraisal approach.
   D. the method used to determine a property's most appropriate capitalization rate.

10. A real estate investor owns a 20-unit apartment building. There are 10 units that rent for $1,000; the other 10 units rent for $1,500. There is a 5% vacancy rate. Additional income from storage facilities is $1,200 annually. What is the effective gross income (EGI)?
    A. $285,231
    B. $286,140
    C. $286,231
    D. $287,543

UNIT 10

Finance

LEARNING OBJECTIVE

When you have completed this unit, you will be able to accomplish the following.

› Describe basic finance concepts and terminology, the various types of real estate financing, and laws affecting financing.

I.   LIEN THEORY VS. TITLE THEORY

A. Lien theory states

1. In lien theory states, equitable and legal title pass to the buyer at closing, and the borrower (mortgagor) gives a mortgage to the lender (mortgagee), pledging the property as collateral (security) for the loan.

    a.   The mortgage is a two-party instrument:

        i.   Mortgagor (borrower), who is giving the mortgage to the lender

        ii. Mortgagee (lender), who is receiving it from the borrower

2. The mortgage creates a lien on the property and is held by the mortgagee (lender) until the loan is paid in full.

    a.   When the loan is paid, the mortgagee (lender) releases its lien with a satisfaction.

    b.   The satisfaction should be recorded in the county in which the property is located, as proof that the lender no longer has an interest in the property.

3. If the mortgagor defaults on the loan, the mortgagee can foreclose.

B. Title theory states

1. In <u>title theory states, legal title does not pass to the buyer at closing</u>.

2. The <u>borrower</u> (buyer) gets equitable title and the right of possession, and <u>conveys</u> bare <u>legal title</u> (naked title—without the right of possession) <u>to a third party trustee using a deed of trust</u>. The trustee holds the deed of trust on behalf of the lender who has the promissory note for the loan on the property.

   a. The <u>deed of trust is a three-party instrument</u>:

      i. Trustor—borrower (buyer)

      ii. Trustee

      iii. Beneficiary—lender

   b. When the loan is paid, the beneficiary notifies the <u>trustee</u>, who <u>returns legal title to the borrower using a deed of reconveyance</u>, also known as a release deed.

   c. The borrower then records the deed of reconveyance in the county in which the property is located, as proof that they now have full legal title to the property.

3. If the buyer defaults on the loan, the trustee can foreclose for the benefit of the lender.

II.   FINANCING INSTRUMENTS

A. Promissory note

1. <u>Evidence of the debt</u> owed, containing of the borrower's promise to repay and the terms of repayment

2. Features may include the following:

   a. Prepayment clause

      i. PREPAYMENT PRIVILEGE allows borrower to prepay the loan early with no penalty

      ii. <u>PREPAYMENT PENALTY requires borrower to pay a penalty for any principal sums repaid to the lender BEFORE they are due</u>

   b. <u>Acceleration clause</u>, which <u>allows the lender to call the loan early when the borrower is in default</u>

3. Promissory note is secured by either a mortgage or a deed of trust

B. <u>Mortgage and deed of trust</u> (security instruments)

1. Contracts that <u>pledge the property as security (collateral) for the loan</u> on the property without the buyer giving up possession of the property

2. This includes the following <u>covenants (promises) made by the borrower</u>, breaking any of which is a default and could cause foreclosure:

    a.   Nonpayment of principal and interest

    b.   Nonpayment of property taxes and special assessment

    c.   Inadequate or no insurance

    d.   Removing improvements that add value to the property without the lender's approval

    e.   Committing waste (not maintaining the property)

    f.   Due-on-sale clause/alienation

        i.   Allows the lender to accelerate the loan if the borrower sells the property without paying off the loan

        ii.   Stops assumption without the lender's consent

3. <u>Includes an acceleration clause</u>, allowing the lender to demand immediate payment of the entire unpaid balance of the loan if the mortgagor is in default

4. Defeasance clause (root word is *defeat*)

    a.   When the loan is paid off (defeated), lender promises to release its interest in the property

III. FORECLOSURE, DEED IN LIEU OF FORECLOSURE, AND SHORT SALES

A. <u>Foreclosure</u>

1. Foreclosure is a legal <u>process whereby property pledged as security for a debt is either taken by a creditor or is sold to pay off the debt.</u>

    a.   If a borrower defaults on a loan, a lender can accelerate the due date (call the loan early) and demand payment of the remaining principal balance and all other payments and costs.

        i.   If the borrower continues in default, the lender can foreclose.

    b.   <u>Insufficient proceeds from a foreclosure sale could result in a deficiency judgment or personal judgment against the borrower.</u> This is known as a default judgment.

    c.   A <u>foreclosure removes all junior liens</u> from a property. <u>Liens superior to the loan, such as taxes and special assessments, remain.</u>

    d.   Foreclosure laws are determined by individual states.

B. Deed in lieu of foreclosure

1. Alternative to foreclosure

    a.   Mortgagor deeds property to the mortgagee

2. Lender does <u>not</u> have to accept

3. Advantage to the lender is avoiding the expense of foreclosing, or ending up owning the property and carrying it as real estate owned (REO) asset

4. Disadvantage to the lender is a deed in lieu <u>does not wipe out junior liens</u>

   a. If lender accepts a deed in lieu of foreclosing, lender takes title subject to any junior liens

C. Short sale

1. Typically occurs when a property owner is either in or facing foreclosure

2. Owner or licensee contacts lender to learn if the lender will consider releasing its interest if the property sells for less than (sells "short" of) the amount owed on the loan

3. Property is then listed, often for a price lower than what is owed on the loan

4. Any <u>offer must be contingent on the lender's approval of the sale</u>:

   a. Even though the lender agreed to consider a short sale, the <u>lender is not obligated</u> to approve one, and <u>may or may not agree to accept a reduced (deficient) price.</u>

   b. The lender may require the seller (original mortgagor) to pay any deficiency.

   c. The seller may have tax consequences, as forgiven debt is considered taxable income in most cases.

IV. FINANCING TERMS

A. <u>Loan-to-value ratio (LTV)</u>

1. This is the <u>maximum percentage of a property's value that the lender will lend.</u>

2. LTV <u>determines the amount of the loan, and whether the borrower will have to pay insurance (PMI or MIP).</u>

3. LTV is <u>always based on the sale price or appraisal, whichever is less.</u>

4. <u>The lower the LTV, the greater the down payment required.</u>

B. Private mortgage insurance (PMI) and mortgage insurance premium (MIP)

1. <u>Private mortgage insurance (PMI)</u> is normally <u>required by lenders on conventional loans with LTVs higher than 80%.</u>

   a. If the borrower defaults, PMI <u>helps protect the lender against loss due to foreclosure, and covers the difference between 80% LTV and the LTV% of the actual loan.</u>

      i. Example: A borrower gets a 95% LTV loan. The PMI covers the dollar amount difference between 80% LTV and 95% LTV.

   b. PMI is <u>paid by the borrower.</u>

      c.   It allows lenders to provide loans to borrowers with LTVs higher than 80%, which translates into lower down payments.

             i.   <u>The higher the LTV, the lower the down payment.</u>

      d.   PMI automatically <u>terminates if a borrower has accumulated 22% equity</u> in the home and is current on mortgage payments.

             i.   This is based on the original purchase price of the home.

             ii.   The lender is not required to consider market appreciation or improvements the borrower has made, but may be willing to do so.

                  ■   The borrower must contact the lender to determine how to proceed, and the lender may require an appraisal.

  2.   The <u>mortgage insurance premium (MIP)</u> is a similar <u>insurance program associated with FHA loans</u>.

      a.   If the borrower defaults, the MIP <u>helps protect the lender against loss due to foreclosure, and covers the entire loan balance</u>.

      b.   Unlike PMI, the <u>MIP is paid by the borrower for the entire life of the loan</u>.

C. <u>Equity</u>

  1.   <u>Market value today – total debt today = equity today</u>

D. **Points and loan origination fee**

  1.   Lenders charge <u>points to increase the yield (profit) on a loan</u>.

      a.   When an interest rate is less than the yield demanded by an investor who will buy the loan, the lender makes up the difference by charging discount points.

      b.   <u>One point = 1% of the loan amount</u>.

  2.   The <u>loan origination fee</u> is what the lender <u>charges to process and issue a loan</u>.

E. <u>Leverage</u>

  1.   This is the <u>use of borrowed money to increase returns on investments</u>.

  2.   The <u>advantage</u> is the <u>borrower can control a large asset with very little of the borrower's own money</u>.

  3.   The <u>disadvantage</u> is the <u>higher risk of default.</u>

      a.   The lower the borrower's equity, the higher the risk of the borrower defaulting.

F. <u>Interest</u>

  1.   This is the <u>percentage of profit the lender wants</u> in return for using the lender's money.

  2.   State laws often control the maximum rate of interest that lenders can charge, depending on the type of loan (e.g., home loan, car loan, student loan).

G. <u>Usury</u>

    1. This is when a lender <u>charges an illegally high interest rate</u>—higher than what's permitted by state law.

        a. States determine which loans will have interest rate ceilings, and what those ceiling are.

H. **Principal, interest, taxes, and insurance (<u>PITI</u>)**

    1. This is the monthly payment made by borrowers that includes the <u>debt service (principal and interest)</u> on their home loan, <u>plus one month's worth of property taxes and one month's worth of the homeowners insurance premium.</u>

        a. The amounts for the property taxes and insurance collected every month by the lender are held by the lender in a borrower's escrow account. The lender then pays the yearly property taxes and insurance premium when they come due.

            i. <u>Lenders require a borrower to acquire and maintain a homeowner's insurance policy (a.k.a. hazard insurance)</u> covering damage or theft in an amount equal to at least 80% of the replacement cost of the property.

           ii. To finance property with federal or federally related mortgage loans, <u>owners in flood-prone areas must also obtain flood insurance.</u>

                ■ Flood insurance is required on all types of buildings for either the value of the property, or the amount of the mortgage loan, subject to maximum limits.

I. <u>Subordination</u>

    1. This is a <u>clause</u> found in some mortgages <u>allowing another lienholder to take higher priority in the public record.</u>

        a. Example: A lender who made a home improvement loan to a property owner who pledged the property as collateral for the loan may "subordinate" its lien position to a new lender in a property refinance.

V.   **METHODS OF DEBT SERVICE (DEBT REPAYMENT)**

A. <u>Fully amortized loans</u>

    1. <u>Each payment pays the interest due and part of the principal balance.</u>

        a. The lender credits each payment to the interest first, then to the principal.

        b. Each succeeding payment goes less to interest and more to reduce the principal balance of the loan.

        c. There is <u>no balloon</u> at the end because the final payment reduces the principal amount to zero.

B. <u>Partially amortized loans</u>

    1. These are similar to fully amortized loans in that each payment pays the interest due and part of the principal balance, but <u>the full amount of principal is not paid off by the end of the term.</u>

    a.   The <u>remaining amount of principal due at the end of the term is paid in one lump sum called a balloon</u>.

    b.   The <u>monthly payment is smaller than a fully amortized loan, but larger than a term/straight/interest-only loan</u>.

C. Term/straight/interest-only loans

    1.   <u>Only interest is paid during the term</u> of the loan.

    2.   It is a <u>small monthly payment (interest only), but a large balloon</u>.

        a.   The full amount of principal is due at the end.

VI.   TYPES OF LOANS

A. <u>Conventional/insured conventional loans</u>

    1.   These are <u>not insured or guaranteed by the government</u>.

    2.   They must meet all the requirements of the secondary market set by Fannie Mae and Freddie Mac for conforming loans.

    3.   They may <u>require private mortgage insurance (PMI) for LTVs higher than 80%</u>.

        a.   The advantage to the buyer is a smaller down payment.

B. <u>FHA-insured loans</u>

    1.   The FHA <u>insures lenders</u> against losses due to foreclosure.

        a.   The <u>FHA does not lend money—approved lenders lend money</u>.

        b.   HUD qualifies lenders to participate in the FHA program.

        c.   Appraisers must be FHA certified.

    2.   There is <u>never a prepayment penalty</u>.

    3.   FHA loans are <u>fully assumable by qualified buyers</u>.

C. <u>VA-guaranteed loans</u>

    1.   The <u>VA guarantees lenders</u> against losses due to foreclosure.

        a.   The <u>VA does not lend money—approved lenders lend money</u>.

        b.   The VA charges a <u>funding fee</u> on each loan to finance their guarantee program.

        c.   HUD qualifies lenders to participate in the VA program.

        d.   Appraisers must be VA certified.

           i.   The <u>VA appraisal is called a certificate of reasonable value (CRV)</u>.

2. <u>Borrowers must meet eligibility requirements</u> set by the VA.

   a. These are <u>available to qualified veterans</u>, active National Guard members, retired military reserve members, and eligible surviving spouses of veterans who died during duty or who passed away due to a disability suffered during service.

   b. <u>Parents of veterans are not eligible.</u>

3. <u>Up to 100% LTV is allowed.</u>

4. There is <u>never a prepayment penalty</u>.

5. <u>Nonveterans who qualify may assume a VA loan.</u>

D. <u>U.S. Department of Agriculture (USDA)/rural loan programs</u>

1. The <u>Farm Service Agency (FSA)</u>, an agency of the Department of Agriculture, offers programs to help families purchase or operate family farms.

   a. The FSA <u>provides programs to assist families with purchasing and improving single-family homes in rural areas</u>.

   b. The FSA does make some direct loans.

   c. The FSA guarantees a percentage of loans made and serviced by private lenders.

   d. The Farm Credit System provides loans to farmers, ranchers, rural homeowners, agricultural cooperatives, rural utility systems, and agribusiness.

E. <u>Amortized loans</u>

1. <u>Each payment in an amortized loan partially pays interest as well as a portion of the principal.</u>

   a. Most mortgages and deeds of trust are amortized loans.

   b. In a fully amortized loan, the lender credits each payment first to the interest due, then to the principal amount of the loan.

F. <u>Adjustable-rate loans (ARMs)</u>

1. The <u>interest rate is tied to a specific economic index and can fluctuate</u> up or down depending on how the indicator fluctuates.

2. Because the interest rate can change, the borrower's loan payment can change (adjust).

3. <u>Index + lender's margin = borrower's interest rate.</u>

   a. For example, a 3% index + 2% margin = 5% borrower's interest rate.

      i. The margin always remains the same, but the index can change.

4. ARMs often include <u>interest and/or payment caps</u>, which helps limit how much the loan payments can change.

G. Bridge loans

1. <u>A bridge loan is a type of short-term loan to cover the period (bridge the gap) between the end of one loan and the beginning of another loan.</u>

2. Here are examples:

    a. A buyer of a new home may get a bridge loan (second mortgage) on their unsold home to fund the purchase of a new home when the seller of the new home won't accept an offer "subject to the sale of the buyer's home".

    b. An investor may get a bridge loan to fund the cost of converting an apartment building to a condominium.

    c. An owner building their own home might get a bridge loan to cover the time between a construction loan and a longer-term amortized loan.

H. Blanket loans

1. A blanket mortgage secures multiple properties in one loan.

2. They are often used in construction lending for development of subdivisions or condominium projects.

3. The loan includes a <u>partial release clause</u> allowing a developer to pay back a portion of the loan and get a release for each lot as they are sold.

I. Package loans

1. A package mortgage <u>includes both real estate and personal property</u> (chattel) as security for the loan.

2. Typically used in the sale of new subdivision loans and the sale of condominiums where furniture and appliances are included in the sale.

J. Reverse mortgages

1. The <u>mortgagee</u> (lender) <u>makes payments to the mortgagor</u> (borrower).

2. Reverse mortgages are <u>used by seniors to obtain money from their equity in the property</u> when they don't want to sell, but they want or need cash.

3. The loan becomes due upon the sale of the property, death of the mortgagor, or at the end of the term agreed to by the borrower and the lender.

K. Subprime loans

1. The <u>borrower pays a higher rate of interest</u> because they fall below "prime" standards as set by the secondary mortgage market and are more likely to default than a "prime" borrower.

L. Owner financing

1. <u>Contract for deed (also called land contract or installment land contract)</u>

a.   A buyer (<u>vendee</u>) and seller (<u>vendor</u>) agree to buyer making a down payment, and then monthly payments of principal and interest for a specific term, at the end of which a balloon payment is typically due.

    i.   <u>The seller (vendor) retains legal title</u> and holds the deed <u>until the contract is fulfilled</u>.

    ii.   <u>The buyer (vendee) gets equitable title and the right of possession.</u>

        ◼   The buyer (vendee) pays all property expenses, including taxes, insurance, maintenance, and so on.

    iii.   <u>The seller (vendor) transfers legal title via a deed when the buyer (vendee) makes the final payment</u>.

2.   Owner financing may occur with residential or commercial transactions, but it is more common with <u>unimproved acreage and farmland sales</u>.

VII.   PRIMARY AND SECONDARY MORTGAGE MARKETS

A.   Primary mortgage market

1.   There are lenders that <u>originate mortgage loans and deal directly with borrowers</u>:

a.   Commercial banks

b.   Credit unions

c.   S&Ls (savings and loans)

d.   <u>Mortgage bankers</u>

    i.   <u>Originate and service loans with their own money</u>

e.   <u>Mortgage brokers</u>

    i.   <u>Act as intermediaries between borrowers and lenders</u>, and don't normally service loans

        ◼   Mortgage brokers <u>don't lend their own money</u>; they put borrowers and lenders together for a fee

B.   Secondary mortgage market

1.   <u>This buys loans (promissory notes secured by mortgages and deeds of trust) from primary market lenders to supplement the mortgage and lending process</u> (i.e., was created to help ensure that the primary market doesn't run out of money).

2.   It <u>sets strict criteria on mortgage loans that can be purchased</u>:

a.   <u>Conforming loans meet these criteria</u>

b.   <u>Borrowers may have to send their monthly payments to a new address if their mortgage loan is sold</u>

3. Using pools of mortgages as collateral, the secondary market creates and sells mortgage-backed securities and bonds to investors.

4. This includes <u>Fannie Mae, Ginnie Mae, and Freddie Mac</u>:

   a. <u>Fannie Mae (Federal National Mortgage Association [FNMA])</u>

      i. Government-sponsored but publicly owned corporation that issues its own common stock

      ii. Buys all types of mortgage loans—conventional, FHA, and VA

      iii. Fannie Mae—<u>largest investor in residential mortgage loans</u>

   b. <u>Ginnie Mae</u> (Government National Mortgage Association [GNMA])

      i. A division of HUD, organized as a corporation but without corporate stock

      ii. <u>Does not buy or sell loans, or issue mortgage-backed securities</u>

         ■ Administers special assistance programs

         ■ <u>Guarantees</u> investment securities issued by private offerors (like banks, mortgage companies and S&Ls), backed by pools of <u>FHA and VA mortgages</u>

   c. <u>Freddie Mac</u> (Federal Home Loan Mortgage Corporation [FHLMC])

      i. Government-sponsored but publicly owned corporation that issues its own common stock

      ii. Primarily <u>buys conventional mortgages</u> and uses them as security for bonds sold on the open market

VIII.   LAWS AFFECTING FINANCING AND LENDING

A.   Truth In Lending Act and Regulation Z

1. Regulation Z of the Truth in Lending Act requires that <u>when a loan is secured by a residence, the lender must disclose the lender's finance charges</u> to the borrower—in other words, the <u>true cost of obtaining credit—APR</u>:

   a. Loan origination fees

   b. Interest rate on the loan

   c. Discount points

   d. Assumption fees

2. <u>APR is the **effective** rate that includes the loan rate PLUS the total amount of the lender's finance charges</u> expressed as a percentage.

3. The APR will always be higher than the interest rate of the loan.

4. The borrower has a <u>three-day right of rescission,</u> but only <u>on home equity loans and refinances.</u>

    a. This right of rescission <u>does not apply when purchasing a first home, a vacation home, or when using a construction loan.</u>

5. With advertising, the <u>price and/or APR are the only specific terms allowed</u> in advertising without triggering full disclosure.

    a. These are <u>triggering items</u> in ads that require full disclosure:

        i. Percentage of down payment

        ii. Amount of any installment payment

        iii. Number of payments

        iv. Time period of payments

        v. Finance charge

        vi. Interest rate of the loan

    b. If any of these terms are used in advertising, the lender must disclose the following:

        i. Cash price

        ii. Required down payment

        iii. Number, amount, and due dates of all payments

        iv. Annual percentage rate

        v. Total of all payments to be made over the life of the loan

        vi. Interest rate of the loan

    c. General terms are okay, like *low down payment.*

    d. Violations include both civil and criminal penalties.

6. Regulation Z applies to all consumer loans, including mortgage loans, but it <u>does not apply to the following</u>:

    a. Loans to corporations

    b. Business or commercial loans

    c. Seller financing

B. <u>Real Estate Settlement Procedures Act (RESPA)</u>

1. Its purpose is to <u>ensure that the seller and the buyer are fully informed of all settlement (closing) costs,</u> and to standardize settlement (closing) practices for one- to four-family properties financed by federally related lenders.

2. It requires an estimate of loan costs at application, and disclosure of actual loan costs before closing.

    a. It requires lenders to give the *Guide to Settlement Costs* booklet and a good-faith estimate of all closing costs at the time of application, or no later than three days after application.

    b. It allows the borrower the right to inspect the Settlement Statement (HUD-1) one day before closing.

3. It <u>prohibits kickbacks among real estate licensees, lenders, and title companies</u>. While a lender cannot pay a broker a fee for referring the client to the lender, <u>payments between cooperating brokers or between real estate salespeople and their employing broker are exempt.</u>

C. <u>TILA-RESPA Integrated Disclosure (TRID)</u>

1. In 2015, key TILA and RESPA disclosures for sellers and buyers were integrated by TRID.

2. Two new disclosure forms were created by the <u>Consumer Financial Protection Bureau (CFPB),</u> which is responsible for the <u>enforcement</u> of the TRID provisions.

3. <u>Loan Estimate (LE)</u>

    a. Provides an <u>accurate description of the costs associated with obtaining the mortgage loan and settlement costs</u>

    b. <u>Must be delivered to the borrower no later than three business days after the lender's receipt of the loan application,</u> and the loan cannot close until at least seven business days after the lender's receipt of that application

4. <u>Closing Disclosure (CD)</u>

    a. Shows the <u>actual loan and settlement costs</u> of the transaction

    b. <u>Must be received by the borrower at least three business days before closing</u>, and the lender must have proof that the buyer received it

    c. <u>If the APR increases, or if a prepayment penalty is added, or if the type of loan changes after the buyer receives the CD, a new CD is required</u>, which could delay closing

5. Applies to all federally related residential mortgage loans <u>EXCEPT</u> the following:

    a. Home equity loans or lines of credit

    b. Mobile homes

    c. Reverse mortgages

    d. Seller financing

D. Equal Credit Opportunity Act (ECOA)

1. This prohibits <u>discrimination in all consumer credit transactions</u> (including mortgage loans) <u>based on an applicant's race, religion, color, sex, national origin, marital status, age, or receipt of public assistance.</u>

    a. Examples

        i. If an applicant otherwise qualifies, a lender cannot refuse to make a loan to retired persons.

        ii. A lender may not deny a mortgage loan to someone because they are or are not married.

        iii. A lender cannot refuse to make a loan to an applicant receiving public assistance/income if the applicant otherwise qualifies.

2. ECOA does not protect minors, a person's sexual orientation, or those with erratic employment histories.

3. ECOA also requires lenders to give an applicant notice of why their credit application was refused.

IX. MORTGAGE FRAUD AND PREDATORY LENDING

A. <u>Mortgage fraud</u>

1. This is the act of <u>inducing or securing a mortgage loan through either implied or expressed deceit.</u>

    a. It includes the entire process of obtaining a residential mortgage, and all the documents involved in that process.

    b. Many states have enacted laws codifying the term *mortgage fraud* and establishing <u>stiff civil and criminal penalties</u> for those found guilty of mortgage fraud.

B. <u>Predatory lending</u>

1. This is an umbrella term for <u>unfair or illegal lending practices.</u>

2. It involves practices by a lender to make loans to people who will be unable to repay the loan.

3. It often occurred in the subprime market.

    a. An example is a subprime loan coupled with down payment assistance (second mortgage) in which the borrower made no down payment (i.e., borrowed 100% of the purchase price). This made the loans more likely to default.

4. Many states now have predatory lending laws that require lenders and loan originators to be licensed, and have enacted penalties for real estate licensees who participate in such schemes.

UNIT 10 REVIEW QUESTIONS

True/False Questions

1. A mortgage impacts the way legal and equitable title to the property is held.
   - A. True
   - B. False

2. A trust deed is signed by the trustor and conveys bare legal title to the beneficiary.
   - A. True
   - B. False

3. A promissory note is the promise of the mortgagor to pay back the loan and agreed-upon interest to the mortgagee.
   - A. True
   - B. False

4. A reconveyance deed and a satisfaction of mortgage both show that a loan has been paid in full, and that the lien has been removed from the property.
   - A. True
   - B. False

5. A package loan packages multiple parcels into one loan.
   - A. True
   - B. False

6. A partial release clause is a typical feature of the reverse mortgage.
   - A. True
   - B. False

7. Promissory notes are sold on the primary mortgage market.
   - A. True
   - B. False

8. Loans are originated in the secondary mortgage market, and sold on the primary mortgage market.
   - A. True
   - B. False

9. The TILA-RESPA Integrated Disclosure (TRID) rule regulates the disclosures that prospective mortgagors must make to prospective mortgagees.
   - A. True
   - B. False

10. A purpose of FHA insurance is that it protects the lender from foreclosure losses should the borrower default on the loan.
    - A. True
    - B. False

11. Private mortgage insurance (PMI) is normally required by lenders on conventional loans with LTVs less than 80%.
    - A. True
    - B. False

12. Usury is when a lender charges an interest rate higher than what's permitted by state law.
    - A. True
    - B. False

13. A short sale occurs when a lender allows a borrower to sell a property for less than what is currently outstanding on the loan.
    - A. True
    - B. False

14. A deficiency judgment might be issued by a court when a property sells at a foreclosure sale for less than what is outstanding on the foreclosing lien.
    - A. True
    - B. False

15. In a contract for deed, the vendor holds legal title and the vendee holds equitable title.
    - A. True
    - B. False

16. A contract for deed is also known as an installment sales contract or a land contract.
    - A. True
    - B. False

17. A contract for deed is a form of seller financing.
    - A. True
    - B. False

18. The vendee does not have the right to possess and occupy the property until the land contract is paid in full.
    - A. True
    - B. False

Multiple-Choice Questions

1. If a borrower was in default on their mortgage payments, the lender could call the entire loan balance due if the loan included
   A. a due-on-sale clause.
   B. an acceleration clause.
   C. a defeasance clause.
   D. a subordination clause.

2. A buyer purchased a single-family residence for $1 million. To finance the purchase, the buyer took out a $800,000 mortgage loan, at a 5% interest rate. The loan was a fully amortized 30-year fixed-rate loan. Which of these terms refers to the interest the homeowner paid to the lender over the term of the loan?
   A. Return on the investment
   B. Return of the investment
   C. Principal
   D. Principle

3. A mortgage using both real and personal property as security is
   A. a blanket mortgage.
   B. a package mortgage.
   C. a dual mortgage.
   D. a wraparound mortgage.

4. A buyer used one real estate agent to both find a home and find a lender able to finance the purchase of the home. Where did the buyer and the lender negotiate the terms of the loan?
   A. Primary mortgage market
   B. Secondary mortgage market
   C. Multiple listing service
   D. FICO score

5. The Real Estate Settlement Procedures Act (RESPA) applies to
   A. federal tax credits, when they are available.
   B. only Federal Housing Administration loans.
   C. only Federal Veteran Administration loans.
   D. federally related mortgage loans.

6. Which lender uses its own money to fund mortgage loans?
   A. Mortgage brokers
   B. Ginnie Mae
   C. Mortgage bankers
   D. The FHA

7. The type of loan that provides for increases in loan payments if interest rates rise is called
   A. an adjustable-rate mortgage.
   B. a bridge loan.
   C. a reverse mortgage.
   D. a straight loan.

8. Under the federal Truth in Lending Act (TILA), which of these are "trigger terms" requiring full disclosure in an advertisement?
   A. The listing price
   B. Monthly payments
   C. The annual percentage rate
   D. HOA dues

UNIT 11

Real Estate Calculations

LEARNING OBJECTIVE

When you have completed this unit, you will be able to accomplish the following.

> Solve math problems using formulas commonly used in the real estate industry.

I.   **MEASUREMENT**

A. **Square footage**

1. Remember these conversions:

a. 12 inches = 1 foot

b. 36 inches = 1 yard

c. 3 feet = 1 yard

d. Inches ÷ 12 = feet (144 inches ÷ 12 = 12 feet)

e. Feet × 12 = inches (12 feet × 12 = 144 inches)

2. The area of a square or rectangle is <u>length × width = area</u>.

3. For example, how many square feet are in a room that is 15 feet × 30 feet?

a. 15 ft. × 30 ft. = 450 sq. ft. (square feet)

B. Acreage total

1. Remember this conversion:

   a. 43,560 sq. ft. = 1 acre

   b. Sq. ft. ÷ 43,530 = acres

   c. For example, 87,120 sq. ft. ÷ 43,560 = 2 acres

   d. Acres × 43,560 = sq. ft.

   e. For example, 2 acres × 43,560 = 87,120 sq. ft.

II.   FINANCE

A. Purchase price and down payment

1. The amount of a down payment may be determined by multiplying the purchase price by the percentage of down payment being made.

2. Down payment in dollars = purchase price × down payment percentage.

3. For example, a 20% down payment on a purchase price of $250,000 is $50,000 ($250,000 × 0.20 (20%) = $50,000). Dividing the down payment by the percentage will result in the purchase price: $50,000 ÷ 0.20 = $250,000.

B. Loan-to-value (LTV) ratio

1. The LTV is the ratio of debt to value of a property. The value for financing purposes is the sale price or the appraised value, whichever is less.

2. LTV = loan amount (the debt) ÷ sales price or appraised value.

3. For example, if a purchaser borrows $80,000 for a purchase of $100,000, the LTV is 80% (80,000 ÷ 100,000 = 0.80 (80%)).

   a. To calculate the amount of funds required for the LTV of 80%:

      i. $100,000 × 0.80 = $80,000

      ii. $100,000 − $80,000 = $20,000 the amount of down payment required from the purchaser

C. Amortization (PITI)

1. A real estate licensee can determine how much of each month's mortgage payment is being applied toward principal and how much is being applied toward interest. A licensee should advise a client to consult with a mortgage broker or lender to discuss mortgage options available.

2. Useful formulas include the following:

   a. Monthly payment − monthly interest payment = amount paid toward principal

   b.   Principal balance × annual interest rate ÷ 12 = <u>one month's interest</u>

   c.   Principal balance − amount paid toward principal = <u>new principal balance</u>

3. For example, assume a 15-year mortgage loan for $150,000 at 3.75% annual interest and a monthly payment of $1,090.50:

   a.   To calculate one month's interest:

      i. 150,000 × 0.0375 (3.75%) = $5,625.00 annual interest ÷ 12 months = first month's interest of $468.75

   b.   To calculate the amount paid toward principal:

      i. $1,090.50 − $468.75 = $621.75

   c.   To calculate the new principal balance after one month's payment:

      i. $150,000 − $621.75 = $149,378.25

4. A <u>loan payment factor</u> can be used to calculate the <u>monthly principal and interest payment</u> on a loan. The payment factor represents the monthly principal and interest payment to amortize a $1,000 loan. The payment factor is based on the annual interest rate and the term of the loan:

   a.   (Loan amount ÷ $1,000) × loan payment factor = monthly PI payment

   b.   Monthly PI payment ÷ loan payment factor = loan amount

5. For example, if a lender uses a loan payment factor of $6.99 per $1,000 of loan amount, the monthly PI (principal and interest) payment on a $301,680 loan amount will be $2,108.74:

   a.   ($301,680 loan amount ÷ $1,000) = $301.68

   b. $301.68 × 6.99 = $2,108.74 (rounded to the nearest cent)

D. Interest

1. Formulas useful in the calculating of interest on a mortgage loan include the following:

   a.   Loan amount (principal) × annual interest rate = <u>annual interest</u>

   b.   Annual interest ÷ annual interest rate = <u>loan amount</u> (principal)

   c.   Annual interest ÷ loan amount (principal) = <u>annual interest rate</u>

2. For example, a parcel of land sold for $335,200. The lender approved a 90% loan at 4.5% interest for 30 years. The appraised value on the parcel was $335,500. The interest paid to the lender in the first monthly payment can be calculated as follows:

   a. $335,200 (<u>sales price is the lesser of the two values</u>) × 90% = $301,680 loan amount

   b. $301,680 × 0.045 = $13,575.60 annual interest

   c. $13,575.60 ÷ 12 = $1,131.30 <u>interest payment</u>

E. Discount points, prepayment penalties

1. Reminder—discount points are charges by a lender to increase the yield on a loan.

    a.   To calculate <u>discount points</u>:

        i.   One point equals <u>1%</u> of loan amount

        ii. Loan amount × <u>points converted to a percentage</u> = amount for points

    b.   Example—a lender charges 3.5 loan discount points on a loan of $80,000, resulting in $2,800 paid for discount points:

        i. $80,000 (loan amount) × 0.035 (3.5 points) = $2,800

    c.   Some mortgage notes contain a <u>prepayment penalty clause. This penalty occurs when principal sums are repaid to the lender before they are due.</u> The penalty may be as little as 1% of the principal sum being prepaid.

    d.   For example, a borrower's remaining balance on a loan is $120,000. The borrower sells the home and prepays the $120,000 to the lender. If the lender charges <u>1% of the principal as a prepayment penalty</u>, the prepayment penalty will be $1,200:

        i. $120,000 (principal balance) × 0.01 (1% penalty) = <u>$1,200.00</u>

F. Banking fees

1. An <u>origination fee</u> is the fee charged by lenders to issue and process a mortgage loan, and the fee is usually computed as a percentage of the amount of the loan.

2. For example, a 2% origination fee on a loan of $100,000 results in a fee of $2,000:

    a. $100,000 (loan amount) × 0.02 (2%) = $2,000

G. Equity in property

1. <u>Equity</u> is the difference between the current value of a property and the current balance of debt on the property.

2. For example, a property owner has a loan balance of $150,000 on a property worth $250,000. The owner's equity in the property is $100,000:

    a. $250,000 (current value of the property) − $150,000 (current loan balance) = $100,000 (the owner's equity in the property)

III.   PROPERTY MANAGEMENT CALCULATIONS

A. Property management and budget calculations

1. The <u>cash flow report</u> is a monthly statement that details the financial status of the property. The steps in determining cash flow are as follows:

    a.   Gross rental income + other income − losses incurred = <u>total income</u>

    b.   Total income – operating expenses = <u>net operating income</u> before debt service (mortgage payment)

    c.   Net operating income before debt service – debt service – reserves = <u>cash flow</u>

2.   The broker prepares a <u>profit and loss statement</u> at a time stated in the property management agreement (monthly, quarterly, semiannually, or annually). The statement provides a <u>general financial picture</u> based on the monthly cash flow reports and does not include itemized information. The formula for determining profit or loss is generally as follows:

    a.   Gross receipts – operating expenses – total mortgage payment + mortgage loan principal = <u>net profit</u>

B. Tenancy and rental calculations

1.   There are steps in calculating <u>monthly rent</u> per square foot for a <u>commercial property</u>:

    a.   Determine the <u>square footage</u> of the rental premises (generally floor space only). To find the square footage, multiply the length by the width.

        i.   For example, when the length is 50 ft. and the width is 30 ft., 50 ft. × 30 ft. = 1,500 sq. ft.

    b.   Find the total <u>annual rent</u>. Multiply the monthly rent by 12 months (1 year).

        i.   For example, when the monthly rent is $3,000, the annual rent is $36,000 ($3,000 per month × 12 months).

    c.   To determine the annual rent per square foot, divide the total annual rent by the <u>total square footage</u>.

        i.   Using the previous calculations, $36,000 ÷ 1,500 sq. ft. = $24 per sq. ft.

    d.   To convert the annual rent per square foot to a monthly rent per square foot, divide the annual rent per square foot ($24) by 12 (months in a year).

        i. $24 ÷ 12 months = $2 per sq. ft.

IV. PROPERTY VALUATION

A. The sales comparison (market data) approach

1.   In this approach, the value of a feature that is <u>present</u> in the subject property but *not* in the comparable property is <u>added</u> to the sales price of the <u>comparable</u>.

2.   A feature that is present in a comparable property but <u>not</u> in the subject property is <u>subtracted</u> from the sales price.

3.   Adjustments are always made to the price of the comparable property.

4.   For example, when a subject property has an attached two-car garage, and one of the comparable properties has no garage, an appraiser may <u>add the value of a garage</u> to the sales price of the comparable. If the same property has one more bedroom than the subject property, an appraiser may subtract the value of a bedroom from the sales price or the comparable. The <u>net adjustments</u> to each

property are added or subtracted to give an <u>adjusted value</u> used in establishing a range of value for the subject property.

5. For example, assume the comparable property sold for $260,000 and there are no other adjustments, and the appraiser values the two-car garage at $20,000 and the extra bedroom at $17,000—the adjusted value for the comparable would be $263,000:

    a. $260,000 + $20,000 (value of a garage) − $17,000 (value of a bedroom) = $263,000 (adjusted value of subject property)

B. Establishing a listing price—the competitive/comparative market analysis (CMA)

1. A CMA is a report by a real estate broker or salesperson of market statistics within a neighborhood to assist a seller in establishing a listing price.

2. The CMA's calculations are basically the same as those used by an appraiser in the <u>sales comparison approach</u>.

3. The CMA is <u>not an appraisal</u>.

4. It compares prices of properties similar to the seller's property that recently sold, those that are currently on the market, and those that did not sell (<u>comparable properties</u>).

5. It determines a <u>value range for the property's sales price</u>—the most probable price the property will bring in an arm's-length transaction under normal circumstances on the open market.

6. It derives a <u>range of value</u> for the property.

7. As in the sales comparison approach, a broker adjusts a comparable property's sales price or listing price based on its features compared to the subject property. <u>Adjustments</u> are made only to the price of a <u>comparable property</u>.

C. Assessed value and property taxes

1. A taxing district establishes a tax rate that is usually expressed in mills. A <u>mill is 1/1,000th of a dollar</u>, or <u>$0.001</u>. A tax rate of 3% on a property's assessed value would be stated as 3% (0.03) and could be expressed as 30 mills or $3.00 per $100 of assessed value, or $30 per $1,000 of assessed value.

2. For example, a property assessed for tax purposes at $160,000 with a tax rate of 3% or 30 mills would have a tax of $4,800:

    a. $160,000 × 0.03 = $4,800

3. In some jurisdictions, an <u>equalization factor</u> is used to correct inequalities in statewide tax assessments. The assessed value of each property in the area is multiplied by that factor, and the tax rate is then applied to the <u>equalized assessment</u>.

4. For example, if an equalization factor of 120% is used in the previous example with a tax rate of 30 mills, then the tax on a property of $160,000 would be $5,760:

    a. $160.000 × 1.20 = $192,000

    b. $192,000 × 0.03 = $5,760

V.   INVESTMENT

A. Net operating income (NOI)

1. To determine the NOI of an income-producing property, calculate the following:

    a. Potential gross income – vacancies and credit loss = effective gross income

    b. Effective gross income – annual operating expenses = annual NOI

2. For example, an office building produces $132,600 of effective gross income. If the annual expenses are $30,600, the NOI is $102,000:

    a. $132,600 – $30,600 = $102,000 NOI

3. Useful formulas in calculating the NOI, the capitalization rate, and the value of an income property are the following:

    a. NOI ÷ rate of return = value

    b. Value × rate of return = NOI

    c. NOI ÷ value = rate of return

B. Capitalization rate

1. The capitalization rate (the cap rate) is the estimated rate of return or yield that an investor will demand for the investment of capital in a property. The value of the property can be determined by dividing the NOI by the capitalization rate.

2. In the previous example, if the capitalization rate is 8.5%, the value of the property will be $1,200,000:

    a. $102,000 ÷ 0.085 = $1,200,000

3. The formulas just listed can be used to calculate the monthly NOI.

4. For example, an investor spends $335,000 for a property that should produce a 9% rate of return (the cap rate). What monthly NOI will the investor receive?

    a. $335,000 × 9% = $30,150 annual NOI

    b. $30,150 NOI ÷ 12 months = $2,512.50 monthly NOI

C. Gross rent and gross income multipliers

1. The gross rent multiplier (GRM) and gross income multiplier (GIM) each relate the sales price of a property to its rental income. The GRM is primarily used for one- to four-unit residential properties. The GIM is primarily used residential properties of five units or more, and for commercial and industrial properties. For practical purposes, the two terms may be used interchangeably.

2. An appraiser uses recent sales and rental dates from at least four comparable properties to determine either a GRM or GIM:

    a. <u>GRM</u> = sales price ÷ gross rent

    b. <u>GIM</u> = sales price ÷ gross income

3. For example, if a home recently sold for $155,000 and its monthly rental income was $1,250, the GRM would be 124:

    a. $155,000 ÷ $1,250 = 124 GRM

4. To estimate the market value of a subject home, the appraiser multiplies the fair market rental of the subject property by the GRM.

5. For example, if the fair market rental of a subject property is $1,750 and the GRM is 124, the estimated value of the subject property would be $217,000:

    a. $1,750 × 124 = $217,000

D. Tax implications on investment

1. A broker should advise a client seeking to purchase an investment property to consult with <u>a tax attorney, CPA, or financial planner</u> on the tax implications of owning and selling that property. The tax benefits of owning investment real estate property depends on <u>current tax laws</u>.

2. There are factors that can have tax implications.

    a. <u>Capital gain</u> is the difference between the adjusted basis of property and the net sale price.

        i. Capital gains generally are calculated as follows:

            ■ Net sale price: sale price – real estate commissions and closing costs = net sale price

            ■ Adjusted basis: basis (original cost) + improvements = adjusted basis

            ■ Net sale price – adjusted basis = capital gain

        ii. For example, some time ago, an investor purchased a single-family home as a rental property for $95,000. The investor sells the property for $200,000 after making $5,000 of improvements. The investor will pay a broker's commission of 7%, and the closing costs will be $800. The capital gain is calculated as follows:

            ■ $200,000 – $14,000 (7% commission) – $800 (closing costs) = $185,200 (net sale price)

            ■ $185,200 (net sale price) – $100,000 (95,000 [original cost] + $5,000) (improvements) = $85,200 (capital gain)

            ■ $185,200 (net sale price) – $100,000 (adjusted basis) = $85,200 (capital gain)

b.   <u>Adjusted basis</u> is the investor's acquisition costs, plus the costs of physical improvements, less the amount of any depreciation claimed as a tax deduction.

c.   Losses from the sale of a real estate investment may be <u>deductible</u>.

d.   <u>Tax credits</u> are available for the renovation of older buildings, low-income housing, and historic properties.

VI.   SETTLEMENT/CLOSING CALCULATIONS

A.   Debits and credits

1.   A closing statement includes each prorated amount either as a <u>debit</u> or a <u>credit</u>.

   a.   A debit <u>takes money</u> from one of the parties to a transaction; it is a charge that a party owes and must pay at closing.

   b.   A credit <u>gives money</u> to one of the parties to a transaction; it is an amount entered in a party's favor.

2.   When a prorated amount involves <u>both the seller and the buyer</u>, it appears <u>twice</u>, as a debit to one party and as a credit to the other party.

3.   When a prorated amount involves one party and <u>someone other than the other party</u>, the amount will be entered <u>once</u> on the closing statement.

4.   Credits to the <u>seller</u> and debits to the <u>buyer</u> in a typical real estate sales transaction may include the following:

   a.   <u>Selling price</u> of the property

   b.   Fuel oil on hand

   c.   Prepaid insurance and tax reserve for mortgage assumed by the buyer

   d.   Refund to seller of prepaid water charges and similar utility expenses

   e.   <u>Prepaid</u> real estate taxes

5.   <u>Debits</u> to seller (that do not appear as credits to the buyer) include the following:

   a.   Payoff of existing mortgage

6.   Credits to the <u>buyer</u> and debits to the <u>seller</u> may include the following:

   a.   Unpaid principal balance if assumed mortgage

   b.   Accrued interest on existing assumed mortgage

   c.   Tenant's security deposit

   d.   Unpaid water and other utility bills

7. Credits to the <u>buyer</u> (that does not appear as a debit to the seller) include the following:

a. Buyer's earnest money

B. Property tax calculations

1. In the closing of a real estate sales transaction, some expenses and income are prorated between the seller and the buyer.

2. Prorations calculate the number of days owed for the expense or the income.

3. The days may be calculated using either a <u>banker's year</u> (also called a statutory year) or a <u>calendar year</u>.

a. <u>Banker's</u> year—the year contains 12 months with each month having 30 days, resulting in a year of <u>360 days</u>.

b. <u>Calendar</u> year—the year contains 12 months with 28–31 days in each month; the total number of days in the year is <u>365</u> (366 in a leap year when February contains 29 days).

4. Prorations are made either <u>through the day</u> of closing or <u>to the day</u> of closing.

a. When prorations are made <u>through the day</u> of closing, the <u>seller</u> is responsible for the day of closing.

b. When prorations are made <u>up to the day</u> of closing, the <u>buyer</u> is responsible for the day of closing.

5. <u>Real property taxes</u> are normally assessed from January 1–December 31 (depending on state or local law) and usually paid in arrears. The <u>seller</u> will owe the buyer for accrued taxes from January 1 through or up to the day of closing if the taxes are paid in arrears. The tax proration will be a <u>debit to the seller</u> and a <u>credit for the buyer</u>.

6. For example, the market value of a home is $115,000. For tax purposes, the home is assessed at 90% of market value. The annual tax rate is $2.50 per $100 of assessed value. The tax year is January 1–December 31. <u>No portion of the annual property taxes have been paid by the date of closing</u>. If the closing is on March 13, what is the prorated amount? (Payments are calculated through the day of closing using a banker's year.)

a. Find the exact number days of accrued taxes from January 1 up to and including the day of closing:

i. 2 months (January and February) × 30 days = 60 days

ii. 60 + 13 days in March = <u>73 days</u>

b. Calculate the annual taxes (market value × assessment ratio = assessed value ÷ 100 × tax rate per hundred = annual taxes):

i. $115,000 × 0.90 = $103,500

ii. $103,500 ÷ 100 × $2.50 = $2,587.50 annual taxes

   c. Find the tax amount per day (annual taxes ÷ 360 days per year = daily taxes):

      i. $2,587.50 ÷ 360 = $7.1875 daily taxes

   d. Compute the prorated tax amount (daily taxes × days owed = tax proration):

      i. $7.1875 × 73 = $524.69 (rounded)

      ii. $524.69 <u>debit</u> to seller; <u>credit</u> to buyer

C. Prorations

1. <u>Interest</u> on a loan is paid in arrears; the monthly payment made on the first day of the month pays interest for the entire previous month.

2. On a new loan, a buyer will not be required to pay any interest at closing.

3. If the buyer <u>assumes</u> a seller's loan, the <u>interest amount</u> will be prorated.

4. For example, a home was purchased on April 4 for $110,000, and the closing was set for the following May 8. The buyer assumed the seller's $93,600 loan balance with an annual interest rate of 6.5%. The monthly payment is $612.82 and due on the first of the month. How much will the interest proration be using a banker's year and prorating through the day of closing?

   a. Find the exact number of days earned of accrued interest:

      i. The seller owes 8 days (May 1–May 8).

      ii. Find the daily interest charge: outstanding loan balance × annual interest rate = annual interest ÷ 360 days = daily interest:

         ■ $93,600 × 6.4% (0.064) = $6,084 annual interest ÷ 360 days = $16.90 daily interest

      iii. Compute the total amount of accrued interest (daily interest × days owed = interest proration):

         ■ $16.90 × 8 = $135.20

         ■ $135.20 debit to seller; credit to buyer

5. Other items in addition to taxes and interest may be prorated at closing:

   a. Unpaid water and other <u>utility bills</u>

   b. <u>Fuel oil</u> on hand (valued at current market price)

   c. <u>Prepaid tax and insurance reserve</u> for mortgage assumed by the buyer

   d. Refund to the seller of <u>prepaid water charges</u> and similar utility expenses

D. Commission and commission splits

1. The full commission in a sales transaction is the <u>percentage of the sales price</u> made as payment to the broker as stated in the listing agreement between the broker and the seller. However, commissions may be paid by either the buyer or the seller in a transaction.

2. There are some useful formulas to determine the amount of a commission:

   a. Full commission × % of full commission of the broker = <u>broker's share</u> of the commission

   b. Broker's share of commission ÷ % of full commission of the broker = <u>full commission</u>

   c. Broker's share of commission ÷ full commission = <u>% of full commission</u> to the broker

3. When an associate broker or salesperson is involved in a transaction and earns a split of the commission as stated in the employment contract with the broker, the following formulas are useful in calculating a commission split:

   a. Broker's share of commission × salesperson's % of broker's share = <u>salesperson's share</u> of commission

   b. Salesperson's share of commission ÷ salesperson's % of broker's share = <u>broker's share</u> of commission

   c. Salesperson's share of commission ÷ broker's share of commission = <u>salesperson's %</u> of broker's share

4. For example, a seller listed a home for $200,000 and agreed to pay a full commission of 5%. The home sold four weeks later for 90% of the listing price. The listing broker agreed to give the selling broker 50% of the full commission and paid the listing salesperson 50% of her share of the commission. The selling broker paid the selling salesperson 60% of his share of the commission. How much commission did the selling salesperson receive?

   a. $200,000 × 90% (0.90) = $180,000 (<u>sales price</u>)

   b. $180,000 × 5% (0.05) = $9,000 (<u>full commission</u>)

   c. $9,000 × 50% (0.50) = $4,500 (<u>selling broker's share</u> of full commission)

   d. $4,500 × 60% (0.60) = $2,700 (<u>selling salesperson's share</u> of selling broker's share)

E. Transfer tax/fees, conveyance tax, recording fees

1. With some exceptions, most deeds are subject to some sort of state and city or county <u>recording tax or fee</u>.

2. For example, the state recording tax is $0.20 per $100 (or fraction of $100) of the consideration paid or the value of the property, whichever is greater, and the county or city recording tax is $0.07 per $100 or fraction of $100. If a home is sold for $425,000, the total fees are $1,147.50, as demonstrated:

   a. $425,000 ÷ <u>100</u> = 4,250 units

   b. 4,250 × <u>$0.20</u> = $850.00 (state recording tax)

    c.   4,250 × <u>$0.07</u> = $297.50 (city or county recording tax)

    d. $850 + $297.50 = $1,147.50 total in recording fees

3. In addition, most deeds are subject to a <u>transfer tax</u> (also called <u>reconveyance fee</u>) paid by the <u>seller</u> and collected at closing; the tax is then <u>paid to the clerk of the county or city</u> where the deed is recorded. In some jurisdictions, the tax is known as a <u>grantor tax</u>.

4. For example, the transfer tax is $0.50 per $500 of the purchase price, or, in the case of an assumption, of the seller's equity in the property being conveyed (the tax may be quoted as $1 per $1,000). If a home sold for $425,000, the transfer tax would be $425, calculated as follows:

    a. $425,000 ÷ 500 = 850 (units) (or $425,000 ÷ 1,000 = 425)

    b.   850 × $0.50 = $425 (the transfer tax) (or 425 × $1 = $425)

F. Seller's proceeds of sale (net to the seller)

1. The seller's proceeds at closing are calculated by subtracting any settlement cost and loan payoffs from the gross amount of the purchase price.

2. For example, if the purchase price of a home is $230,000, the seller's proceeds could be calculated as follows:

Contract sales price	$230,000.00
Minus	
Total settlement charges to seller	− $15,565.00
■ Real estate commission:	$13,800.00
■ Title examination fees:	$20.00
■ Attorney's fees:	$600.00
■ Title insurance:	$560.00
■ Recording and transfer fees:	$25.00
■ Survey:	$200.00
■ Pest inspection:	$100.00
■ Tax stamps:	$260.00
Minus	
Payoff of first mortgage loan	− $115,736.60
Real estate taxes	− $1,581.20
Total reduction amount due to seller	− $132,882.80
Total cash due at closing to seller	$97,117.20

G. Buyer funds needed at closing

1. The buyer's funds due at closing are calculated by subtracting any funds paid for or on behalf of the buyer from the gross amount owed by the buyer.

2. For example, if the purchase price of a home is $230,000, the buyer's cash required at closing could be calculated as follows:

Contract sales price	$230,000.00
Plus	
Total settlement charges paid from borrower's fund	+ $9,959.35
■ Loan origination fee:	$2,300.00
■ Loan discount:	$3,680.00
■ Interest paid in advance:	$611.85
■ Hazard insurance premium for one year:	$690.00
■ Hazard insurance reserves (escrow):	$115.00
■ County property taxes reserves (escrow):	$2,012.50
■ Attorney's fees:	$500.00
■ County recording fee:	$50.00
Minus	
Amounts paid for or on behalf of buyer	
■ Earnest money	– $46,000.00
■ Principal amount of new loan	– $184,000.00
■ County taxes unpaid by seller	– $1,581.20
Total amount due from borrower	$239,959.35
Total amount paid by/for borrower	($231,581.20)
Total cash due at closing from borrower	$8,378.15

UNIT 11 REVIEW QUESTIONS

True/False Questions

1. One mile is 640 acres.
   A. True
   B. False

2. One acre is the equivalent of 43,560 square feet.
   A. True
   B. False

3. One discount point is 1% of the purchase price.
   A. True
   B. False

4. The mortgage ratio of 80%/20% was always based on the appraised value of the property.
   A. True
   B. False

5. Leverage is an advantage for an investor because the investor can—without putting much money down—control an entire property.
   A. True
   B. False

6. Equity is what is left after debt charged to a property is deducted from the property's market value.
   A. True
   B. False

7. For a property manager to calculate effective gross income, the property manager would subtract vacancy and collection losses from potential gross income.
   A. True
   B. False

8. A property manager calculating net operating income for an investor would subtract operating expenses and debt service from effective gross income.
   A. True
   B. False

9. Deducting expenses from income equals cash flow.
   A. True
   B. False

10. To calculate net operating income for income-generating real estate, multiply the capitalization rate by the value.
    A. True
    B. False

11. When using the gross rent multiplier (GRM), multiply the rent times the GRM to find the value of the property.
    A. True
    B. False

12. A buyer purchases a house for $100,000 and obtains a purchase money mortgage for $80,000. If the buyer pays one discount point, the discount point will be for $1,000.
    A. True
    B. False

13. Commission divided by commission rate equals sales price.
    A. True
    B. False

14. The formula for gross scheduled income is the monthly rent for each unit multiplied by 12 minus operating expenses.
    A. True
    B. False

15. The formula to calculate net operating income is the capitalization rate of return multiplied by the property value.
    A. True
    B. False

16. To calculate the capitalization rate of return on income-producing property, divide the net operating income by the value of the property.
    A. True
    B. False

17. Prepaid property taxes will be prorated on the settlement closing statement as a seller credit and a buyer debit.
    A. True
    B. False

18. Tenant security deposits will be prorated on the settlement closing statement for a purchase transaction involving a one- to four-unit residential dwelling property.
    A. True
    B. False

19. It is irrelevant to proration calculations as to which party will be responsible for the day of the close of escrow.
    A. True
    B. False

20. If there is an existing mortgage lien on the purchased property, a payoff will always be listed on the closing statement.
    A. True
    B. False

Multiple-Choice Questions

1. Which of these is the correct way to calculate the number of square feet in a square mile?
   A. 640 × 640 =
   B. 5280 × 5280 =
   C. 4280 × 4280 =
   D. 1000 × 1000 =

2. How many acres are in a square mile?
   A. 640
   B. 43,560
   C. 40
   D. 160

3. A buyer purchased two parcels of land. One was 1 square mile and the other contained 10 acres. If the land cost $2,500 an acre, what was the cost of the land?
   A. $1,265,000
   B. $1,625,000
   C. $1,526,000
   D. $1,600,000

4. An investor leases 12 apartments for a total monthly rental of $3,000. If this figure represents an 8% annual return on the investment, what was the original cost of the property?
   A. $450,000
   B. $360,000
   C. $45,000
   D. $36,000

5. Which of these property management calculations is correct?
   A. Income − expenses = net worth
   B. Assets − liabilities = cash flow
   C. Both of these
   D. Neither of these

6. To calculate an investor's net operating income from an apartment building, a property manager would consider all of these EXCEPT
   A. debt service.
   B. potential annual gross income.
   C. bad debt.
   D. vacancies.

7. A loan is originated for $900,000, and that was 80% of the appraised value. What was the appraised value of the house?
   A. $1,000,000
   B. $1,125,000
   C. $1,200,000
   D. $1,500,000

8. If a buyer obtains a mortgage for $50,000 and pays 4 discount points, how much will the buyer be charged by the lender at closing for the points?
   A. $6,000
   B. $200
   C. $2,000
   D. $600

9. An income-producing apartment building has 20 units. Each unit rents for $1,000. How is gross scheduled income calculated?
   A. 20 × $1,000 =
   B. 20 × $1,000 × 12 =
   C. Both of these
   D. Neither of these

10. If an investment property is worth $500,000 and the capitalization rate of return is 4%, what is the net operating income?
    A. $10,000
    B. $20,000
    C. $30,000
    D. $40,000

11. Prorated items that represent prepaid expenses of the seller should be shown on the settlement statement as
    A. a credit to the seller and a debit to the buyer.
    B. a debit to the seller and a credit to the buyer.
    C. a credit to the buyer.
    D. a debit to the seller.

12. For a purchase transaction, all of these are considered a credit to the buyer on a settlement closing statement EXCEPT
    A. prepaid taxes.
    B. an earnest money deposit.
    C. a new mortgage.
    D. a good-faith deposit.

UNIT 12

Broker Only Topics

LEARNING OBJECTIVE

When you have completed this unit, you will be able to accomplish the following.

> Discuss problems and responsibilities related to a principal broker.

I.   FORMS OF OWNERSHIP

A.   Property ownership held in trust

1. <u>Legal title</u> to a property may be transferred by the grantor (or trustor) to a trustee.

2. The trustee holds and manages the property for the benefit of another, <u>the beneficiary</u>.

3. The beneficiary holds <u>equitable title</u>.

4. A <u>land trust</u> is originated by the owner of a property with real estate as the <u>only asset</u>.

5. The legal and equitable title is in the trustee's name under a <u>deed of trust</u>.

6. The <u>beneficiary</u> is usually the trustor, the person creating the trust.

7. The beneficiary has the <u>rights to possession, income, and proceeds of sale</u> of the property.

8. A land trust generally is created for a <u>definite term</u>, such as 20 years.

9. Land trusts are commonly established among <u>multiple owners</u> to seek protection against the effects of divorce, judgments, or bankruptcies of the other owners.

II.   TRANSFER OF TITLE

A. Cloud on title and suit to quiet title

1. A <u>cloud on title</u> is any unreleased lien, or encumbrance that may <u>impair the marketability of title</u> of the property, or cast doubt on the <u>title's validity</u>.

2. Clouds on title may include the following:

   a.   A contract for deed has not been removed from the record, and buyer has defaulted

   b.   A prior conveyance that has an <u>incomplete legal description</u>

   c.   A recorded option not exercised but still appearing on the record

   d.   A mortgage paid in full without any <u>satisfaction of the mortgage</u> recorded

   e.   An heir with a <u>questionable claim</u> to the property

   f.   A deed not signed by one or more heirs

   g.   A property sold without the wife's <u>release of dower</u> interest

   h.   A dropped <u>pending litigation</u> not removed from the record

   i.   A lessee in default having an option to purchase the property

3. A <u>title search</u> usually reveals a cloud on title.

4. A cloud of title may be removed by a <u>quitclaim deed</u>.

5. A property owner may also initiate a court action known as <u>suit to quiet title</u> or <u>quiet title action</u>.

   a.   <u>All parties</u> with a possible claim or interest in the property must join in the suit.

   b.   Once a judgment or decree of the court has been recorded, a proper <u>notice of the claimant's right</u> and interest in the property is established.

III.   LEASING AND PROPERTY MANAGEMENT

A. Property manager's fiduciary responsibilities

1. Property management agreement

   a.   Leasing property (manager works with property owner to set rents and lease rates)

      i.   Rental rates are influenced by supply and demand. A broker engaged as a property manager should conduct a detailed survey of the competitive space available in the neighborhood, especially similar properties.

ii. The property manager's decision on rental rates must consider the following:

- That the rental income must be sufficient to cover the property's <u>fixed charges and operating expenses</u>

- That the rental income provides a <u>fair return</u> on the owner's investment

- That the rental rate is in line with <u>prevailing rates</u> in comparable buildings

- That the current <u>vacancy rate</u> is a good indicator of how much of a rent increase is warranted

iii. Rental rates for <u>residential</u> space are usually stated as a monthly rate <u>per unit</u>.

iv. For <u>commercial and industrial</u> spaces, the rent is usually stated in either annual or monthly rates <u>per square foot</u>.

IV.   PRACTICE OF REAL ESTATE

A.   Advertising and technology

1. Supervision practices

a.   Licensees

i. A real estate broker is defined as a person <u>licensed</u> to represent another who wishes to buy, sell, exchange, or lease real property <u>and charge a fee</u> for those services.

ii. A real estate broker should have a <u>written employment agreement</u> with every licensed associate broker, salesperson, community association manager, property manager, or other affiliate as determined by state law.

iii. The employment agreement defines the affiliate as an <u>employee</u> or an <u>independent contractor</u>.

iv. The broker is <u>liable</u> for the acts of any affiliate within the scope of the employment agreement.

v. A broker is required to <u>supervise</u> the actions of any licensed affiliate, either personally or by delegating supervision to an individual office manager (usually an associate broker) or a firm's supervising associate broker.

vi. In general, supervising of a firm's affiliates involves the following:

- Establishing and distributing either in print or electronically a <u>company policy manual</u> defining the policies and procedures for handling trust accounts, submitting offers, fair housing, environmental issues, hiring of unlicensed personnel, office duty, contract forms, multiple listing service membership and fees, and other business issues

- Regular review of all offers and contracts drafted by the company's affiliates

- Offering fair housing training and ethics training for all affiliates

- Required monthly reconciliation of all trust accounts

b. Unlicensed personnel

  i. State laws determine if <u>real estate assistants</u> (a.k.a. personal or professional assistants) must have a real estate license.

  ii. In many states, <u>unlicensed personnel</u> may act as real estate assistants.

  iii. Real estate assistants are usually hired by <u>individual licensees</u> or groups of licensees in a real estate firm.

  iv. Most states require that a broker and an affiliated licensee each have a <u>written employment agreement</u> with any unlicensed assistant working in the firm outlining the <u>specific duties and responsibilities</u> of the assistant.

  v. The broker is ultimately responsible for the actions of all unlicensed assistants.

  vi. While state laws may vary, <u>common duties</u> permitted for unlicensed personnel include

  ▪ clerical and administrative functions;

  ▪ office management;

  ▪ telemarketing;

  ▪ market strategy development;

  ▪ direct contact with clients and customers, provided the assistant does not engage in any activity <u>reserved for a licensed</u> broker or salesperson;

  ▪ setting up and hosting open houses, provided the assistant provides customers only with <u>written information</u> from the listing broker or agent about the property; and

  ▪ managing the flow of documents in all aspects of the real estate transaction.

V.   REAL ESTATE CALCULATIONS

A. Investment

1. Appreciation

  a. Appreciation is the <u>increase in value</u> of a property due to market conditions. The appreciation may be temporary or permanent.

  b. A real estate broker may need to know the basics of calculating an investment, but the broker should always advise the client to consult a <u>CPA or investment counselor</u> for a professional <u>estimate of property appreciation</u>.

  c. To find the <u>change in value</u> of a property:

  i. The change in value = new value (listing or sale price) – old value (original purchase price).

  ii. For example, the change in value = $250,000 – $200,000 = $50,000 (an appreciation of 25%).

d.   To calculate the <u>future value</u> of a property:

    i.   Find the <u>current appreciation rate</u> in the neighborhood or city (rate may be available from news sources, REALTOR® associations or industry associations, or local planning departments).

    ii.   Find the <u>future growth factor</u>:

       ■   Future growth = $(1 + \text{average annual appreciation rate})^{\text{years}}$

       ■   Years = number of years a purchaser or owner plans to hold onto the investment

       ■   For example, the average appreciation rate in City A is 6%, and the investment will be sold in 10 years. The future growth factor will be 1.79, as demonstrated:

         –   Future growth = $(1 + 0.06)^{10}$

         –   Future growth = 1.79

    iii.   Find the <u>future value</u> (multiply the future growth factor by the property's current value):

       ■   Future value = (future growth factor) × (current value)

       ■   For example:

         –   Future value = (1.79) × ($300,000)

         –   Future value = $537,000

         –   In 10 years, property will be worth $537,000

2.   Depreciation

    a.   In the cost approach to value used by appraisers, depreciation is the <u>loss in value</u> due to any cause or condition that adversely affects the value of a property.

    b.   For investment properties, depreciation calculations are used to determine the loss in value of property for <u>tax purposes</u>. Depreciation allows a rental property owner to deduct the costs from taxes of buying and improving a property over its useful life.

       i.   Rental property owners use depreciation to <u>deduct</u> the purchase price and improvements from a tax return.

       ii.   Depreciation <u>commences</u> as soon as the property is available for use as a rental.

       iii.   Most U.S. residential property is depreciated at a rate of <u>3.636%</u> each year for <u>27.5 years.</u>

       iv.   Only the <u>value of buildings</u> is depreciated; land is not depreciated.

    c.   <u>Depreciation tables</u> are available online for calculation purposes.

    d.   An investment property depreciation calculation involves the following calculations:

       i.   <u>Purchase price</u> – land value = <u>building value</u>

ii. Building value ÷ <u>27.5</u> = annual allowable depreciation deduction

iii. For example, assume the value of land on which a fourplex investment property is $90,000 and the purchase price of the property is $350,000. The depreciation will be $9,455 a year, as shown:

■ $350,000 − $90,000 = $260,000 building value

■ $260,000 ÷ 27.5 years = $9,454.55 ($9,455) a year in depreciation

UNIT 12 REVIEW QUESTIONS

True/False Questions

1. The depreciation allowance on a principal dwelling residence is 27½ years.
   A. True
   B. False

2. Under a trust arrangement, the trustor holds and manages the property for the benefit of another.
   A. True
   B. False

3. A land trust is originated by the owner of a property with real estate as the only asset.
   A. True
   B. False

4. The beneficiary in a trust has the rights to possession, income, and proceeds on sale of the property.
   A. True
   B. False

5. A land trust is usually created for an indefinite term.
   A. True
   B. False

6. A deed not signed by one or more heirs would create a cloud on the title.
   A. True
   B. False

7. An unreleased lien, or encumbrance, is a cloud on the title that may cast doubt on the title's validity.
   A. True
   B. False

8. A cloud on title may be removed by a quitclaim deed.
   A. True
   B. False

9. A quitclaim deed is not sufficient evidence to remove a cloud on the title.
   A. True
   B. False

10. A broker engaged as a property manager should conduct a detailed survey of the competitive space available in the neighborhood, especially similar properties.
    A. True
    B. False

11. Rental rates for residential space are usually stated as a yearly rate per unit.
    A. True
    B. False

12. A broker is required to personally supervise the actions of any licensed affiliate.
    A. True
    B. False

13. Appreciation is the increase in value of a property due to market conditions. The appreciation may be temporary or permanent.
    A. True
    B. False

Multiple-Choice Questions

1. When a property is held in a trust, which party holds legal title?
   A. Beneficiary
   B. Grantor
   C. Trustor
   D. Trustee

2. A defect or cloud on the title to a property may be removed by
   A. paying cash for the property at closing.
   B. obtaining quitclaim deeds from all interested parties.
   C. filing an action to register the title.
   D. bringing a suit of foreclosure against the property.

3. What is the effect of a cloud on a property's title?
   A. It invalidates the title.
   B. It prevents the property from being sold.
   C. It enables the local government to take possession of the property.
   D. It impairs the marketability of the property.

4. Rental rates for residential space are usually stated as
   A. an annual or monthly rate per square foot.
   B. a percentage of total available space.
   C. an annual rate per room.
   D. a monthly rate per unit.

5. While state laws may vary, an unlicensed personal assistant would be prohibited from
   A. performing clerical and administrative functions.
   B. negotiating an offer to purchase a property.
   C. developing a market strategy.
   D. managing the flow of documents in a real estate transaction.

6. A residential investment property has a land value of $180,000 and the purchase price of the property is $700,000. What is the yearly depreciation using a useful life of 27½ years?
   A. $5,200 per year
   B. $6,545 per year
   C. $18,910 per year
   D. $25,455 per year

SALESPERSON PRACTICE EXAM

1. A farmer is growing a crop of corn on a family farm. The same family has owned the land for 50 years. The corn is not yet ripe enough to harvest. All of these are correct EXCEPT
   A. if the farmer sells the entire farm and does not exclude the corn from the sale, the corn will transfer to the buyer with a bill of sale.
   B. if the farmer sells the growing crop of corn, the farmer will give the buyer a bill of sale.
   C. the government could take the family farm through its power of eminent domain.
   D. if the farmer sells the entire farm, the farmer will give the buyer a deed.

2. For which of these, if sold, will the seller NOT give the buyer a bill of sale?
   A. An unattached house
   B. An easement
   C. A potted 25-foot tree
   D. An inflatable swimming pool

3. If a seller wants to keep any of these, they must all be excluded from the purchase contract EXCEPT
   A. an installed chandelier.
   B. a 750-pound piano in a living room.
   C. hydraulic lifts in the garage floor.
   D. apples growing on an apple tree.

4. The total amount of a loan encumbering a parcel of real estate is more than the current fair market value of the property. This loan has a due-on-sale acceleration clause in the boilerplate language of the financing instrument. What element of value will MOST be affected by this?
   A. Underwater mortgage
   B. Transferability
   C. Demand
   D. Usefulness

5. Who is MOST likely to pay to terminate an appurtenant easement?
   A. The holder of the dominant tenement
   B. The holder of the servient tenement
   C. The city where the property is situated
   D. None of these

6. Several years ago, a seller of a single-family residence planted a tree in the backyard to commemorate the birth of a child. The seller placed a restriction into the deed that the tree not be cut down as long as it remained alive. This deed restriction
   A. is considered a zoning variance.
   B. violates federal fair housing laws.
   C. is an example of a public restriction.
   D. is an example of a private restriction.

7. Which of these BEST describes a section of land described using the rectangular survey method?
   A. 640 acres
   B. 320 acres
   C. 160 acres
   D. 40 acres

8. Which is typically the BEST method for describing a parcel of land with a lot of curves and angles?
   A. The rectangular survey system method
   B. The government survey system method
   C. The metes and bounds method
   D. The lot, block, and subdivision method

9. Which of these is NOT a freehold estate?
   A. Life estate
   B. Fee simple
   C. Fee simple determinable
   D. Estate at will

10. All of these are incorrect regarding a fee simple defeasible estate EXCEPT
    A. it might be terminated automatically and be a violation of the condition.
    B. it features the maximum control or use of real estate known under the law.
    C. it is a nonfreehold estate of possession.
    D. it is measured by a person's existence.

11. A less-than-freehold estate
    A. features the maximum control over realty known under the law.
    B. allows a nonowner to possess the property.
    C. lasts forever.
    D. requires the lessor to pay rent.

12. Which of these estates is common for residential lessees?
    A. Fee simple estate
    B. Fee simple defeasible estate
    C. Periodic estate
    D. Estate at sufferance

13. In a state where joint tenancy is legal, how does the last living survivor hold title to the property?
    A. As last joint tenant
    B. In severalty
    C. Joint and several liability
    D. Tenancy in common

14. Two people—in a business relationship only—own a parcel of real estate concurrently. None of these ways of holding title would be available to these two individuals EXCEPT
    A. tenants in common.
    B. tenants by the entirety.
    C. community property.
    D. community property with right of survivorship.

15. Which of these is NOT a necessary element of a valid deed?
    A. In writing
    B. Grantor signature
    C. Grantee signature
    D. Description of the property

16. This deed conveys no grantor warranties or promises. It is used to clear up clouds on title, and it is also used when the grantor wants no future liability for the transfer. It is called
    A. the special warranty deed.
    B. the quitclaim deed.
    C. the general warranty deed.
    D. a sheriff's deed.

17. River, the owner of a parcel of real estate worth $5 million, executed a deed to transfer ownership to Dakota, a business rival. Dakota refused to accept the deed. Who holds title to the property?
    A. Dakota holds title to the real estate.
    B. River and Dakota are now joint owners of the real estate.
    C. River still holds title to the real estate.
    D. There is insufficient evidence provided to answer the question.

18. The deed that provides the greatest protection to the buyer is a
    A. quitclaim deed.
    B. special warranty deed.
    C. general warranty deed.
    D. bargain and sale deed.

19. A buyer financed the acquisition of a home with a purchase money mortgage. Thirty years after the purchase of the real estate, one title insurance policy no longer offered any coverage to the insured. The buyer still owned the property, but had only paid for title insurance one time, at the closing. Which of these policies MOST likely will no longer offer any coverage?
    A. The mortgagee's policy of title insurance
    B. The owner's policy of title insurance
    C. The real estate agent's policy of title insurance
    D. Both the mortgagee's policy and the owner's policy

20. Historically, why were real estate property taxes favored by government authorities?
    A. Because property taxes could result in an escheat to the government
    B. Because realty cannot be hidden by owners
    C. Because property could be taken by eminent domain, if property taxes were not paid
    D. Because property taxes were part of the government's police powers

21. Ten years ago, an owner added an extra bathroom to a home. The owner did so quietly, without getting any of the required local permits. The city finally discovered the extra bathroom and demanded the owner either bring the extra bathroom up to code or demolish it. This is an example of government
    A. overreach.
    B. escheat.
    C. police power.
    D. eminent domain.

22. In the covenants, conditions, and restrictions (CC&Rs), a developer prohibited homeowners in a new subdivision from keeping wild animals as pets. If challenged in court, this subdivision restriction will MOST likely be
    A. upheld.
    B. struck down as arbitrary and capricious.
    C. struck down as police power overreach.
    D. struck down as eminent domain overreach.

23. If a property is situated in an area designated by either the federal or state government as a wetland, then
    A. development would be prohibited.
    B. development would be regulated.
    C. hazard insurance would be unavailable.
    D. emergency services would be unavailable.

24. Which of these hazards is considered an environmental hazard in a parcel of real estate with a newly constructed single-family residence?
    A. A property located in a 100-year flood zone
    B. Radon gas caused by the breakdown of uranium in the soil
    C. A property located in a seismic hazard zone
    D. A property located in a wildfire zone

25. An owner of commercial property wants to use a portion of the property for a use not permitted by local zoning regulations. The local municipality's approval of the owner's request could be in the form of all of these EXCEPT
    A. a special use permit.
    B. a special exception.
    C. a conditional use permit.
    D. an amendment.

26. In a state where dual agency is legal, which of these pairs would NOT be in a dual agency relationship with a real estate broker?
    A. Vendor and vendee
    B. Lessor and lessee
    C. Vendor and lessee
    D. Optionor and optionee

27. Which of these lists contains only the fiduciary duties an agent owes to clients?
    A. Obedience, loyalty, disclosure, confidentiality, accounting, reasonable skill and care
    B. Obedience, loyalty, disclosure, consideration, accounting, reasonable skill and care
    C. Obedience, loyalty, disclosure, confidentiality, acceptance, reasonable skill and care
    D. Offer, loyalty, disclosure, confidentiality, acceptance, reasonable skill and care

28. Emmerson is a real estate broker, and has been friends with Charlie for 20 years. They verbally agree that Emmerson will sell Charlie's home. Emmerson competently finds a buyer for the property. After the sale is complete, Charlie refuses to pay Emmerson's commission. In a lawsuit filed promptly by Emmerson against Charlie, who will likely prevail?
    A. Emmerson, because Charlie violated the statute of limitations
    B. Charlie, because the agreement violated the statute of frauds
    C. Emmerson, because the work was performed competently
    D. Charlie, because an agency can be terminated by the principal

29. One of these agencies, when created, creates fiduciary duties owed by the agent to the principal, with typically no chance of the agent being compensated. It is
    A. a secret agency.
    B. a special agency.
    C. a general agency.
    D. an implied agency.

30. An associate licensee brought a listing into the real estate brokerage firm. The associate licensee did all the work related to the listing. Because the broker of record was busy, the seller and the broker of record never met. The broker of record unexpectedly died from a heart attack. What is the status of the listing agreement?
    A. The associate licensee can continue to market the property.
    B. The seller and the associate licensee must decide the status of the listing.
    C. The listing agreement remains between the associate licensee and the seller.
    D. The listing agreement terminated with the death of the broker of record.

31. A listing agent knew the septic system of a listed property needed to be repaired. The listing agent promised the seller to disclose the needed repairs to any prospective buyer who asked. However, none of the prospective buyers asked about the condition of the septic system. The listing agent
    A. acted properly, given that no one asked about the condition of the septic system.
    B. acted properly, given that the repair of septic systems was beyond the scope of the listing agent's professional knowledge.
    C. failed to reveal a material fact about the subject property.
    D. breached the fiduciary duties owed to prospective buyers.

32. A broker told a buyer that a home they were purchasing was "in a desirable neighborhood." After purchasing the home, the buyer learned there had been several crimes recently in the neighborhood. The broker's statement to the buyer is considered
    A. puffing.
    B. fraud.
    C. misrepresentation.
    D. deception.

33. A seller and a listing agent enter into a written net listing in a state where this type of listing is legally permitted. The listing agent promptly and competently finds a buyer. The listing agent was not paid for the transaction. Which of these reasons would MOST likely explain this lack of agent compensation for the transaction?
    A. The listing agreement violated the statute of frauds.
    B. The property sold for less than the net profit the seller wanted.
    C. The listing agreement neglected to set forth the agent's compensation.
    D. The listing agreement violated the statute of limitations.

34. In writing, a seller told a listing agent not to market the property on the multiple listing service (MLS). The listing agent complied. The listing agent
    A. violated the terms of the MLS.
    B. violated federal fair housing laws.
    C. violated ethical norms for real estate professionals.
    D. did nothing wrong.

35. An owner hired a real estate broker. The broker had one job. The position was advisory only. The broker had no authority to bind the owner to the broker's decisions. All of these could fall within this description EXCEPT
    A. a property manager under a property management contract.
    B. a listing agent under an exclusive right-to-sell agreement.
    C. a selling agent under a buyer representation agreement.
    D. a listing agent under a reserved seller agreement.

36. A lease agreement is a bilateral contract between which of these?
    A. The lessee and the lessor
    B. The lessee, the lessor, and the property manager
    C. The lessee and the property manager
    D. The lessor and the property manager

37. For which of these can an owner of residential rental property have the property manager lawfully deny housing to a prospective tenant?
    A. The prospective tenant has a history of arson.
    B. The prospective tenant—clean and sober for five years—was convicted of drug dealing.
    C. The prospective tenant has a spotty employment history and low credit score.
    D. All of these can happen.

38. To make a client feel more comfortable, a real estate licensee showed the client homes only in neighborhoods where other members of the client's religion lived. The real estate licensee did this without discussing the matter with the client. The client ultimately purchased one of the homes shown by the selling agent. The selling agent
    A. showed empathetic customer service skills.
    B. behaved ethically.
    C. engaged in steering.
    D. engaged in redlining.

39. Which of these is an example of redlining?
    A. Immediately denying a loan application on the basis of where a property is located
    B. Immediately denying a loan application on the basis of the FICO score of the applicant
    C. Immediately denying a loan application on the basis of the applicant's income
    D. Immediately denying a loan application on the basis of the applicant's reliance on public assistance

40. All the tenants of an apartment building belonged to the same race. The owner of the apartment building wanted a more racially balanced tenant population. To achieve this goal, the owner rejected tenant applications from members of that race. This was
    A. in violation of federal fair housing laws.
    B. proper, if the current tenants approved.
    C. proper, as long as no other races were rejected.
    D. an acceptable exception to federal fair housing laws.

41. An old three-story office building was demolished, and a new three-story office building was recently constructed. The old building did not have an elevator. Under the federal Americans with Disabilities Act (ADA), is the new three-story building required to have an elevator?
    A. No—under the ADA, a three-story office building is not required to have an elevator.
    B. No—unless the new office building is used for medical offices.
    C. Yes—provided the elevator will not exceed 10% of the construction costs.
    D. Yes.

42. During a time when there was tremendous competition for listings, a real estate broker posted a listing on the multiple listing service (MLS). The compensation was 1% of the purchase price, and the listing agent offered 40% of the compensation to the selling agent. This MLS listing was
    A. proper.
    B. proper as to the 1% commission, but improper as to the 40% split offered to the selling agent.
    C. proper as to the 40% split offered to the selling agent, but improper as to the 1% commission.
    D. improper.

43. An associate licensee placed an advertisement that did not state a real estate licensee was involved with the transaction. A prospective buyer called the phone number listed on the advertisement, expecting to speak directly to the buyer. The associate licensee apologized for the error and said the advertisement would immediately be pulled. The associate licensee
    A. ran a blind advertisement.
    B. ran a blind advertisement but legally rectified the error by apologizing.
    C. did nothing wrong.
    D. did nothing wrong, provided the seller later ratified the advertisement.

44. A real estate broker had a trust account that typically held over $100,000. The real estate broker gave an employee, an unlicensed assistant, access to $25,000 in the trust account. The real estate broker should have a fidelity bond for
    A. $25,000.
    B. $30,000.
    C. $50,000.
    D. the typical aggregate trust fund liability.

45. The broker of record at a large brokerage firm required all associate licensees to check the computer system before associate licensees took prospective buyers to see any listed properties. This was a written rule in the brokerage firm's policy manual created to prevent undisclosed dual agency. An associate licensee took a prospective buyer to see a property listed on the MLS and neglected to check the brokerage firm computer system. The broker of record fired the associate licensee. This action by the broker of record was
    A. acceptable.
    B. unethical.
    C. illegal.
    D. illegal if the property was located in a state where dual agencies were lawful.

46. Party A forced Party B to sign a contract. Party B subsequently rejected the contract in court and was released from any further contractual duties. What is this type of contract called?
    A. Valid
    B. Voidable
    C. Void
    D. Ad valorem

47. Two old friends met for dinner. One friend made a verbal offer on a property. The other friend immediately accepted. The two shook hands over the agreement for the sale of the parcel of real estate. If one of them ends up suing the other over this agreement, who will MOST likely win the legal action?
    A. The prospective buyer
    B. The prospective seller
    C. Both have equal chance at winning the lawsuit
    D. Neither

48. A prospective buyer made an offer on a single-family residence. The seller accepted the offer and communicated acceptance. The buyer, however, did not make a good-faith deposit. What impact will the absence of a good-faith deposit have on a purchase contract for residential property?
    A. The absence of a good-faith deposit will have no impact on the purchase contract.
    B. The absence of a good-faith deposit will make the purchase contract void.
    C. The absence of a good-faith deposit will make the purchase contract voidable.
    D. The absence of a good-faith deposit will make the purchase contract unenforceable.

49. Which of these is an example of undue influence?
    A. An adult child convincing an elderly parent to sell against the parent's best interests
    B. Convincing a client to accept an offer merely because it promises faster compensation for the agent
    C. Convincing a client to make an offer merely because it will result in compensation for the agent
    D. All of these

50. A prospective buyer made an offer on a single-family residence. The seller rejected the offer and made a counteroffer. The buyer rejected the counteroffer. The seller then accepted the original offer and communicated acceptance to the buyer. Which of these is correct?
    A. The seller and buyer are now in contract with each other.
    B. A former offer can be accepted after being rejected by an offeree.
    C. A rejection permanently terminates an offer.
    D. Communication of acceptance of a previously rejected offer reinstates the offer.

51. Which of these is NOT an essential element of a contract?
    A. Consent
    B. Capacity
    C. Writing
    D. Lawful purpose

52. A listing agent presented three offers to a seller. The seller was moving out of state and was very motivated to sell the property as quickly as possible. Assuming all other things are equal, which of the offers will the listing agent advise the seller to accept?
    A. An all-cash, noncontingent offer
    B. A noncontingent offer
    C. An offer to enter into a land contract
    D. "Time is of the essence"

53. An option for the rental of vacation property was given by the optionor to the optionee. The optionee, having found a more desirable vacation rental property, decided not to exercise the option. The optionor sued the optionee for not exercising the option. In the lawsuit, who is MOST likely to prevail?
    A. The optionor, because the optionee did not exercise the option
    B. The optionor, because the optionee did not perform
    C. The optionee, because there was no performance
    D. The optionee, because neither party made promises to each other

54. A vendor and vendee entered into a contract with each other for the sale of 40 acres of agricultural land. The vendee took possession of the property and started making payments to the vendor. When the last payment was made under the contract, the vendee received a deed to the property from the vendor. Before receiving a deed from the vendor, what title did the vendee hold under this arrangement?
    A. Legal title
    B. Equitable title
    C. Legal title and equitable title
    D. No title

55. Because of damage caused by a heavy storm, a purchase contract needed to be amended. Both the buyer and the seller were represented by real estate agents. The seller had previously signed a listing agreement with the seller's agent, and the buyer had previously signed a buyer representation agreement with the buyer's agent. Who signed the amendment to the purchase contract?
    A. The seller and the buyer
    B. The seller and the seller's agent
    C. The seller's agent and the buyer's agent
    D. The seller, the seller's agent, the buyer, and the buyer's agent

56. A city is exercising its power of eminent domain to widen a busy two-lane street. One property owner has lived on the street for over 50 years and loves the home. An appraiser is brought in to appraise the home for condemnation purposes. All of these will be considered by the appraiser EXCEPT
    A. the emotional value of the home.
    B. the home's amenities.
    C. the value of the land.
    D. the condition of the roof.

57. An owner of a single-family residence—located near federally protected wetlands—is refinancing a purchase money mortgage. The loan is conditioned on an appraisal. Which of these forms is the appraiser MOST likely to use?
    A. Narrative report
    B. Self-contained report
    C. Summary report
    D. Environmental impact report

58. Which of these acronyms shows the essential elements of value?
    A. TILA
    B. RESPA
    C. DUST
    D. TRID

59. Two listed homes on the same street were built around the same time. They both have the same basic amenities and were equally maintained. The house with the lower asking price sold first. Which principle of value explains this scenario?
    A. The principle of highest and best use
    B. The principle of supply and demand
    C. The principle of conformity
    D. The principle of substitution

60. A prospective buyer met with a real estate broker. The prospective buyer said to the real estate agent, "Find me the worst home in the best neighborhood." Out of these choices, what principle of value does this statement MOST closely reflect?
    A. Regression
    B. Progression
    C. Highest and best use
    D. Substitution

61. A single-family residence, serving as a home for the current owner, is located in a subdivision with 50 other single-family residences. However, only the subject property was designed by a famous architect. The other properties in the subdivision are unremarkable tract homes. Which method is the appraiser MOST likely to use when appraising the home designed by the famous architect?
    A. The income approach
    B. The market data approach
    C. The cost approach
    D. The sales comparison approach

62. When would an appraiser subtract something from the sales price of a comparable?
    A. When the subject property had the same amenity
    B. When the comparable had an amenity the subject property lacked
    C. When the subject property had an amenity the comparable lacked
    D. With the replacement cost new

63. In the income approach, which of these correctly states the relationship between net operating income, rate of return, and value?
    A. Rate of return × net operating income = value
    B. Value × net operating income = rate of return
    C. Rate of return × value = net operating income
    D. Principal × assessed value = net operating income

64. This is a two-party instrument that buyers sign when taking out a loan to purchase real estate. It is not used for all-cash deals and has no impact on the title. What is this two-party instrument called?
    A. A deed of trust
    B. A mortgage
    C. A promissory note
    D. A deed

65. A borrower paid one of these when taking out a loan to purchase a parcel of realty. The borrower paid this so that the lender would lower the interest rate. This also benefited the lender by increasing the lender's yield. What is this called?
    A. A loan origination fee
    B. A discount point
    C. A mutual mortgage insurance premium
    D. A title insurance premium

66. When real estate is sold under an installment land contract, the vendee's interest in the property is
    A. a legal title interest.
    B. an equitable title interest.
    C. kept by the mortgagor until the full purchase price is paid.
    D. held by the mortgagee until the full purchase price is paid.

67. A subdivider got a loan to build 40 homes in a new residential subdivision. The loan encumbered all 40 properties. The lender agreed that the loan could be repaid as the new homes were sold, and that the lender would release each lot from the loan when sold. What was the name of the loan?
    A. Partial release
    B. Blanket mortgage
    C. Package mortgage
    D. Reverse mortgage

68. This is a negotiable instrument that is transferred from seller to buyer when a mortgage loan is sold onto the secondary mortgage market. It is signed by the mortgagor during loan origination, and is not recorded in the public records. What is the name of this financing instrument?
    A. A promissory note
    B. A mortgage
    C. A deed of trust
    D. An endorsed check

69. The federal government allows major institutional lenders to charge prospective borrowers for which of these disclosures?
    A. The Loan Estimate
    B. The Closing Disclosure
    C. Both of these
    D. Neither of these

70. A silent second is a type of mortgage fraud perpetrated in a purchase transaction by the buyer and the seller against a lender. The buyer and seller intentionally deceive the lender about
    A. the appraised value of the encumbered land and improvements.
    B. the number of liens on the encumbered property.
    C. the creditworthiness of the buyer.
    D. the creditworthiness of the seller.

71. During a recession, a borrower sold a property with the help of a listing agent. The property sold for less than what was currently owed on the only mortgage encumbering the property. The lender approved the sale but required the borrower to pay the difference. What BEST describes this scenario?
    A. Deficiency judgment
    B. Subordination agreement
    C. FSBO
    D. Short sale

72. A mile is a unit of distance. How many acres are in a mile?
    A. 5,280
    B. 640
    C. 43,560
    D. None

73. A buyer purchased land described in the government survey method. The buyer purchased a quarter-quarter section and a quarter section. How much land did the buyer purchase?
    A. 40 acres
    B. 80 acres
    C. 160 acres
    D. 200 acres

74. A buyer purchased a commercial office building for $5 million. The lender required the buyer to put 20% down. How much was the buyer's purchase money mortgage?
    A. $2 million
    B. $3 million
    C. $4 million
    D. $5 million

75. An investor wanted to earn a 5% rate of return on income-producing property. A recently listed building had a net operating income of $245,000. What should the investor offer on the property to realize this rate of return?
    A. $1,900,000
    B. $3,900,000
    C. $4,900,000
    D. $5,900,000

76. A property manager is asked to report the effective gross income (EGI) on investment property to the owner. The office building has potential gross rental income of $250,000 annually. The vacancy rate is 7%. There is additional monthly income of $750 from the business center and the vending machines. What is the EGI?
    A. $140,860
    B. $200,870
    C. $240,870
    D. $240,890

77. If a 10-unit residential apartment building has a net operating income (NOI) of $300,000 and a capitalization rate of return of 6%, what is its value?
    A. $3,000,000
    B. $4,000,000
    C. $5,000,000
    D. $6,000,000

78. An investor purchased a residential property as a principal residence. The property was appraised at $400,000. The land was valued at $100,000, and the improvements were valued at $300,000. To finance the purchase of the property, the investor got a mortgage loan of $320,000. How much of a depreciation allowance can the investor take on this property on a yearly basis?
    A. Nothing
    B. $11,328
    C. $10,909
    D. $10,000

79. Which of these will NOT be prorated between a buyer and a seller on the settlement closing statement?
    A. Property taxes
    B. A payoff of the seller's mortgage
    C. HOA dues
    D. None of these will be prorated

80. On a closing settlement statement, what is the commission owed to the listing broker?
    A. Debit to the seller
    B. Debit to the buyer
    C. Credit to the seller and a debit to the buyer
    D. Credit to the buyer

BROKER PRACTICE EXAM

1. A homeowner went to a garden nursery to purchase a small tree. After bringing it home, the homeowner placed the tree on the backyard patio. The following weekend, the homeowner planted the tree. Several years later, the homeowner listed and sold the property, excluding the tree from the purchase contract. Before moving out, the homeowner uprooted the tree from the backyard and immediately placed it in the moving van. All of these are incorrect EXCEPT
   A. the tree was chattel when it was purchased, and real estate when it was on the patio.
   B. the tree was chattel when it was uprooted, and real estate when it was purchased.
   C. the tree was real estate when it was on the patio, and chattel when it was in the moving van.
   D. the tree was chattel when it was purchased, and real estate when it was planted.

2. An agricultural property had a growing crop of wheat. All of these are incorrect EXCEPT
   A. the tenant farmer must leave the growing crop of wheat upon termination of the lease.
   B. the seller of the farm must leave the wheat, unless it is included in the deed.
   C. the seller of the farm must leave the wheat, unless it is excluded from the purchase contract.
   D. the doctrine of lis pendens prohibits the buyer of the farm from keeping the wheat.

3. The owner of a dominant tenement had the right to cross over a neighbor's property to get to the only road in the area. The government built a new road, and the dominant tenement owner began to use the new road. After several months, the servient tenement owner went to the dominant tenement owner to see about terminating the easement. The owner of the dominant tenement refused to terminate the easement without being paid. Which of these is incorrect?
   A. The servient tenement owner can unilaterally terminate the now unused easement.
   B. The servient tenement owner can sign a deed terminating the now unused easement.
   C. Because of the new road, the easement is terminated through operation of law.
   D. All of these are incorrect.

4. All of these result in a split between legal title and equitable title EXCEPT
   A. a deed of trust.
   B. a mortgage.
   C. a land contract.
   D. a revocable living trust.

5. Which of these easements are only for contiguous properties?
   A. Easement in gross
   B. Appurtenant easement
   C. Both of these
   D. Neither of these

6. A homeowner contracted to build a swimming pool in the backyard. While the swimming pool was being constructed, the homeowner got a loan from a relative, and the relative promptly and properly filed the mortgage loan in the public records. After the swimming pool was completed, the homeowner neglected to pay the contractor. The contractor then filed a mechanic's lien on the property for the unpaid work on the swimming pool. Finally, the homeowner did not pay the property taxes that became due and delinquent after the mechanic's lien and the mortgage were filed for the record. In the event of homeowner default, which of these choices shows the MOST likely order in which these liens will be paid?
   A. Property taxes, mechanic's lien, mortgage
   B. Mechanic's lien, mortgage, property taxes
   C. Mortgage, property taxes, mechanic's lien
   D. Property taxes, mortgage, mechanic's lien

7. Which of these is NOT a parcel of real estate?
   A. One township
   B. 23,040 acres
   C. One rod
   D. 640 acres

8. Based upon their respective acquisition deeds, Neighbor A and Neighbor B both claim a 5-foot strip of land in between their contiguous properties. In the event the neighbors litigate this strip of land, the judge will MOST likely
   A. decide the two parcels of land both contain the contested 5 feet of land.
   B. order a survey to determine the correct legal descriptions of the two parcels.
   C. split the contested land evenly between the two neighbors.
   D. find for the owner who acquired the property first.

9. A corporation purchased a parcel of real estate in fee. There were no conditions in the deed. Assuming that no laws are broken, for how long can the corporation continue to own the property?
   A. A corporation can hold title to real estate indefinitely.
   B. A corporation can only hold title to real estate for 100 years.
   C. A corporation can only hold title to real estate for 99 years.
   D. A corporation can only hold title to real estate for 51 years.

10. A deed conveying a property to a city stated that the city must use the land as a park, that the park must have an aquarium, and the aquarium must—at all times—have at least 250 living fish. All of these are incorrect EXCEPT
    A. it is illegal to have more than one condition in a deed.
    B. a deed cannot be conditioned upon a required minimum number of living animals.
    C. a conveyance of real estate to a governmental entity cannot be qualified with conditions.
    D. the property conveyed to the city was a fee simple defeasible freehold estate.

11. The owner of a condominium unit wanted to make sure a current spouse had a place to live for life. However, after the current spouse died, the owner of the condominium unit wanted the condominium to go to an adult child from a former marriage. Of these choices, what would BEST accomplish the owner's goals?
    A. A deed of trust
    B. A life estate for the current spouse and a remainder to the adult child
    C. A life estate for the current spouse with a reversionary interest to the grantor
    D. A life estate for the current spouse, pur autre vie, and a remainder to the adult child

12. A very desirable retail rental property was offered for lease. The improvements had many desirable amenities, including a view of a nearby lake, and it was located near an upscale neighborhood. The lease stated that the lessee would be responsible for a base rent plus payment of property insurance, property taxes, and maintenance. When the lessee is responsible for these types of charges to the property, what is this type of lease called?
    A. Ground
    B. Net
    C. Variable
    D. Sale-leaseback

13. An investor, with a leased fee estate, listed a single-family residence for sale. The lessee was halfway through a five-year lease. The property sold at over the listing price, and escrow closed in 60 days. Which, if any, of these is correct?
    A. The new owner can move in immediately following the closing.
    B. The lessee held a leased fee estate under the prior owner, but now holds a nonfreehold estate.
    C. The lessee must vacate the premises following proper notice of the sale.
    D. None of these are correct.

14. Five unrelated friends purchased a parcel of real estate. They are holding title as tenants in common. To finance the purchase, the friends took out a purchase money mortgage on the property. How are they MOST likely responsible for paying the mortgage?
    A. Jointly
    B. Severally
    C. Jointly and severally
    D. Payment will depend upon their respective ownership shares in the property

15. Two people owned a parcel of real estate as joint tenants. They were taking a cab to the airport and were involved in a car crash. One died at the scene, and the other joint tenant died an hour later in the hospital. Which of these is correct?
    A. Because the joint tenants were in the same car crash, their heirs will split the property 50-50.
    B. Because the joint tenants died so close to the same time, their heirs will split the property 50-50.
    C. The heirs of the joint tenant who died in the hospital will inherit the entire property.
    D. The heirs of the joint tenant who died at the scene will inherit the entire property.

16. A competent seller delivered a deed to a buyer for the listed property. The buyer accepted the deed, and title transferred to the buyer. The deed was in writing, signed by the seller, contained a description of the property, conveyancing words, and designated the buyer by name. All of the following were a required part of a valid deed EXCEPT
    A. a competent seller.
    B. acceptance by the buyer.
    C. a written deed.
    D. a description of the property.

17. A seller listed a property. The preliminary report of title insurance indicated that the deed from a former owner had never been filed for the record. The former owner stated that a deed had been signed before the close, but promised to do whatever was necessary to cure the cloud on title on the seller's property. Which of these will clear the cloud on the seller's title without any promises or warranties being made by the former owner?
    A. A general warranty deed
    B. A special warranty deed
    C. A quitclaim deed signed by the former owner
    D. A quitclaim deed signed by the former owner and the seller

18. What is TRUE of an abstract of title?
    A. It can only be prepared by an attorney.
    B. It is an historical summary of all conveyances and encumbrances that have ever been recorded on a property.
    C. It includes the names of missing heirs to the property.
    D. It indicates any forged documents.

19. A seller sells a parcel of realty to Buyer A. Buyer A does not record the deed. The seller then sells the same parcel of realty to Buyer B. Buyer B immediately records the deed. Buyer B knows about the earlier deed to Buyer A, but also knows that Buyer A has not recorded the deed. If this occurred in a race-notice state, who owns the property?
    A. Buyer A
    B. Buyer B
    C. The seller
    D. Buyer A and Buyer B, as tenants in common

20. A buyer purchased a parcel of commercial real estate. A major institutional lender financed 80% of the appraised value and conditioned the loan on the purchase of a lender's policy of title insurance. This was the only title insurance policy that was issued for the purchase transaction. After the closing, the title insurance company discovered that it had missed the deed showing the seller was not in fact the owner of the property. The title insurance company will issue a check to
    A. the buyer.
    B. the lender.
    C. the buyer and the lender.
    D. neither the buyer nor the lender.

21. A city changed the zoning in an entire area. The change in zoning erased the value of a particular parcel of real estate. The owner sued the city for the lost value and won. The name of the lawsuit was
    A. inverse condemnation.
    B. interpleader.
    C. lis pendens.
    D. a quiet title action.

22. Jordan purchased a property in a new residential subdivision. The purchase was the first deed out from the developer and the deed stated that the transfer obligated Jordan to conform with covenants, conditions, and restrictions (CC&Rs) for the subdivision. Several years later, Jordan decided to sell the property. The deed from Jordan to the buyer did not contain any reference to the CC&Rs. The buyer
    A. can ignore the CC&Rs as violating ownership rights inherent in real estate.
    B. must conform to all of the subdivision's CC&Rs.
    C. does not have to conform to the private CC&Rs.
    D. must conform to the subdivision's lawful CC&Rs.

23. If an improvement is built in a 100-year flood zone, it means that
    A. the property will be flooded at least once a century.
    B. the lender will typically condition a loan on special flood insurance coverage.
    C. homeowners insurance will cover improvement damages caused by floodwaters.
    D. the property will always be situated in a flood zone.

24. An individual was considering buying a single-family residence (SFR) or renting one unit in a duplex. Both properties were built in 1975. All of these statements related to federal lead-based paint (LBP) rules are incorrect EXCEPT
    A. the individual must be offered the opportunity to test for LBP for both properties.
    B. the individual must be offered the opportunity to test for LBP for the duplex, but not for the SFR.
    C. the individual must be offered the opportunity to test for LBP for the SFR, but not for the duplex.
    D. federal LBP rules only apply to residential dwellings built before January 1, 1968.

25. Who regulates construction of mobile homes?
    A. Local municipalities in building codes
    B. The governmental entity responsible for determining proper affixture
    C. HUD
    D. All of these

26. Which of these pairs is in an agency relationship?
    A. Optionor; optionee
    B. Vendor; vendee
    C. Lessor; lessee
    D. Grantor; attorney-in-fact

27. A seller hired a real estate broker to sell a home. The seller privately told the broker the lowest acceptable offer the seller would accept ($1 million), the seller's motivation for selling (a leaky roof), and the only terms amenable to the seller (noncontingent offers) Which of these is TRUE?
    A. Because of the fiduciary duty of disclosure, the listing agent must disclose the leaky roof.
    B. Because of the fiduciary duty of obedience, the listing agent must not disclose the leaky roof.
    C. Because of the fiduciary duty of confidentiality, the listing agent must not disclose the lowest acceptable offer.
    D. Because of the fiduciary duty of loyalty, the listing agent must disclose the leaky roof.

28. A listing agent did not bring a listing agreement to a meeting with a seller. The seller had a power of attorney (POA) document, and the listing agent and seller decided to use that instead of the listing agreement. Which of these is correct?
    A. Like the listing agreement, the POA always includes agent compensation.
    B. Like the listing agreement, the POA establishes an agency relationship.
    C. Like the listing agreement, the POA prohibits the agent from making decisions to bind the principal.
    D. Like the listing agreement, the POA is advisory only.

29. A seller and a listing agent entered into a listing agreement for a commercial property. Two days later, the improvements burned down. What is the status of the listing agreement?
    A. The listing agreement will pause until the improvements are rebuilt.
    B. The listing agreement will terminate.
    C. The listing agreement will terminate, provided the seller agrees.
    D. The listing agreement will still be in effect.

30. In a real estate brokerage firm, an associate licensee brought in multiple listings. Which of these will terminate these listing agreements?
    A. The death of the associate licensee
    B. The insanity of the associate licensee
    C. The associate licensee filing for bankruptcy
    D. None of these

31. Real estate licensees owe a duty of disclosure to principals and third parties. All of these related to disclosure are incorrect EXCEPT
    A. because of respondeat superior, the duty of disclosure to a principal is much broader.
    B. because of respondeat superior, the duty of disclosure to a third party is much broader.
    C. because of vicarious liability, the duty of disclosure to a third party is much broader.
    D. because of vicarious liability, the duty of disclosure to a principal and third party are equal.

32. A seller and a real estate broker entered into a written listing agreement. The seller stated the profit the seller wanted to gain from the transaction, and both parties agreed that the broker's commission would be anything above that amount. The real estate broker than helped the seller establish a listing price for the property. All of these are correct EXCEPT
    A. this is referred to as a net listing.
    B. this is referred to as a seller reserved listing.
    C. many states have banned this type of listing because of potential conflicts of interest.
    D. the real estate broker may find a buyer and still receive no compensation from the transaction.

33. A property not listed with the multiple listing service (MLS) is known as which of these?
    A. Pocket listing
    B. Whisper listing
    C. Off-market listing
    D. All of these

34. An investor purchased income-producing residential rental property. Originally, the investor planned on managing the property without professional assistance. However, when the investor advertised the vacant units, no prospective tenants called or emailed to express an interest. Reluctantly, the investor hired a property manager to manage the investment property. To set the rent, the property manager would consider all of these EXCEPT
    A. property market data.
    B. averages from the surrounding area.
    C. location.
    D. federal fair housing laws.

35. Both the listing agent and the property manager serve as agents and owe fiduciary duties to their principals. Which of these statements is correct?
    A. The listing agent is a general agent, while the property manager is a special agent.
    B. The listing agent can bind the principal, while the property manager cannot.
    C. The exclusive listing agent serves for a specified term, while the property manager does not.
    D. The scope of the listing agent's and the property manager's authority is advisory only.

36. An owner of income-generating residential rental property sold the property to an investor. Several current tenants asked the property manager about the status of their leases now that the property was under new ownership. All of these responses from the property manager are incorrect EXCEPT
    A. the status of the leases depends on how the new owner wants to develop the property.
    B. the leases will immediately need to be renegotiated with the new owner.
    C. the new property owner bought the property subject to the current leases.
    D. because of the leases, the new property owner purchased the property as a nonfreehold estate.

37. An investor purchased a 10-unit residential apartment building. The new owner of the income-producing property, clean and sober for 20 years, told the property manager not to check prospective tenants for past or current drug use, convictions for drug manufacturing, or convictions for drug dealing. Which of these statements can the property manager lawfully make to the property owner?
    A. Renting to current drug users violates federal fair housing laws.
    B. Renting to convicted drug dealers violates federal fair housing laws.
    C. Renting to convicted drug manufacturers violates federal fair housing laws.
    D. The property manager cannot make any of these statements.

38. An investor purchased a 20-unit apartment building as investment property. A property manager was hired to manage the 20-unit residential building. Construction of the building had been completed on January 1, 1978. Who, if anyone, will get a lead-based paint (LBP) warning?
    A. No one
    B. The investor
    C. The prospective tenants
    D. The property manager

39. Which of these is NOT a protected class under federal fair housing laws?
    A. Religion
    B. Color
    C. Victims of violence
    D. National origin

40. A 59-year-old retiree submitted an application for a rental vacancy at an apartment designated as senior housing. The retiree was rejected. All of these are valid reasons for the application being denied EXCEPT
    A. the senior housing was limited to tenants older than the 59-year-old retiree.
    B. the rent was beyond the retiree's ability to pay.
    C. the retiree had a history of violence against other tenants.
    D. the retiree did not match the racial mix in the complex.

41. In its covenants, conditions, and restrictions (CC&Rs), a homeowners association (HOA) limited the dogs that residents could own based upon breed and weight. All of these are incorrect EXCEPT
    A. this CC&R is always illegal.
    B. this CC&R is proper, provided the dog is not a service animal.
    C. this CC&R violates the homeowners' fundamental property rights.
    D. this CC&R is in violation of federal fair housing laws.

42. A privately owned company with 10 employees was not open to the public. The company complied with all provisions of the Americans with Disabilities Act (ADA). Which of these statements is correct?
    A. ADA compliance is mandatory for companies with 10 employees or more.
    B. ADA compliance was voluntary.
    C. ADA compliance was a legal requirement for this company because of yearly sales.
    D. ADA compliance was legally required because of square footage.

43. A newly licensed real estate associate had marketing material made and included the word *REALTOR®* on all business cards. Why would the business cards need to be reprinted without this word?
    A. The associate specialized only in commercial property and manufactured homes.
    B. The associate was not an active member of a specific professional organization.
    C. The associate was not the broker of record.
    D. The associate was not sufficiently experienced.

44. An advertisement placed by a real estate brokerage firm promised both future buyers and sellers a $100 rebate if these parties used the services of the brokerage firm and escrow closed within six months of the advertisement. Under federal law, this advertisement was
    A. illegal, because it violated consumer protection law.
    B. legal, provided disclosures were made to the appropriate parties.
    C. illegal, because it violated federal antitrust law.
    D. legal, as long as both the seller and the buyer to each transaction received a rebate.

45. A real estate brokerage firm treats associates as independent contractors by not withholding taxes, not providing benefits, and compensating associates based on results. The brokerage firm, however, holds meetings—related to changes in federal, state, and local laws—and requires the attendance of all associates. One associate told the brokerage firm that the associate would not be attending the mandatory meetings, but would be researching any changes in the law on an individual basis. If the associate will not attend the mandatory meetings related to recent legal changes, the brokerage firm will likely
    A. research to see if the associate has the background to individually research the law.
    B. engage in risk management/effective supervision and fire the associate.
    C. change the associate's status from independent contractor to employee.
    D. make the meetings related to legal changes voluntary for all associates.

46. A real estate broker was married to an unlicensed assistant at the brokerage firm. The real estate broker trusted the unlicensed assistant, allowing this person access to the brokerage firm trust fund and not following applicable rules for trust fund handling and transaction records. This was
    A. acceptable because of the marital relationship between the broker and the unlicensed assistant.
    B. unacceptable because of the broker's duty to supervise employees at the brokerage firm.
    C. acceptable because the broker has a duty to supervise employees at the brokerage firm.
    D. unacceptable because it violates the Sherman Antitrust Act.

47. A homeowner said to a neighbor, "If you paint my pantry closet on Saturday, I will pay you $100 dollars." On Saturday, the neighbor had to unexpectedly drive his child to a weekend soccer game. In a lawsuit promptly filed by the homeowner against the neighbor because of the unpainted pantry closet, who is likely to prevail?
    A. The homeowner
    B. The neighbor
    C. The homeowner, provided the contract was later put in writing
    D. The neighbor, because of the statute of familial obligations

48. Which of these agreements is a unilateral contract?
    A. An open listing agreement
    B. A seller reserved listing agreement
    C. An exclusive right-to-sell listing agreement
    D. A purchase contract for real estate

49. Two parties entered into a written agreement for the manufacture and delivery of an illegal substance. The two parties negotiated a purchase price of $2 million. In the event the manufacturer does not deliver, what will the other party NOT legally be allowed to do?
    A. Ask for a return of the deposit
    B. Find an alternative source
    C. File a lawsuit for compensatory damages
    D. All of these

50. Two parties enter into a contract. Behind the scenes, Party A threatened to break Party B's arm if Party B didn't sign the contract. Party B signed the contract, and the agreement is still ongoing. What type of contract is this?
    A. Valid
    B. Voidable
    C. Void
    D. Executed

51. A seller and a buyer enter into a verbal purchase contract for a home. There was an offer made by the buyer. It was accepted in a timely manner by the seller, who communicated acceptance to the offeror. One week before the closing, the seller decided not to sell the property to the buyer. What legal options are typically available to the buyer?
    A. Punitive damages
    B. Compensatory damages
    C. Specific performance
    D. Nothing

52. A buyer and seller entered into a contract for the purchase of residential real estate. The buyer conditioned the contract on being able to build an accessory dwelling unit (ADU) in the backyard. A contractor determined that an ADU could not be built because of a large public utilities easement running at the rear of the property. For having kept the property off of the market for two weeks, what will the seller receive?
    A. Liquidated damages
    B. The good-faith deposit
    C. The earnest money deposit
    D. Nothing

53. This agreement starts off as a unilateral contract. Only one party, the owner of real estate, is making a promise. If the other party walks away, the promisor will not be able to sue, but can keep _____.
    A. the option fee
    B. the good-faith deposit
    C. the liquidated damages
    D. the rent

54. A vendor and vendee enter into an installment sales contract. During the contract, the vendee has all of these EXCEPT
    A. equitable title.
    B. legal title.
    C. the right of possession.
    D. the right to record the installment sales contract.

55. In a sale of a parcel of real estate, the seller is represented by a listing agent, and the buyer is represented by a selling agent. One contract, the seller reserved listing agreement, needs to be amended. Who would sign this amendment?
    A. The seller and the listing agent
    B. The buyer and the selling agent
    C. The two real estate agents
    D. The seller, the buyer, and the two real estate agents

56. Four appraisers appraised the same duplex dwelling on the same date and for the same function. All of these are incorrect EXCEPT
    A. all appraisals have the same function.
    B. if the four opinions of value don't match, it's an indication of appraiser error.
    C. the purpose is the reason for the appraisal; the function of the appraisal is an estimate of value.
    D. the value estimates of the four appraisals will likely vary from each other.

57. A developer purchased a large parcel of vacant land with the intention of building a new residential subdivision. The developer wanted the appraiser to draw as complete a picture of the real estate as possible. What appraisal report form would the developer require?
    A. Narrative
    B. Self-contained
    C. Both of these
    D. Neither of these

58. Which of these is a complete and correct list of the essential elements of value?
    A. Demand, utility, scarcity, transferability
    B. Demand, scarcity, cost, transferability, utility
    C. Demand, location, scarcity, transferability
    D. Scarcity, transmutability, utility, demand

59. A homeowner added an in-ground swimming pool to the backyard, and an additional bathroom to existing space within the home. The swimming pool cost $50,000, but only added $40,000 to the market value of the property. The bathroom cost $12,000, but added $17,000 to the market value of the property. Which of these is correct?
    A. The bathroom is an example of progression.
    B. The swimming pool is an example of progression.
    C. The swimming pool is an example of contribution (increasing returns).
    D. The bathroom is an example of contribution (increasing returns).

60. Two married buyers with a lot of small children, but a limited budget, met with a real estate agent to discuss available properties. The real estate agent showed them several listed properties. Which of these properties would BEST meet the married buyers' current dwelling needs?
    A. A large house in a neighborhood of small, older properties
    B. A small house in a neighborhood of remodeled, large, upscale properties
    C. The worst house, not up to code, in the best neighborhood
    D. Unimproved land in an area zoned for residential properties

61. Which of these appraisal methods is MOST like the product real estate brokerage firms provide to residential buyers (to help them determine a reasonable offer) and residential sellers (to help them determine a reasonable list price)?
    A. The cost approach
    B. The income approach
    C. The sales comparison approach
    D. The replacement cost approach

62. An appraiser was hired to appraise a historic church. The property was not generating any revenue. The owner of the property wanted to know the cost of building an exact replica of the church. What appraisal method would the appraiser MOST likely select?
    A. The market data approach
    B. The reproduction cost approach
    C. The replacement cost approach
    D. The income approach

63. Which of these income-producing properties has a 9% rate of return?
    A. A property listed for $500,000 with a net operating income of $15,000
    B. A property listed for $500,000 with a net operating income of $25,000
    C. A property listed for $500,000 with a net operating income of $35,000
    D. A property listed for $500,000 with a net operating income of $45,000

64. An owner of a parcel of real estate wants to take out a loan using the realty as collateral. However, the owner does not want the loan to have any impact on how title to the property is held. What loan document should the prospective borrower insist upon signing?
    A. A trust deed
    B. A mortgage
    C. An option
    D. A subordination

65. A buyer got into a bidding war with other prospective buyers and ended up submitting the winning bid of $1.2 million for a very desirable property. The appraisal came in with an estimate of $1 million. The buyer is not getting a loan that is either guaranteed or insured by any government program. The lender agreed to finance 80% of the purchase. What is the MOST likely amount a lender will be willing to finance for this purchase transaction?
    A. $1.2 million
    B. $1 million
    C. $960,000
    D. $800,000

66. A partial release clause is MOST common in which of these types of loans?
    A. A package loan
    B. An air loan
    C. A blanket loan
    D. A purchase money loan

67. A loan that enables older homeowners to convert part of the equity in their homes to cash without having to sell, transfer title, or incur a new monthly loan payment is a
    A. subprime loan.
    B. reverse mortgage.
    C. term loan.
    D. bridge loan.

68. Which of these is correct regarding the loan disclosures required of major institutional lenders under the federal TILA-RESPA Integrated Disclosure (TRID) rule?
    A. The Loan Estimate must be sent within three business days of receiving the loan application.
    B. The Closing Disclosure must be delivered at least three business days before the closing of the loan.
    C. The Closing Disclosure time frame can be waived upon a bona fide financial emergency of the borrower.
    D. All of these statements are correct.

69. During a national recession, a lender approved a short sale of a residential home. The outstanding loan balance was $450,000. The fair market value of the property was $440,000. What was the sales price of the property?
    A. $445,100
    B. $450,000
    C. $450,001
    D. $475,000

70. Agricultural property was described using the government survey method. A buyer purchased the east half of one section and the northwest quarter of a contiguous section. How many acres did the buyer purchase in total?
    A. 320 acres
    B. 480 acres
    C. 960 acres
    D. Impossible to calculate from the information given

71. An investor purchased a single-family residence for $1 million to use for rental purposes only. The land was valued at 40%, and the improvements were valued at 60% of the total purchase price. How much could the investor take each year as a depreciation allowance on the investment property?
    A. $10,256.41
    B. $14,545.45
    C. $15,384.61
    D. $21,818.18

72. A property manager has been asked by an investor to research the purchase of a single-family residence for investment purposes. The list price of a property is $1 million. The investor already owns a single-family residence that cost $750,000 and generates $7,500 in monthly rent. The investor is satisfied with this rate of return. Which of these would, per the property manager, provide the same acceptable rate of return?
    A. $1,000
    B. $5,000
    C. $7,500
    D. $10,000

73. An income-producing commercial office building had a net operating income of $475,000 and a rate of return of 8%. What was its value?
    A. $4,750,000
    B. $5,750,000
    C. $5,937,500
    D. $9,370,000

74. Each unit in a 10-unit residential apartment building rents for $1,500 a month. There is an onsite laundry facility and rental storage spaces that bring in an additional $1,000 a month. The building has a 5% vacancy rate. What is the effective gross income (EGI) for this income-producing property?
    A. $172,100
    B. $182,400
    C. $191,100
    D. $192,400

75. A duplex owner lives in one unit and rents the other for $600 a month, due on the first of the month. The owner sells the property, and the closing is scheduled for April 21. How will the rent be prorated if the seller has the day of closing?
    A. The seller owes the buyer $180.
    B. The buyer owes the seller $200.
    C. The seller owes the buyer $400.
    D. The buyer owes the seller $420.

ANSWER KEY

Unit 1
True/False Questions

1. **B** Items like garage door openers and house keys are adapted to the use of a specific property and are considered real property.

2. **A**

3. **B** Chattel (a.k.a. personal property) is not attached to the realty, and would not need to be excluded from the purchase contract.

4. **B** Because of the legal doctrine of emblements, the growing crop of wheat belongs to the tenant farmer, even after the lease ends.

5. **A**

6. **A**

7. **B** A license is the *revocable* permission by an owner of real estate, allowing another person to use the land without it being a trespass.

8. **B** Even a tree limb growing over a joint fence—without touching the property—can encroach on a neighboring property owner's air rights.

9. **A**

10. **A**

11. **B** The party giving up an interest in real estate signs the deed—here, that would be the owner of the dominant tenement.

12. **A**

13. **B** In the government survey system, the grid is formed by a base, a meridian, ranges, and tiers.

14. **A**

15. **A**

16. **B** In the rectangular survey system, a section of land is one square mile and contains 640 acres.

17. **A**

Multiple-Choice Questions

1. **C** Easements transfer with the land. Trade fixtures belong to tenants. Freestanding stoves and refrigerators are personal property and transfer to the buyer only if they are included in the purchase contract.

2. **B** Trade fixtures must be removed from the property on or before the lease expires. The tenants are responsible for any damage caused by the removal of the fixtures. Those that are not removed become the property of the landlord.

3. **D** House keys are adapted to the use of a specific property and are considered real property.

4. **D** A license is revocable permission by an owner of real estate that allows another person to use the land without it being a trespass. The other answer choices are incorrect. A prescriptive easement is established, among other things, without the permission of the owner—here, the fact pattern states that the owner of the northern parcel crossed over the southern parcel with the permission of the owner. An appurtenant easement over the southern parcel would need to be established formally and in writing. The facts inform us that this was an informal, verbal arrangement between neighbors. An easement in gross involves only one parcel of real estate, while in this fact pattern, there are two (the northern "landlocked" parcel without road access, and the southern parcel with road access).

5. **A** The priority of liens generally date back to when they are filed for the public record; however, real estate taxes and special assessments take priority over all other liens.

6. **B** An encroachment is the unauthorized use of a property without the consent of the owner. It might be a building intruding upon (or trespassing on) the neighboring parcel. Even a one-inch encroachment is a serious issue that should be addressed with an experienced real estate attorney as soon as the encroachment is discovered, hopefully before making an offer on the property. While the laws governing encroachments vary by state, there is a limited statutory period to take the encroaching property owner to court. The other answer choices are incorrect. An owner is benefitted by the right to access a neighbor's land to get to a street. Per the U.S. Supreme Court, a deed restriction limiting the races to whom the property could be sold no longer has any force and effect in any part of the United States [*Shelley v. Kraemer*, 334 U.S. (1948)]. Finally, a lis pendens is a document recorded to show there is a lawsuit pending on a property. A withdrawal of lis pendens indicates the lawsuit has been dropped or withdrawn.

7. **A** When a seller reserves a portion of the property, it means that portion of the property is not included in the sale. Here, the seller divided up the property into the west half and the east half and reserved—or kept—the west half of the property. That meant the seller was selling only the east half of the property. The seller also reserved an easement over the south 10 feet of the east half (the property being conveyed).

8. **C** In a metes and bounds legal description, the point of beginning starts the description of a particular parcel of real estate. The other answer choices are incorrect. A metes and bounds legal description will very frequently start at some permanent reference point *outside* the boundaries of a particular parcel of real estate. This external reference point will appear in the legal description with the words *starting at* or *commencing at*. This might be a government spike in the middle of a nearby road or a large, immovable natural object near the subject property. *Base and meridian* are terms used in the government survey system.

9. **C** A developer developing a new residential subdivision in a suburban area would likely use the lot and block method legal description. Typically, the developer is required to create and record the plat map before building. *Note:* The lot and block method is also called the lot and tract method; the lot, block, and tract method; or the lot, block, and subdivision system.

Unit 2
True/False Questions

1. **A**

2. **B** The fee simple defeasible estate is an estate of ownership with one or more conditions that—if violated—may result in a loss of title.

3. **B** The life tenant under a life estate holds a freehold estate of ownership that will terminate upon the death of the measuring human life.

4. **B** A leased fee estate is an estate of ownership that the lessor (owner) rents to a lessee (tenant).

5. **B** An estate for years does not need to be for multiple years; it must have a specific start date and a specific termination date.

6. **A**

7. **B** Ownership in severalty is ownership by one person or one entity.

8. **A**

9. **B** Only married couples can hold property as tenants by the entirety.

10. **A**

Multiple-Choice Questions

1. **C** In an estate at sufferance, a tenant occupies the premises without the landlord's consent or other legal agreement with the landlord.

2. **D** A fee simple defeasible estate is an example of a freehold estate of ownership that can be inherited from the owner and might last forever. The fee simple defeasible estate is one in which there is a condition that might result in the loss of title (e.g., "Person A to Person B, for as long as the property is used as a park"). If Person B never stops using the property as a park, Person B will not lose title to the property because of the condition. The other answer choices are incorrect as they relate to leasehold estates held by tenants.

3. **B** In an estate from period to period (also called a periodic estate), the tenancy period automatically renews for an indefinite period of time with the timely payment of rent.

4. **C** The fact pattern describes a tenancy at will (a.k.a. an estate at will). This is a leasehold estate—with no fixed period of time—that can be terminated at any time by either party. Multiple states have prohibited or regulated this type of leasehold estate because it can traditionally be terminated without notice. The other answer choices are incorrect. The estate (or tenancy) for years is a leasehold estate with a definite start and termination date. The periodic tenancy renews automatically upon payment of rent until proper notice is given. This type of leasehold estate is especially prevalent for residential property. The estate at sufferance is the lowest estate in land—it is what a holdover tenant has if that tenant stays on the leasehold property beyond the end of the lease.

5. **C** Ownership in severalty is ownership of real estate by a sole person or entity. The only answer choice that shows sole ownership is ownership by a multinational corporation. The other answer choices are incorrect. Even though each answer choice starts with the word *one*, these incorrect answer choices show two people. If owned in severalty, only one person can be on title.

6. **B** Tenancy in common is a form of ownership in which multiple owners concurrently own the same parcel of real estate. When Person C wrote her will, she made the other co-owners her devisees. Now, Person A and Person B each own 50% of the property as tenants in common. Several terms in this fact pattern are related to wills. Dying *testate* means dying after executing a will. A *devisee* is a person who will inherit real estate per the terms of a will. The other answer choices are incorrect. If the property were held in a joint tenancy, then the property would not pass per the provisions of a will. It would pass automatically through operation of law to the survivors. A property owned in severalty is owned by one person or entity: even after Person C's death, there are still multiple owners of the property. Finally, if the property had been held in a trust, it would have passed to Person A and Person B per the terms of the trust, not via a will.

Unit 3
True/False Questions

1. **B** Per the statute of frauds, a deed must be in writing.

2. **A**

3. **B** A special warranty deed warrants title only during the term of the grantor's ownership.

4. **B** A quitclaim deed contains no warrants or promises.

5. **B** For title to transfer, the deed must be delivered by the grantor to the grantee.

6. **B** Title transfers when a valid deed is delivered by the grantor and accepted by the grantee.

7. **A**

8. **B** A lender's policy only protects the lender—if the borrower wants coverage, the borrower must purchase an owner's policy of title insurance.

9. **B**

10. **B** A mortgagee's policy (that is, a lender's policy) of title insurance protects only the lender.

11. **A**

Multiple-Choice Questions

1. **C** Proof of heirship is not a requirement for a valid deed.

2. **B** A title transferred by a quitclaim deed provides no warranties. It transfers whatever interest the grantor currently has in the property.

3. **D** Delivery was effective when the deed was given to the settlement officer. The general rule is that delivery must be made when the grantor is alive and has the intention of conveying the property to the grantee. However, there is an exception to this rule when the deed has been delivered to an agent of the grantor. The settlement officer (in some states, referred to as an escrow officer) is a dual agent of both the seller and the buyer in a purchase transaction—delivery was complete when the executed deed was given to the settlement officer.

4. **A** The priority of liens is usually determined by the order in which they are filed or recorded.

5. **A** If a general warranty deed was given, there may be recourse through the previous owner. *Note:* A mortgagee's policy of title insurance only protects the lender (the mortgagee) and only while a mortgage loan is outstanding.

Unit 4
True/False Questions

1. **B** Zoning is part of the government's police power.

2. **A**

3. **A**

4. **B** The fourth power is property taxes. Ad valorem is a Latin term that means *according to value*. The term is frequently used in relation to property taxes, but is not the name of the power itself.

5. **B** Zoning laws are local and not state or national.

6. **B** Private deed restrictions that discriminate against protected classes are illegal, but other deed restrictions on residential properties are legal.

7. **B** Ad valorem taxes are based on the assessed value of the property, not on the current market value.

8. **A** Some property may be exempt from taxes, such as schools, parks, hospitals, or property owned by a government jurisdiction or religious and charitable organizations.

9. **A** This is sometimes referred to as being "grandfathered in."

10. **B** Building codes, not zoning laws, specify construction standards required when erecting or repairing buildings.

11. **A**

12. **B** The development of wetlands is regulated—not prohibited—by federal and state law.

13. **B** An environmental hazard is one that human beings bring to the property, typically through modern methods of construction and installation.

14. **B** For properties built before January 1, 1978 (i.e., target housing), only prospective buyers must be given the opportunity to test for lead-based paint.

15. **A**

16. **B** Radon gas is created naturally through the breakdown of uranium in the soil.

17. **B** No privately owned real estate is shielded from the government's power of eminent domain.

18. **A**

19. **A**

Multiple-Choice Questions

1. **D** Condemnation is the legal process by which governments exercise their power of eminent domain. It is not one of the four governmental powers. The four governmental powers are police power, eminent domain, taxation, and escheat (memory aid: PETE).

2. **D** No privately owned real estate is shielded from the government's power of eminent domain.

3. **B** Eminent domain is the right of the government to "take" (acquire) privately owned real estate for public use.

4. **D** To implement and enforce the master plan, local governments enact zoning laws and ordinances covering items such as permitted uses of land, lot sizes, types of structures, building heights, setback distances, the style and appearance of structures, structural density, and the protection of natural resources.

5. **C** If a state mandates the disclosure of material facts or property defects, prospective buyers would need to be informed that a property was situated in a floodplain zone.

6. **B** Brownfield sites are frequently abandoned properties with toxic and/or environmental hazards. The other answer choices are incorrect. Wetlands are geographic areas inundated or saturated with surface water, and development of these areas is frequently subject to both federal and state regulation. Greenfields are undeveloped land, typically agricultural property located outside of city limits. Beigefields is a made-up word.

7. **D** Agents are not expected to be experts in the area of hazardous substances, but they should have a basic knowledge so all parties in the transaction can make informed decisions.

8. **B** For residential properties of one to four units built before 1978, federal law requires that LBP warnings [and an Environmental Protection Agency (EPA) pamphlet] be given to prospective buyers and tenants. An opportunity to test for LBP, however, must only be given to prospective buyers. *Note:*

No one is legally required to remove LBP if it is discovered on the subject property.

9. **B** The fact that the owner could earn more money if the owner wasn't made to comply with zoning is not a valid reason to grant relief from zoning regulations.

10. **D** The police power of the state is its authority to create regulations to protect the public health, safety, and general welfare of its citizens.

Unit 5
True/False Questions

1. **B** The listing is a contract owned by the broker.

2. **A**

3. **B** Agents must only obey lawful commands of the principal.

4. **B** Both the listing agreement and the POA establish an agency relationship between an agent and a principal.

5. **B** Fiduciary duties are owed by the agent to the principal. The promise to use due diligence to fulfill the terms of the listing contract is the promise that the listing agent makes to the principal (seller).

6. **A**

7. **B** An exclusive listing agreement is a bilateral contract. The seller is promising to pay the broker, if a buyer is found. The listing broker is promising to use due diligence to find a buyer.

8. **A** Listing agreements can be terminated a number of ways including agreement of the parties.

9. **B** Although state law varies, typically, any interest in a property held by an agent involved in a transaction must be disclosed to interested parties.

10. **B** An implied agency *does* result in fiduciary duties being owed from the agent to the principal.

11. **A**

12. **B** Agencies can be created by an expressed agreement or implied through a party's actions.

13. **B** The listing contract is by and between the seller and the broker of record at the brokerage firm. Because the seller is not a party to the contract, the death of the seller won't terminate the listing contract.

14. **A**

15. **A**

16. **A**

17. **B** The duty of disclosure to a third party is typically limited to a disclosure of material facts about a property and any conflict of interest. The fiduciary duty of disclosure that an agent owes a principal is much broader.

18. **B** Although state law varies, a listing agent is not generally allowed to conceal known defects about the listed property from interested parties.

19. **A**

20. **A**

21. **A**

22. **A**

23. **B** Commissions are typically split 50/50, but there is no MLS law stating they must be.

24. **A**

25. **A**

26. **A** A dual agency occurs when one broker represents two principals in the same transaction. Dual agencies must always be disclosed.

Multiple-Choice Questions

1. **D** The purchase and sale agreement is a contract between the seller and the buyer. It does not establish an agency relationship between a principal and an agent, as all the other answer choices do.

2. **C** A listing agreement does not allow the broker to act *in place* of the seller. The listing agreement usually establishes a special agency, and this is an advisory position only—it allows the broker to act *on behalf* of the seller. For example, a broker can solicit offers on behalf of the seller, but the listing agreement does not permit the broker to act in place of the seller and accept an offer. *Test-taking tip*: When two answer choices are very close to each other, pay special attention to them. This is frequently what the question is testing.

3. **B** If an agent hears something related to the scope of the agency, it's as though the principal has heard it. That is why the agent (the listing broker) has a

fiduciary duty of disclosure about the closing of the train station to the principal (the seller). What the seller will do with that information one week before closing is irrelevant to this practice test question. *Note:* Fiduciary duties are owed by the agent to the principal. Unless there is a dual agency (prohibited in multiple states), a listing broker is not in an agency relationship with a buyer and does not owe the fiduciary duty of disclosure to the buyer.

4. **B**   The listing broker is the agent of the seller. The seller is the broker's client.

5. **D**   The agent would need to disclose all of these to the prospective buyer. All of these choices represent a potential conflict of interest between the buyer's agent and the buyer. *Note:* In some states, a dual agency—where the seller's agent also serves as the buyer's agent—is illegal.

6. **B**   An implied agency is created accidentally or unintentionally by the actions or speech of the parties. When the listing broker advised the prospective buyer/friend regarding how to raise a credit score and how to submit a winning offer, the listing broker established an implied agency relationship. Because the listing broker was already in an agency relationship with the seller, this resulted in an undisclosed, dual agency relationship.

7. **C**   The death of a buyer would not terminate the fiduciary duties established in a listing agreement. A listing agreement is by and between a seller and a listing broker. Because a buyer is not a party to the listing agreement, the buyer's death would not affect the listing agreement or the fiduciary duties set forth in the listing agreement.

8. **D**   A listing agreement typically terminates if the improvements are destroyed. *Note:* An important characteristic of land is that it is—at least in theory—considered physically indestructible.

9. **C**   Vicarious liability is the responsibility created not because of the broker's actions but because of the relationship between the broker and affiliates. A real estate broker is vicariously liable for the acts of an associate broker or salesperson even if the broker did nothing to create liability.

10. **D**   None of these choices are correct. Most states legally require listing agents to disclose materials defects to prospective buyers, even when ordered by the principal to lie or keep silent. The listing broker (the agent) does not owe any fiduciary duties to a prospective buyer (a third party), only to the seller

(the principal). The duty to disclose the material facts or defects to prospective buyers is a legal requirement of many states—it is *not* a fiduciary duty.

11. **D**   This is a net listing. A net listing is where the seller states a certain, specified net amount to be made from the sale of the listed property, and the broker agrees to receive as compensation anything above that stated amount. This type of listing is illegal or discouraged in many states.

12. **B**   The net listing agreement is discouraged or banned outright by multiple states because of the potential conflict of interest between the seller (principal) and the listing broker (agent). *Note:* A dual agency is not a type of listing agreement. Rather, it describes a situation where the seller's broker also serves as the buyer's broker in the same purchase transaction. The dual agency has also been banned by multiple states.

13. **B**   Real estate brokers belonging to the MLS usually split commissions evenly with the buyer's agent, but there is no legal requirement for them to do so. The other answer choices are incorrect. FSBO is an acronym meaning *for sale by owner*. A listing broker might post a property on the MLS for a FSBO owner with a flat fee or entry-only MLS. This is only a posting of the property and would not include any other services.

14. **D**   Personal property (chattel goods) that the seller does not want included as part of the sale of real estate would not be listed on the multiple listing service.

Unit 6
True/False Questions

1. **B**   A property manager's duties include staying current on the rental rates at nearby rental properties.

2. **A**

3. **A**

4. **B**   The fiduciary duty of obedience is owed only for lawful commands—excluding tenants of a particular race is illegal under federal fair housing laws.

5. **B**   The property manager is a general agent and typically has a limited authority to bind the owner to property management decisions like signing tenants.

6. **A**

7. **A**

8. **B** Sufferers from HIV/AIDS are protected under the handicapped and disability classifications of federal fair housing laws.

9. **B** Both the listing agent and the property manager (also an agent) owe the fiduciary duty of confidentiality to their respective principals.

10. **A**

11. **B** Fiduciary duties are only owed by the agent to the principal.

Multiple-Choice Questions

1. **D** A property manager would not evaluate the owner's estate planning paperwork. Estate planning in advance of a property owner's death would be evaluated by an attorney, not by a property manager.

2. **B** The typical property manager acts on behalf of the property owner as a general agent. A general agent is authorized to perform multiple acts on behalf of the property owner. General agents have a limited ability to bind the property owner to their decisions (e.g., finding and signing well-qualified tenants, hiring and paying people to repair the units).

3. **B** Constructive eviction is wrongful conduct by a landlord that interferes with the tenant's use and enjoyment of the property allowing the tenant to vacate the property and end all lease obligations.

4. **D** The ADA requires private accommodations open to the public be accessible to people with handicaps or disabilities. This law pertains to properties managed either by the owner or by a property manager.

5. **A** Under the terms of a ground lease, any improvements added by the tenant become the owner's/lessor's property at the end of the lease.

6. **C** Addison, the property manager, must disobey to keep from violating federal fair housing laws. The property manager should inform the owner that limiting prospective tenants on the basis of religion would be illegal for both the owner and the property manager. The other answer choices are incorrect. The fiduciary duty of obedience does not include illegal activity. There are certain federal exemptions when an owner is occupying a unit on the property, but these federal exemptions are for one- to four-unit residential properties. Finally, the property manager (the agent) owes fiduciary

duties only to the principal (the owner), not to the tenants.

Unit 7
True/False Questions

1. **A**

2. **A**

3. **B** An owner of rental housing is allowed to exclude tenants based upon their ability to afford paying the rent.

4. **B** Prohibition of discrimination on the basis of race is also found in the Civil Rights Act of 1866.

5. **B** One of the primary goals of the ADA was to make public accommodations accessible to handicapped and disabled people.

6. **B** Making new construction for public accommodations ADA compliant has nothing to do with the financial status of the builder.

7. **A**

8. **A**

9. **B** The practice of encouraging property owners to sell or rent their homes by claiming that protected classes of people are moving into the neighborhood, which will have a negative impact on property values is blockbusting. Steering is channeling home seekers to particular neighborhoods.

10. **B** One of the primary goals of the ADA was to make public accommodations accessible to handicapped and disabled people. This pertains primarily to commercial property.

11. **A**

12. **B** Exaggerating a property's benefits is called puffing.

13. **A**

14. **A**

15. **B** Discrimination on the basis of sex is prohibited under both state (typically) and federal fair housing laws.

16. **A**

17. **B** While state law varies, the broker of record has the authority and legal responsibility to supervise associate licensees, whether or not the brokerage firm withholds taxes.

18. **A**

19. **A**

20. **A**

21. **B** Puffing is an exaggerated form of sales talk that no reasonably prudent buyer would rely upon to make a decision. Look for statements that cannot be measured objectively, such as, "This house has the most beautiful view in the subdivision."

Multiple-Choice Questions

1. **A** There are circumstances in which the Fair Housing Act does not apply to single-family homeowners, but none of these exceptions apply when an owner uses the services of a real estate broker.

2. **D** It is discriminatory to change the list price based upon the race of prospective buyers.

3. **B** Those individuals who are receiving treatment for alcoholism are protected under the ADA.

4. **B** The owner of a commercial building could refuse to make changes to the "first-come, first-serve" parking to accommodate a disabled tenant. Under reasonable accommodations, a commercial landlord would be expected to delegate a parking space for a disabled tenant.

5. **D** Sex is a class covered by the federal Fair Housing Act while other classes are protected under state fair housing laws.

6. **B** This practice is called blockbusting. Steering restricts freedom of choice for buyers, testing is done to enforce fair housing laws and redlining is denying loans or insurance to people in certain areas, regardless of their qualifications.

7. **D** Although the exact laws vary from state to state, a real estate salesperson cannot work independently; the salesperson must work under the authority of a real estate broker.

8. **D** State law varies. However, in general, while an unlicensed employee may oversee the brokerage firm business, the managing broker will have ultimate responsibility for the licensed and unlicensed employees at the brokerage firm.

9. **B** Fair housing laws do not prohibit where brokers may solicit listings. Discrimination occurs when the broker treats people differently because they are members of a protected class.

Unit 8
True/False Questions

1. **B** An executed contract is one where all tasks have been completed by all parties to the contract.

2. **B** A contract for an unlawful purpose is void from its inception.

3. **A**

4. **B** Only the victim of the other party's bad behavior can go to court to exit a voidable contract.

5. **B** Consideration is the exchange of value.

6. **A**

7. **A**

8. **B** A unilateral contract is the exchange of a promise for performance.

9. **B** A sales contract is a bilateral contract.

10. **B** Until the parties to a contract agree on all terms, there is no contract.

11. **B** A sales contract is by and between the seller and the buyer—only these two parties would sign the sales contract.

12. **B** If a buyer exits a sales contract via a valid contingency, the buyer will not be subject to legal or financial liability and will typically get any deposit back.

13. **B** The reverse is true—the owner is the optionor and the potential buyer is the optionee.

14. **B** The option fee is nonrefundable. It is what the owner receives in exchange for keeping the property off the market while the potential buyer decides whether or not to buy.

15. **B** An option contract is a unilateral contract.

16. **A**

17. **B**   Only the parties to a contract would sign an amendment to a contract. The listing agreement is a contract by and between the seller and the seller's broker.

18. **B**   To keep parties to a contract on track with a transaction, contracts usually have a *time is of the essence* clause in them. If a party does not comply with the time frame specified in the contract, the party—absent some legal reason—would be in breach of contract.

19. **A**

20. **A**

Multiple-Choice Questions

1. **C**   The MLS is an agreement between brokers, not between an agent (seller's broker) and a principal (seller).

2. **A**   A listing contract terminates with the death of either party.

3. **A**   There are four essential elements of a contract: consent, capacity, consideration, and lawful object/purpose (memory aid: Co-Ca-Co-La).

4. **D**   None of these laws will protect the friend who wants to proceed with the verbal agreement to buy the parcel of real estate. Per the statute of frauds, a contract for the sale of real estate must be in writing to be enforceable in a court of law.

5. **C**   Consideration is anything of value that the parties to a contract agree on.

6. **A**   A sales contract with no contingencies is a valid, enforceable contract.

7. **B**   An option is a unilateral agreement in which the owner promises to keep the property off of the market during a specific period of time while the prospective buyer decides either to buy or not. The option sets the sales price and option term, but it also gives the buyer the option not to buy the property. If the buyer decides not to buy, an option contract does not allow the seller to sue (recourse). Sellers agree to option contracts because they receive a typically nonrefundable option fee from the buyer.

8. **B**   In an option contract, the optionee is the prospective vendee (or buyer).

9. **C**   The legal title is transferred to the buyer at the closing, not equitable title.

10. **B**   The document that modifies an existing contract is an amendment. An addendum is an item that is added to a contract, such as an addendum for a long legal description or a report. Ad valorem is a term used in property taxes, meaning *according to value*. Accretion is an addition to property through natural causes, such as the action of a river.

11. **C**   The seller and the buyer are the only two parties to the purchase contract. The agents are not parties to the contract and would sign neither the purchase contract nor any amendment to the purchase contract.

Unit 9
True/False Questions

1. **A**   A federally related loan is any real estate financial transaction involving a federally regulated lender or financial institution.

2. **A**

3. **B**   To complete an appraisal, one must be a licensed appraiser.

4. **B**   Market value is the most probable price a property will sell for if put on the market today. Market price is a historical fact—it was the purchase price for the property at one point in the past.

5. **A**

6. **B**   Even though real estate professionals can charge a fee for a CMA, they must be certain the CMA cannot be considered an appraisal, and may not be used in the financing of a property transaction.

7. **A**

8. **B**   The principle of substitution is the basis of the market data approach, but it is also used in the cost approach and the income approach.

9. **B**   For appraisers, the most important aspect to an improvement is not what it cost, but what it adds (or detracts) from the market value of the property.

10. **A**

11. **A**

12. **A**

13. **B**   The cost approach—not the market data approach—uses either the reproduction cost or the replacement cost.

14. **A**

15. **B**   There are four ways to estimate the cost of new construction: the quantity survey method, unit-cost-in-place method, cubic or square foot method, and the index method.

16. **A**

17. **B**   Debt service (repaying the principal and interest on a loan) is considered an ownership expense, not an operating expense.

18. **A**

Multiple-Choice Questions

1. **C**   Economic (external) obsolescence are negative factors not on the subject property, such as environmental, social, or economic forces, which are always incurable because the loss in value cannot be cured by spending money on the property.

2. **D**   The value of an ADU depends upon numerous factors, including the area in which the subject property is located. Affluent owners may want a master bedroom and bathroom, particularly if they have young children. Furthermore, even if it complies with the law, wealthy individuals may not want to share a portion of their private residence with tenants. Finally, if the market for rental properties is depressed, this may impact the value the ADU adds to the subject property.

3. **B**   The cost approach to estimating value is the most effective method for new construction and special-purpose or single-purpose buildings.

4. **D**   Here is the rule for supply and demand: price moves *opposite* of supply, and price moves *with* demand. This is true for both prices and rents.

5. **C**   The principle of substitution is used in all approaches to value because it requires the appraiser to determine whether the estimated value is correct for the actual market. Conformity is used only if a property does not conform to the neighborhood. Contribution is used to determine how much value improvements add. Scarcity is an element of value, not a principle.

6. **B**   Per the principle of conformity, the value of a property tends to move toward its surroundings. The value of an underimproved property (the worst house) will increase if located in an expensive area (the best neighborhood). This is progression.

7. **C**   Especially for the sales comparison method (a.k.a. market data approach), the appraiser relies on the market price of comparable properties that recently sold. The market may have changed since the date a comparable property sold.

8. **C**   Adjustments are never made to the subject property—only to the comparable properties.

9. **C**   Reconciliation (a.k.a. correlation) is where the appraiser looks at all three approaches to value. The final estimate or opinion of value of the subject property will not be an average of these three approaches. Rather, the appraiser will rely most heavily on the approach most appropriate for the particular property being appraised.

10. **B**   The calculation is 10 × $1,000 × 12 = $120,000. Then, 10 × $1,500 × 12 = $180,000.

    So, $300,000 (potential gross rental income) + $1,200 (extra income) = $301,200.

    The result is $301,200 − $15,060 (5% for vacancies) = $286,140 (EGI).

Unit 10
True/False Questions

1. **B**   A mortgage is merely a lien, and has no impact on legal or equitable title.

2. **B**   A trust deed (a.k.a. a deed of trust) is signed by the trustor (borrower)—but conveys bare legal title not to the beneficiary (lender), but to the trustee.

3. **A**

4. **A**

5. **B**   A package loan includes both real estate and personal property as collateral for the loan. A blanket loan encumbers multiple parcels of land in one loan.

6. **B**   The partial release clause is a typical feature of the construction loan, allowing a developer to pay back a portion of the loan and get a release for each lot as they are sold.

7. **B** Promissory notes are sold on the secondary mortgage market.

8. **B** The reverse is correct. Loans are originated in the primary mortgage market, and sold on the secondary mortgage market.

9. **B** The TRID rule regulates the disclosures that prospective mortgagees (lenders) must make to prospective mortgagors (borrowers).

10. **A**

11. **B** Private mortgage insurance (PMI) is normally required on loans with LTVs <u>more</u> than 80%. If the borrower defaults, PMI helps protect the lender against loss due to foreclosure, and covers the difference between 80% LTV and the LTV% of the actual loan

12. **A**

13. **A**

14. **A**

15. **A**

16. **A**

17. **A**

18. **B** The vendee holds equitable title during the land contract—that includes the right to possess and occupy the property while paying off the land contract.

Multiple-Choice Questions

1. **B** An acceleration clause allows the lender to call the loan early when the borrower is in default.

2. **A** Return *on* the investment is the profit the lender will make from lending money to the buyer. The other answer choices are incorrect. Return *of* the investment is the buyer paying back the principal loan amount of, here, $800,000. A principle is not a financing term: it is a basic truth. *Note:* This looks like a math problem, but the numbers are here to distract you from what is a simple vocabulary question. When you get a question like this, it may be helpful to read the actual question you need to answer, before reading the fact pattern.

3. **B** A package mortgage includes both real estate and personal property (chattel) as security for the loan. This type of loan is used, for example, for the purchase of furnished vacation homes.

4. **A** The primary mortgage market is where loans are negotiated and created (i.e., originated).

5. **D** RESPA covers one- to four-unit residential loans financed by a federally related mortgage loan.

6. **C** Mortgage bankers originate and service loans with their own money.

7. **A**

8. **B** Per the TILA, the total number and/or the dollar amount of monthly payments in an advertisement would trigger the full disclosure requirement. An advertisement can only show the asking price and/or the annual percentage rate (APR) without triggering the need for a full disclosure. *Note:* This rule does not include any payment to third parties like homeowners associations or property tax collectors.

Unit 11
True/False Questions

1. **B** One mile is a distance equaling 5,280 feet. One *square* mile is an area that contains 640 acres.

2. **A**

3. **B** One discount point is 1% of the loan amount.

4. **B** A mortgage ratio of 80%/20% meant that the lender was willing to lend 80% of the appraised value or the purchase price, whichever was less.

5. **A**

6. **A**

7. **A**

8. **B** Debt service (repaying a loan's principal and interest back to a lender) is not included in operating expenses.

9. **A**

10. **A**

11. **A**

12. **B**   Discount points are 1% of the loan amount, not the purchase price—here, the discount point that the buyer pays the lender will be for $800.

13. **A**

14. **B**   The formula for gross scheduled income is the monthly rent for each unit multiplied by 12.

15. **A**

16. **A**

17. **A**

18. **B**   Security deposits of tenants—held (not owned) by the current owner of the rental property—are not prorated.

19. **B**   To perform proration calculations, it is essential to know whether the seller or the buyer is responsible for closing day. Traditionally, the buyer is responsible for the day of the close, as that is typically the day that ownership transfers from the seller to the buyer.

20. **B**   If the buyer is assuming the mortgage or buying the property "subject to" the mortgage, then the payoff will *not* be listed in the settlement/closing statement. *Note:* Be very careful with words like *always* and *never* on test questions.

Multiple-Choice Questions

1. **B**   A mile is 5,280 feet. (*Note:* Memorize this for the exam.) To calculate an area, the formula is width times length. Here, because a square has the same width and height, the formula is 5,280 feet × 5,280 feet. *Note:* There are 640 acres in a square mile.

2. **A**   There are 640 acres in a square mile. In the rectangular survey system, each (classic) township is 36 square miles. The township is further divided into 36 sections, each having an area of one square mile (640 acres). *Note:* There are 43,560 square feet in one acre.

3. **B**   640 + 10 = 650 acres × $2,500 = $1,625,000. (*Note:* 1 square mile = 640 acres.)

4. **A**   The original cost of the property was $450,000. Here is how to reach this answer: $3,000 × 12 = $36,000; so, $36,000 ÷ 8% = $450,000.

5. **D**   Neither of these is correct. Income – expenses = cash flow; assets – liabilities = net worth.

6. **A**   Debt service on a loan encumbering the rental property is considered an ownership expense of the investor; it is not factored into the calculation of the net operating income.

7. **B**   The calculation is $900,000 ÷ 80% = $1,125,000.

8. **C**   The calculation is $50,000 × 4% = $2,000. *Note:* A discount point is 1% of the loan amount.

9. **B**   The formula for gross scheduled income is the monthly rent for each unit multiplied by 12.

10. **B**   The formula to calculate net operating income is the capitalization rate of return × property value.

11. **A**   Prorated prepaid expenses of the seller (like prepaid property taxes) are reflected on the settlement statement as a credit to the seller and a debit to the buyer.

12. **A**   For a purchase transaction, seller prepaid taxes would be a prorated credit to the seller, and a debit to the buyer.

Unit 12
True/False Questions

1. **B**   Homeowners are not allowed to take a depreciation allowance on their homes. A depreciation allowance for residential rental property is 27½ years.

2. **B**   The trustee holds and manages the property for the benefit of another. Not the trustor.

3. **A**

4. **A**

5. **B**   A land trust generally is created for a definite term, such as 20 years.

6. **A**

7. **A**

8. **A**

9. **B**   A cloud on title may be removed by a quitclaim deed or suit to quiet title.

10. **A**

11. **B** Rental rates for residential space are usually stated as a monthly rate per unit. For commercial and industrial spaces, the rent is usually stated in either annual or monthly rates per square foot.

12. **B** A broker is required to supervise the actions of any licensed affiliate, either personally or by delegating supervision to an individual office manager (usually an associate broker) or a firm's supervising associate broker.

13. **A**

Multiple-Choice Questions

1. **A** Legal title to a property is transferred by the grantor (or trustor) to a trustee for the benefit of the beneficiary.

2. **B** A cloud on title may be removed by a quitclaim deed. A property owner may also initiate a court action known as suit to quiet title or quiet title action.

3. **D** A cloud on title is any unreleased lien, or encumbrance that may impair the marketability of title of the property or cast doubt on the title's validity.

4. **D** Rental rates for residential space are usually stated as a monthly rate per unit. For commercial and industrial spaces, the rent is usually stated in either annual or monthly rates per square foot.

5. **B** A personal assistant may not perform an activity requiring a real estate license, which is typically defined as performing activities for another who wishes to buy, sell, exchange, or lease real property.

6. **C** $700,000 – $180,000 = $520,000 value of the building

$520,000 ÷ 27.5 years = $18,909.10 ($18,910) per year in depreciation

Salesperson Practice Exam

1. **A** If the farmer sells the entire farm and does not exclude the growing corn from the sale, the farmer will give the buyer a deed, not a bill of sale. The other answer choices are incorrect. A bill of sale is given from the seller to the buyer of personal property. It is basically a receipt. It is true that the growing crop is still attached through the stalk to the land. However, because of constructive severance (the intent to sever the crop from the land as soon as it is ripe), the buyer of only the growing crop would receive a bill of sale, not a deed.

2. **B** An easement is an interest in real estate, and it must be transferred with a deed. The other answer choices are incorrect. Personal property (a.k.a. chattel) is sold with a bill of sale. *Note:* When the house is sold unattached to land, it is considered personal property.

3. **B** A grand piano is considered personal property (also known as chattel) and, therefore, would not need to be excluded from the purchase contract.

4. **B** Because of the due-on-sale clause in the loan, the loan will need to be paid in full when the property is sold. If the property is underwater—meaning there is more debt on the property than it is currently worth—it is unlikely to attract a buyer. *Note:* Underwater mortgage describes the situation. It is not an element of value.

5. **B** The holder of the servient tenement is most likely to pay to terminate an appurtenant easement. An appurtenant easement has two parcels of land associated with it. There is the dominant parcel (this property benefits from the appurtenant easement) and the servient tenement (this property is burdened with an easement).

6. **D** This is an example of a private (meaning nongovernment) restriction on real estate. The example in the fact pattern is of a private—not a public—restriction.

7. **A** In the rectangular survey method of land description, a section of land is 640 acres (one square mile).

8. **C** The metes and bounds method of land description is the best method to describe an irregularly shaped parcel of land.

9. **D** The estate at will is a less-than-freehold estate (also known as a leasehold estate). It is held by a tenant when there is no formal lease or rental agreement. The estate at will can traditionally be terminated by either the landlord or the tenant at any time and without any notice. *Note:* This type of leasehold estate is now either limited or prohibited by multiple states.

10. **A** A fee simple determinable can terminate automatically but a fee simple subject to a condition subsequent to the right of reentry or power of termination must be exercised.

11. **B** A less-than-freehold estate is a leasehold estate. The tenant (lessee) is permitted to possess the property owned by the landlord (lessor), typically in exchange for rent.

12. **C** The periodic estate is a type of leasehold estate that continues for a specified time period, typically month to month. This tenancy can be renewed automatically upon payment of rent, until terminated by either party providing proper notice. It is commonly used for residential properties.

13. **B** When one person holds title to real estate, that individual is said to hold title in severalty (also known as an estate in severalty). This is sole ownership by one individual—here, it is the last surviving joint tenant.

14. **A** Of these answer choices, only tenants in common would be available to these two people owning a parcel of real estate concurrently. The other choices, when they are permitted by state law, are only allowed for married couples and sometimes for registered domestic partners.

15. **C** The signature of the party (the grantee) receiving the interest in the real estate is not a required element of a valid deed.

16. **B** The quitclaim deed conveys no grantor warranties or promises. It is used to clear up clouds on title, and when the grantor wants no future liability for the transfer.

17. **C** For title to transfer, a valid deed must be delivered (by the grantor) and accepted (by the grantee). Here, Dakota, the grantee, refused to accept the deed. Therefore, River still holds title to the real estate. *Note:* Why would someone refuse to accept a deed for a property worth $5 million? It could be polluted, with the projected cleanup costs higher than the property's current fair market value.

18. **C** A general warranty deed provides the greatest protection to the grantee (the buyer) in the transfer of real property and includes five covenants (promises) made by the grantor.

19. **A** After a loan is paid in full, the lender's policy of title ceases to offer any coverage to the lender. A lender is a mortgagee. The other answer choices are incorrect. Typically, an owner's policy of title insurance insures the owner until title is transferred. The premium for title insurance for both the lender's policy and the owner's policy is paid only one time, typically at the closing. *Note:* There is no real estate agent's policy of title insurance.

20. **B** In contrast to other assets, real estate is just about impossible to hide from the tax authorities.

21. **C** Under the government's police power, the government has the right to enact and enforce building codes to enhance public health and safety. Ordering the owner to bring the extra bathroom *up to code* means that the owner must make the unpermitted addition reach the minimum health and safety standards imposed upon new construction in that city.

22. **A** Developers frequently put limitations on homeowners as to what types of pets they can keep in a subdivision. Sometimes, these restrictions are related to the number of pets, the breeds of dogs, and the maximum weight per pet. A private CC&R prohibiting a wild animal as a pet would not typically be struck down.

23. **B** Development of wetlands is regulated at both federal and state levels. Development isn't prevented in these areas, but it is controlled through the issuance of permits regulating the type of the project and any necessary dredging.

24. **B** Radon gas, created naturally through the breakdown of uranium in the soil, is considered an environmental hazard. An environmental hazard is one that human beings brought to the property. While radon gas occurs naturally, it is an environmental hazard because modern methods of construction and installation now trap radon gas in buildings.

25. **D** An amendment (a.k.a. rezoning) is a term typically used to describe a zoning change that affects an entire area.

26. **C** A dual agency is where a real estate broker serves as the agent for both parties to a transaction. A vendor (buyer) and a lessee (tenant) are not typically two parties to the same transaction.

27. **A** A fiduciary relationship imposes one of the highest trust relationships known under the law upon the agent. The agent owes fiduciary duties to the principal. These fiduciary duties owed by the agent to the principal can be summarized as obedience, loyalty, disclosure, confidentiality, accounting, and reasonable skill and care.

28. **B** A listing agreement is one of the contracts that must be in writing to satisfy the statute of frauds. Because the agreement between these two parties was verbal, it is unlikely that the real estate broker will be allowed to proceed with a lawsuit for the unpaid commission.

29. **D** An implied agency relationship is typically created accidentally or unintentionally. It may be created as a result of speech or actions of one or more parties to an agency relationship. Because there is nothing in writing related to compensation, this agency relationship may result in fiduciary duties owed to a principal without any realistic expectation of agent compensation.

30. **D** A listing agreement is a contract by and between the broker of record and the seller. This contract is terminated by the death, mental incapacity, or bankruptcy of either of these two parties.

31. **C** The listing agent had an affirmative duty to disclose to third-party buyers that the septic system needed to be repaired, whether asked about it or not. The other answer choices are incorrect. The listing agent merely had to disclose the repair of the septic system, not explain how the repair should be completed. Finally, fiduciary duties are owed by an agent to a principal. Here, the fact pattern tells us this is a listing agent (owing fiduciary duties to the seller). No fiduciary duties were owed to any prospective buyers.

32. **A** Puffing is not illegal. Puffing is an exaggerated form of sales talk that will be dismissed or ignored by the reasonably prudent buyer. Superlative statements about the quality of a property that should not be considered assertions of fact.

33. **B** The property sold for less than the net profit the seller wanted. In this type of listing agreement, the seller sets a net profit to be realized from the sale. Anything over that net price will be the agent's compensation. Anything at—or below—this net price will result in the agent not earning anything on the transaction. *Note:* This type of listing agreement is illegal or discouraged in many states because of the potential conflict of interest between the listing agent and the seller. For example, the listing agent might be inclined to push the seller to set a low list price to enhance the listing agent's prospects for greater compensation.

34. **D** The listing agent did nothing wrong by complying with the seller's written instructions to not market the property on the MLS.

35. **A** The property manager position is an example of a general agency. Under a general agency, the real estate broker serving as a property manager typically has multiple jobs and a limited ability to bind the principal (the owner) to the decisions of the agent (the real estate broker). A general agency is typically associated with an ongoing business. The other answer choices are incorrect. A listing agent and a selling agent are examples of a special agency. A special agent has one job, no authority to bind the principal to the decisions of the agent, and is advisory only.

36. **A** A lease is a bilateral contract between the lessee (the tenant) and the lessor (the owner of the rental property). This is true even if the tenant never meets the owner of the rental property and only interacts with the property manager.

37. **D** Federal fair housing laws allow property owners and property managers to decline an application when the applicant's past behavior might put other tenants at risk. Arson and a conviction for drug dealing are two examples of risky behavior. Federal fair housing laws do not prohibit denying an applicant housing on the basis of erratic employment and a low credit score.

38. **C** The selling agent engaged in steering. Steering is illegal under federal fair housing laws. A real estate licensee engages in steering when directing a client to or away from a particular geographic neighborhood as a means of discrimination. The intent to make the client feel more comfortable is irrelevant.

39. **A**   Redlining is illegal under federal fair housing laws. Before redlining became illegal, lenders used to put up maps in lending offices and would encircle certain geographic areas with red lines. If a loan applicant's property was within those red lines, the application would be declined immediately. The effect of redlining was discrimination against loan applicants on the basis of race or ethnicity. Before denying a loan, lenders and creditors are now legally required to consider each application on its merits.

40. **A**   Discrimination against individuals on the basis of race is illegal under federal fair housing laws. There are no exceptions allowing discrimination on the basis of race in the sale or rental of housing.

41. **D**   The new three-story office building must have an elevator to be ADA compliant.

42. **A**   The MLS listing was proper. There is no minimum commission rate; lower rates are advantageous to consumers. Usually, commissions on the MLS are split 50-50, but there is no law or MLS rule stating they must be.

43. **A**   An advertisement for a listed property must legally include some sort of notification to inform prospective buyers that a real estate licensee is involved in the transaction. The other answer choices are incorrect. An apology is an insufficient response to breaking a law. The seller's later approval does not absolve the licensee from breaking the law.

44. **A**   The fidelity bond should be for the amount the unlicensed employee can access—here, that amount is $25,000. A fidelity bond is a type of crime insurance product protecting employers from the fraudulent activities (theft) of employees. *Note:* Although laws in different states vary, in some states, this type of fidelity bond is a legal requirement.

45. **A**   Firing the associate licensee was acceptable supervisory behavior on the part of the broker of record. Dual agencies are illegal in many states. Even in states where they are legal, they need to be disclosed to both parties in advance, and frequently, both parties must consent to the dual agency in writing.

46. **B**   This is a voidable contract. A voidable contract looks valid, but it may be disaffirmed by one party who was the victim of the other party's bad behavior. Examples of bad behavior include fraud, misrepresentation, undue influence, duress (use of force), menace (threat of force), and so on. Until the disadvantaged party takes action to reject the voidable contract, the contract proceeds as though valid. *Note:* The term ad valorem means *according to value.* It is typically used in regard to property taxes.

47. **D**   A purchase contract for real estate must be in writing to satisfy the statute of frauds. If the agreement is not in writing (and signed by the party to be charged in the lawsuit), it is highly unlikely that a lawsuit will be allowed by a court to proceed.

48. **A**   The absence of a good-faith deposit will have no impact on the purchase contract: a good-faith deposit is not a legally required element of a valid contract.

49. **D**   All of these are examples of undue influence. Undue influence is misusing a position of trust to induce the other party into making decisions not in their best interests.

50. **C**   Legally, a rejection permanently terminates an offer.

51. **C**   A writing is not required for all contracts—some verbal contracts are enforceable in a court of law.

52. **A**   Assuming all other things are equal, the listing agent will most likely advise the seller to accept the all-cash, noncontingent offer. A noncontingent offer is good for sellers. Why? A contingency allows a buyer to exit a purchase contract without legal or financial liability. Common contingencies include problems such as the following: the buyer not getting a loan, the appraisal, the home inspection report, the title insurance report, the pest control report, the sale of the buyer's current residence, and so on. *Note:* "Time is of the essence" is not an offer; it is a clause in a contract requiring timely completion of contract duties.

53. **C**   The option is a unilateral contract—only one party makes a promise and must honor it if the other party decides to perform. Here, the optionee decided against exercising the option, meaning that the prospective tenant decided to not rent the property. The optionor (that is, the party making the promise) will have no grounds for a lawsuit, but can keep the option fee.

54. **B** Before receiving a deed, the vendee held equitable title to the property. This fact pattern describes a land contract (a.k.a. a contract for deed). During the term of the land contract, the seller (the vendor) holds legal title, and the buyer (the vendee) holds equitable title. Someone holding equitable title has the right to possess, occupy, and enjoy the property. When the land contract is paid in full, the seller will give a deed to the buyer. Thereafter, the buyer will hold both legal and equitable title. *Note:* Memorize the terms *vendor* and *vendee* for your exam.

55. **A** The seller and the buyer would sign an amendment to the purchase contract. A purchase contract is by and between a seller and a buyer. If the purchase contract must be amended, the amendment would be signed by the parties to the contract.

56. **A** An appraisal is an opinion or estimate of value. That value is expressed in monetary terms. The emotional value of the property to the current owner will not be factored into the appraiser's estimate of value.

57. **C** The appraiser is most likely to use the summary report form. Here, the appraiser summarizes the data in the appraiser's workfile and shows the estimate or opinion of value. *Note:* An environmental impact report (EIR) evaluates the impact of a proposed project on the environment—it is not a type of appraisal.

58. **C** DUST is an acronym for the essential elements of value, which are demand, utility, supply, and transferability. The other answer choices are incorrect. TILA stands for the federal Truth in Lending Act; RESPA stands for the federal Real Estate Settlement Procedures Act; TRID stands for the federal TILA-RESPA Integrated Disclosure rule.

59. **D** The principle of substitution posits that, all other things being equal, the less expensive home will sell before the more expensive home. The principle of substitution also applies to rentals. *Note:* This is the most important principle in appraisals.

60. **B** The principle of progression posits that underimproved property increases based upon where the property is situated. Per this principle, the value of the "worst home" rises because of its location in the "best neighborhood."

61. **C** The appraiser is most likely to use the cost approach when appraising the home designed by a famous architect. The other answer choices are incorrect. The market data approach (a.k.a. the sales comparison approach) will not be useful to the appraiser—even if nearby homes have recently sold, they would not help the appraiser determine the value of the unique subject property. The income approach will not be useful either, as there is no indication in the fact pattern that the subject property is generating income.

62. **B** An appraiser would subtract from the sales price of a comparable when the comparable had an amenity the subject property lacked. For example, the comparable has a fireplace in the primary bedroom, and the subject property does not. The appraiser would subtract the value of a fireplace from the sales price of the comparable.

63. **C** The correct formula is rate of return × value = net operating income.

64. **B** A mortgage is a financing instrument signed by a borrower when taking out a loan and using a parcel of realty as security. The mortgage is a two-party instrument: there is the borrower (mortgagor) and the lender (mortgagee). The mortgage—in contrast to the deed of trust—has no impact on title to the property, as during the lifetime of the loan, the borrower continues to hold legal and equitable title.

65. **B** Borrowers pay discount points because, if they do, lenders will lower the interest rate on the loan. Discount points increase the original lender's profit (yield). *Note:* One discount point equals 1% of the loan amount.

66. **B** The buyer's interest in the property in a land contract is an equitable title interest, but the seller retains legal title. A land contract is not a mortgage.

67. **B** When one loan encumbers multiple lots, it is called a blanket mortgage. The other answer choices are incorrect. A partial release is typically a clause in the blanket loan that will release an individual lot from the loan as the developer sells the lot and pays back a portion of the loan. A package mortgage is when both real estate and personal property (chattel) are included as collateral for the loan. A reverse mortgage is offered to a senior homeowner—it only encumbers the senior homeowner's home.

68. **A** A promissory note—signed by the borrower—is evidence of the debt and the borrower's promise to repay the loan and the agreed-upon interest. It is a negotiable instrument, meaning it can be bought

and sold while the loan is outstanding. *Note:* An endorsed check is also a negotiable instrument, but it is not necessarily related to mortgage loans.

69. **D** The federal government doesn't allow lenders to charge prospective borrowers for either the Loan Estimate or the Closing Disclosures. *Note:* These disclosures reveal the true cost of borrowing loan money.

70. **B** A silent second is when the buyer and seller agree to let the seller finance a portion of the down payment. The buyer and seller do this without informing the lender, who is typically financing a large portion of the purchase price. This is mortgage fraud because it does not allow the institutional lender to get an accurate picture of the buyer's future debt load. Carrying two loans on a property may be beyond the ability of a buyer to repay and may lead to borrower default.

71. **D** A short sale describes a situation where a lender allows the borrower to sell the property for less than what is owed under a mortgage loan. Some lenders require the borrower to make up the deficiency, and some do not. The other answer choices are incorrect. A deficiency judgment is issued by a judge during a judicial foreclosure. A subordination agreement is an agreement between lenders, as it artificially reorders the priority of liens. *FSBO* means for sale by owner.

72. **D** A mile (5,280 feet) is a distance or a length. An acre is an area of land. There are 640 acres in a *square* mile—a square mile is an area of land.

73. **D** A section of land has 640 acres: this is one square mile. A quarter section has 160 acres. A quarter-quarter section has 40 acres. The buyer purchased 200 acres in total.

74. **C** The purchase money mortgage was for $4 million; $5,000,000 × 80% = $4,000,000.

75. **C** To realize a 5% rate of return, the investor should offer $4,900,000 on the listed property.

   The formula is $245,000 (net operating income) ÷ 5% (rate of return) = $4,900,000 (price).

76. **C** The EGI is the result of all incomes minus any losses due to vacancy, bad checks, and so on.

   Here is the formula: $250,000 (potential gross income) + $9,000 [$750 (other income) × 12] = $259,000.

   So, $259,000 − $18,130 (vacancies at 7% [0.07]) = $240,870.

77. **C** The value of the property is $5,000,000.

Here is the formula: $300,000 (NOI) ÷ 6% (rate of return is 0.06) = $5,000,000 (value).

78. **A** The investor will not be able to take any depreciation allowance on this property. A depreciation allowance is a tax advantage allowed only for business and investment properties. The test question states that this was the investor's principal residence (i.e., the investor's home).

79. **B** A payoff of the seller's mortgage will appear as a debit on the seller's side, but it will not appear as a credit on the buyer's side. The other answer choices are incorrect. Prepaid property taxes and prepaid HOA dues may be prorated so that each party only pays for those days they own the property.

80. **A** The commission owed to the seller's broker is a debit to the seller on a closing settlement sheet.

Broker Practice Exam

1. **D** Chattel is movable personal property. When the tree was purchased, on the patio, uprooted, and in the moving van, it was chattel. When it was planted in the backyard, it was considered part of the real estate. That was why the seller had to exclude it from the purchase contract. Normally, a tree planted on the property is considered part of the real estate and would transfer with the deed.

2. **C** The seller of the farm must leave the growing wheat, unless it is excluded from the purchase contract. The growing wheat is attached to the land and typically would transfer with the deed, unless excluded from the purchase contract. The other answer choices are incorrect. The legal doctrine of emblements allows a tenant farmer to cultivate and harvest a growing annual crop, even after the lease has ended. A growing crop of wheat would not be included in a deed. There is no doctrine of lis pendens: a lis pendens is a document that is filed in the public records to notify "all the world" that the property is the subject of an ongoing lawsuit.

3. **D** All of these statements are incorrect. The servient tenement owner cannot unilaterally terminate an easement, whether used or not. The servient tenement owner would not sign a deed: it would be signed by the party conveying the interest in the land (i.e., the dominant tenement owner). The creation of the new road does not automatically terminate the easement for ingress and egress to the old road.

4. **B** A mortgage is a voluntary lien that has no impact on either legal or equitable title to the owner's property. The mortgage is a financing instrument that a borrower signs when getting a loan and using a parcel of real estate as security or collateral for the loan. The other answer choices result in a split between legal title and equitable title.

5. **D** Neither of these easements must be for contiguous (touching) properties. With an easement in gross, there is only one property, the servient tenement. With an appurtenant easement, the properties do not need to be touching or contiguous. For example, a dominant tenement owner can have an appurtenant easement over several properties to have road access. The dominant tenement owner's property may not be contiguous with the parcel immediately adjacent to the road.

6. **A** The most likely order in which these liens will be paid is (1) property taxes, (2) mechanic's lien, and (3) mortgage lien. A lien for property taxes jumps to the senior (#1) position. The ability to impose property taxes (and senior lien priority status) is one of the government's fundamental powers related to real estate. While the laws related to mechanics' liens (a.k.a. construction liens) vary between the states, the priority of the lien typically dates back to when labor was first performed or materials were first delivered. Because property taxes jump to the senior position and mechanics' liens typically jump to when labor was performed or materials were delivered, the mortgage lien will probably be paid last.

7. **C** A rod is a 16.5 feet—it is a distance between two points, and it cannot be a parcel of real estate. A parcel of real estate is an area of land, like a township or a certain number of acres.

8. **B** The judge would most likely order a survey to determine the correct legal description for each parcel of real estate. *Note:* Two separate parcels of real estate cannot legally share land with each other.

9. **A** A corporation with a fee simple absolute estate of ownership can hold title to real estate indefinitely. Ownership without a specific termination date or any conditions is one of the advantages to owning realty in fee simple absolute.

10. **D** The property conveyed to the city was a fee simple defeasible freehold estate. A fee simple defeasible estate is an estate of ownership (freehold) with conditions. It is legal to have more than one condition in a deed, and it is also legal to convey real estate to a governmental entity with conditions in the deed. State law varies. In general, however, while it may be unusual to convey property to a governmental entity conditioned upon a required minimum number of living animals to be kept on the real estate, it is not currently illegal.

11. **B** Of these choices, the best way to accomplish the owner's goal is to create a life estate for the current spouse and a remainder to the adult child. Usually, life estates are created through a deed signed by the current owner. The other answer choices are incorrect. A deed of trust (a.k.a. a trust deed) is a loan document signed by a borrower. A life estate with a reversionary interest would mean that, after the current spouse died, the property would revert back to the current owner. The term pur autre vie means a life estate that would only last as long as the life of someone other than the life tenant. However, that would not accomplish the owner's goals—if the other person died before the current spouse, the current spouse would not have a place to live for life.

12. **B** In a net lease, the lessee pays a base rent and one or more charges to the property. You might also call this lease a triple-net lease, as the tenant is responsible for three charges to the property. *Note:* With a net lease, the owner of the leasehold property is still financially responsible for capital improvements.

13. **D** None of these are correct. A buyer takes title to a property subject to any ongoing lease. The buyer will not have the right of possession until the five-year lease is over. An owner renting real estate to a tenant has a leased fee estate of ownership. A tenant has a nonfreehold estate of possession (i.e., a leasehold estate). Notice of the sale will not terminate the lease. The new owner acquired title subject to the five-year lease.

14. **C** The five concurrent owners will most likely have joint and several liability for paying the mortgage, paying property taxes, and paying homeowners insurance. *Joint and several liability* means that any one of them individually (severally) and all of them jointly are responsible for making the payment. For example, if four owners were out of the country, the one owner still in the country would be responsible for making the *entire* mortgage payment.

15. **C** At the time of death in the hospital, the survivor owned the entire property, so the heirs of the survivor will inherit the entire property.

16. **B**   Acceptance by the grantee (the buyer) of the deed is required for the transfer of title, but it is not a part of a valid deed.

17. **C**   A quitclaim deed contains no promises or warranties. When this deed is used, it's as though the grantor is stating to the grantee: "Anything I currently own in this property, if anything, I convey to you." *Note:* A deed is signed only by the party conveying an interest in real estate—here, that would be the former owner, not the seller.

18. **B**   An abstract of title is prepared by an abstractor, and includes all recorded liens and encumbrances and lists the records searched. It does not indicate forgeries and interests that are unrecorded or that could be discovered by an actual property inspection.

19. **A**   In a race-notice state, a subsequent purchaser for value who records first will own the property, unless the subsequent purchaser had notice of the earlier conveyance. Because Buyer B had notice of the earlier conveyance to Buyer A, Buyer A will own the property.

20. **B**   A title insurance company will pay a claim (for something like a missed deed) to the insured party. Here, the insured party was the lender. If a buyer wants title insurance coverage, the buyer must purchase an owner's policy of title insurance.

21. **A**   An inverse condemnation action is a lawsuit filed by an owner of real estate when a government exercises its police power and erases the value of the owner's property. The argument is that the government should have exercised its power of eminent domain and paid the owner just or fair compensation for the property. These lawsuits are rarely successful, unless the value of the property has basically been erased by government action. *Note:* Inverse condemnation is also known as reverse condemnation.

22. **D**   CC&Rs are filed in the public records and run with the land. Even if the deed from Jordan to the buyer did not reference the CC&Rs and the buyer never read the CC&Rs, the buyer will still be bound by them. The buyer would not, however, be bound by illegal CC&Rs (e.g., racial restrictions).

23. **B**   For a property located in a 100-year flood zone, a lender will typically condition the loan on the owner acquiring a government-backed policy of flood insurance. The other answer choices are incorrect. A property located in a 100-year flood zone has a 1% chance—each year—of being flooded. Homeowners policies typically exclude damage caused by floodwaters when the

properties are located in flood zones. Flood zones are determined by maps: if natural or human-made conditions change, a property may be either placed into or removed from a flood zone.

24. **C**   The individual must be offered the opportunity to test for LBP for the single-family residence (the property listed for sale), but not the duplex (the rental property). Federal LBP laws apply to target housing, defined as a residential dwelling (of one to four units) built before January 1, 1978. An opportunity must be given to prospective buyers of target housing to test for LBP. There is no law requiring landlords to give prospective tenants the right to test for LBP. *Note:* Prospective buyers and prospective tenants must both be given an Environmental Protection Agency (EPA) pamphlet on the dangers of lead.

25. **C**   The construction of mobile homes (a.k.a. manufactured homes) is regulated by the federal Department of Housing and Urban Development (HUD).

26. **D**   The person executing a power of attorney (a.k.a. a letter of attorney) is in an agency relationship with the agent. The principal is frequently called the grantor and the agent is called an attorney-in-fact. *Note:* The agent does not need to be a lawyer or an attorney.

27. **C**   Because of the fiduciary duty of confidentiality, the listing agent must not disclose the lowest acceptable offer. Fiduciary duties are owed by the agent (here, the seller's broker) to the principal (here, the seller). The leaky roof would be disclosed to prospective buyers because of the listing agent's legal responsibility to be honest and disclose material facts to third-party buyers. However, no fiduciary duties are owed to third-party buyers. The duty of obedience that the seller's broker owes to the seller does not extend to what is illegal in many states: it is illegal in many states for a listing agent to remain silent about a material defect like a leaky roof. Finally, the listing agent does not owe third-party buyers the fiduciary duty of loyalty. Loyalty is owed by the listing agent to the seller, but that fiduciary duty of loyalty does not extend to illegal activities (such as remaining silent about a material defect).

28. **B**   The listing agreement and the POA both establish an agency relationship.

29. **B**   Destruction of the premises (e.g., fire or a natural disaster) will terminate a listing agreement.

30. **D**   A listing agreement is a contract by and between the broker of record at the brokerage firm and a seller. The associate licensee is not a party to the listing agreement. Therefore, the death, insanity, or bankruptcy of the associate licensee will not affect the listing agreement. *Note:* The death, insanity, or bankruptcy of the real estate broker of record (or the seller) will, however, terminate the listing agreements.

31. **A**   Respondeat superior (and vicarious liability) basically mean that the law will hold the principal legally and financially responsible for the actions and speech of an agent acting within the scope of the agent's authority. Because of respondeat superior (vicarious liability), the agent's fiduciary duties to a principal are much broader than any duties owed to a third party. Agents do not owe third parties fiduciary duties. The legal doctrine of respondeat superior is why it is so risky for a principal to hire an agent, and that is why the law requires agents to fulfill their fiduciary duties. Another reason why the fiduciary duty of disclosure is so much broader with a principal is that, when the agent hears or sees something, it's as though the principal has seen or heard it. The much narrower (nonfiduciary) duty of disclosure for a third party is usually related to disclosing material facts concerning the subject property.

32. **B**   This is a net listing, not a seller reserved listing. Many states have prohibited or discouraged net listings because of the potential conflict of interest between the seller and the agent. For example, the agent might encourage the seller to set too low a list price so the agent can make a higher commission. Finally, if the seller sets a specific net profit, and the property sells for that amount, the real estate broker can end up not making anything—even though a buyer was found for the subject property.

33. **D**   A property not listed on the MLS is known by all of these terms. It is a way of marketing exclusive properties, and it occasionally has been used to violate fair housing laws.

34. **D**   Federal fair housing laws would apply to rental properties across the nation and would not be a helpful way to determine the ideal rent amount that would generate income for the investor at a level prospective tenants could afford.

35. **C**   The exclusive listing agent serves for a period of time that must be specified in the listing agreement. The property manager, part of an ongoing business, may not have a specific termination date when property management services will no longer be needed by the principal.

36. **C**   A purchaser of real estate buys subject to the leases currently on the property. This is known as a leased fee estate, an estate of ownership. The new owner can negotiate to end the current leases early (e.g., cash for keys), but cannot evict the current tenants based solely on the transfer of ownership. *Note:* An estate of ownership is known as a freehold estate, and a leasehold estate is known as a nonfreehold estate.

37. **D**   Renting residential property to current drug users, convicted drug manufacturers, or convicted drug dealers is not in violation of federal fair housing laws. Landlords and property managers are typically permitted to exclude these groups of prospective tenants, but they are not legally required to do so.

38. **C**   Federal rules related to LBP require that prospective tenants of a one- to four-unit residential property be given warnings if the property was undergoing construction before January 1, 1978. Since construction was completed on January 1, 1978, that indicates that construction was ongoing before this date. The investor would not have been given a warning because the purchase was for a 20-unit apartment building—anything over 4 units is considered commercial, not residential, and no LBP warnings need be given to the buyer.

39. **C**   Victims of violence are not currently a protected class under federal fair housing laws. They may, however, have the right to pursue legal action against a landlord or property manager if they are evicted or denied housing because someone perpetrated domestic violence against them. The list of protected classes under federal fair housing laws includes race, religion, color, national origin, sex, family status, and handicap/disability.

40. **D**   Discrimination on the basis of race in the sale and rental of housing is never permitted under federal fair housing laws. *Note:* There is age 55+ senior housing and 62+ senior housing. For 62+ senior housing, all residents must be at least age 62 or older.

41. **B**   Limitations by breed and weight are fairly common in CC&Rs. However, under the federal Americans with Disabilities Act (ADA), service animals cannot be restricted based upon either breed or weight.

42. **B**   For private companies not open to the public and with 15 or fewer employees, compliance with the ADA is voluntary.

43. **B**   REALTOR® is a registered trademark of the National Association of REALTORS® (NAR). Only active members of the NAR are legally permitted to use this word on any professional marketing material.

44. **B** Provided the appropriate disclosures are made, federal law does not prohibit a real estate broker giving rebates to either buyers or sellers. The other answer choices are incorrect. These rebates protect consumers and enhance competition by lowering the cost of buying and selling real estate. The rebates do not violate federal antitrust law. The real estate broker would not need to give a rebate to both a seller and a buyer if, for example, one of those parties were represented by a real estate broker from another brokerage firm.

45. **B** The employing broker—the broker of record—has a legal duty to supervise associate licensees, no matter how the brokerage firm pays them. This supervision includes keeping associate licensees knowledgeable about changes in federal, state, and local law. Making it mandatory for real estate associates to attend meetings related to changes in pertinent law can minimize the exposure of the brokerage firm to risk.

46. **B** The broker of record at the brokerage firm has the supervisory responsibility to ensure that trust funds and trust accounting records are handled properly by every employee at the firm. The marital relationship between the employing broker and the unlicensed assistant does not relieve the broker of the duty to supervise the handling of funds belonging to clients.

47. **B** The neighbor will likely prevail in the lawsuit. This is a unilateral contract: one party (here, the homeowner) is making a promise, but only has to honor that promise if the other party performs (here, the neighbor, by painting the pantry closet). The neighbor never made a promise to paint the pantry and will not face legal or financial liability for doing something else. The other answer choices are incorrect. Apart from those contracts that must be in writing to satisfy the statute of frauds, verbal contracts are typically legal. There is no statute of familial obligations—that is a made-up law.

48. **A** An open listing agreement between a seller of real estate and multiple real estate brokers is a unilateral contract. In a unilateral contract, only one party is making a promise, and that one party only has to honor the promise if the other party performs. Here, only the seller is making a promise, and one of those brokers must perform and find a buyer in order for the seller to have to pay the commission to that one broker. If the seller finds the buyer, none of the brokers will receive a commission. The other answer choices are incorrect— they are all bilateral contracts where the parties are exchanging promises with each other.

49. **C** One essential element of a valid contract is a lawful purpose. If the purchase agreement is for an illegal substance, it is void from its inception.

50. **B** A voidable contract is one where a party to the contract has misbehaved behind the scenes—the victim of the misbehavior can go to court to be released from contractual obligations. The contract itself, however, may look valid, and it is treated as valid until the victim goes to court and asked to be relieved of all further contractual obligations. Here, Party B is the victim of Party A's threats. Here are some common examples of misbehavior with voidable contracts: duress (force), menace (threat of force), undue influence (taking advantage of a position of trust), and fraud (intentional deceit). *Note:* An executed contract is one where every duty has been completed. The question states that the agreement is still ongoing.

51. **D** The buyer will most likely have no legal options because this is a verbal contract for the purchase of real estate. The statute of frauds requires certain contracts be in writing to be enforceable in a court of law. While there is some variation between the states, a contract for a purchase of real estate is overwhelmingly included as one of the contracts where a writing—signed by the party to be charged in the lawsuit—is required.

52. **D** If a prospective buyer exits a purchase contract via a valid contingency, the buyer will not be subject to financial or legal liability. In fact, the buyer will typically get back any deposit. The other answer choices are incorrect. Liquidated damages must be agreed to by both parties, but are only available to the seller when the buyer does not have a valid reason for exiting the purchase contract. *Test-taking tip*: A good-faith deposit and an earnest money deposit are synonyms. Because there is no option allowing you to pick both answer choices, neither can be the correct answer choice.

53. **A** An option for the purchase or lease of real estate is a unilateral contract. Only the owner of the property is making a promise that, if the option is exercised, the owner will sell or lease at the agreed-upon terms. If the optionee decides not to exercise the option, then the optionor is limited to keeping the option fee. Note: A lease is a bilateral contract.

54. **B** During an installment sales contract (a.k.a. a land contract), the vendee does not have legal title to the property. When the installment sales contract is paid in full, the vendor will convey legal title to the vendee via a deed.

55. **A** A listing agreement is a contract by and between the seller and the listing agent (the seller's agent). Any amendment to this contract would be signed by the two parties to that contract.

56. **D** Appraisals done on the same date and for the same function will most likely vary from each other. An appraisal is not a scientific process, and the appraisers may be using different comparables and making different adjustments. The other answer choices are incorrect. The purpose of an appraisal is to arrive at an estimate of opinion of value. The function of the appraisal is the reason it is being completed (e.g., purchase, refinance, insurance, divorce, condemnation, IRS depreciation allowance challenge).

57. **C** The narrative report (a.k.a. the self-contained report) is the most comprehensive and expensive appraisal report. It is completed for some large commercial projects when the owner or the lender wants information about the property and the surrounding areas. The appraiser includes—and explains—everything in the appraiser's workfile.

58. **A** The essential elements of value are demand, utility, scarcity, and transferability.

59. **D** Per the principle of contribution, the value of an improvement is not what it costs, but what it adds to the market value of the property. The bathroom is an example of increasing returns because it added more than it cost to the property's market value. The swimming pool is an example of decreasing returns because it cost more than it added to the property's market value.

60. **A** The principle of regression posits that a large home in a neighborhood of small homes will decline in value because of where it is located. Therefore, the buyers could get a larger house than they could get in an area where all the homes are large. *Note:* The "worst house in the best neighborhood" is typically a small, older home in a neighborhood of remodeled, upscale properties. Here, the answer choice states that the home is not even up to the local building codes.

61. **C** The sales comparison approach and the comparative market analysis (CMA) both rely on the sales prices of recently sold properties in the same general area. The appraiser uses "comparables" and adjusts the sales prices of the comparables to arrive at an estimate or opinion of value of the subject property. The appraiser would only use recently sold comparables in the sales comparison approach. In the CMA, however, real estate licensees might also include the list prices of properties still on the market, pocket listings, and properties recently withdrawn from the market.

62. **B** The cost approach is the method used by appraisers when appraising historic, special use, or new construction (when no comparables are available). The reproduction cost approach is used to calculate how much it would cost to build an exact replica of the improvements on the property. In the real world, the reproduction cost is almost never used, but it is very frequently tested on real estate exams.

63. **D** The formula is net operating income ÷ value (or price) = rate of return.
So, $45,000 (net operating income) ÷ $500,000 (list price) = 9% (rate of return)

64. **B** A mortgage is a financing instrument used when an owner (or a buyer) is using a parcel of real estate as security for a loan. The mortgage is a lien on the property, and while it impacts the title, it does not change how title to the property is held. That is why states that only use mortgages are called lien theory states. A trust deed is also a financing instrument used when an owner (or a buyer) is using a parcel of real estate as security for a loan. However, the trust deed does have an impact on title to the property: the borrower conveys (bare) legal title to the trustee for the lifetime of the loan. That is why states that use trust deeds are called title theory states.

65. **D** The loan-to-value ratio (a.k.a. the mortgage ratio) is based on the purchase price or the appraised value, whichever is less. Here, the appraisal came in at $1 million, lower than the winning offer of $1.2 million; 80% of $1 million is $800,000.

66. **C** A partial release clause is most common in a blanket loan. The blanket loan is typically taken out by a developer. The partial release clause allows individual lots to be released from the blanket loan as the developer sells each lot and pays back a portion of the loan. *Note:* Individuals can also get blanket loans, and the parcels do not have to be contiguous.

67. **B** Reverse mortgages are used by seniors to obtain money from their equity in the property when they don't want to sell, but they want or need cash. The loan becomes due upon the sale of the property, death of the mortgagor, or at the end of the term agreed to by the borrower and the lender.

68. **D** All of these statements are correct.

69. **A** A short sale occurs when a lender is willing to let the owner sell the property for less than what is needed to pay off the outstanding mortgage loan. Here, the outstanding loan amount is for

$450,000. The only dollar amount that is "short" of this outstanding loan amount is $445,100.

70. **B** In the government survey system, a section of land is one square mile and contains 640 acres. One-half of a section contains 320 acres. A one-quarter section contains 160 acres. *Note:* The term *contiguous* means touching or adjacent. So, 320 acres + 160 acres = 480 acres.

71. **D** The calculation is $600,000 (improvement value) ÷ 27.5 (years) = $21,818.18 (annual depreciation allowance).

The depreciation allowance for residential investment property is taken on the value of the improvements divided over a period of 27½ years. The other answer choices are incorrect. The depreciation allowance is never permitted on land: land does not depreciate, meaning it never wears out and needs to be replaced. *Note:* The depreciation allowance for commercial properties is taken over 39 years.

72. **D** The "1% rule" is frequently used by real estate investors. The rule posits that the return on real estate investment should be equal to—or greater than—a 1% return on the purchase price. Here, a 1% return on a $1 million property would be $10,000.

73. **C** The value is $5,937,500. The formula is net operating income ÷ rate of return = value. So, $475,000 (net operating income) ÷ 8% [rate of return (0.08)] = $5,937,500 (value).

74. **B** The calculation is $1,500 × 10 = $15,000 × 12 = $180,000 (potential gross income).
$1,000 × 12 = $12,000 (other income).
$180,000 + $12,000 = $192,000.
$192,000 − $9,600 (vacancies at 5%) = $182,400.

75. **A** The seller always owes the buyer rent because rent is paid in advance by the tenant. The seller will owe the buyer for the portion of the month the buyer will own the property. With the seller having the day of closing, the buyer is owed for nine days of rent.